Achieving

QTS

Primary
Mathematics
Teaching Theory and Practice

Achieving
QTS

Primary
Mathematics

Teaching Theory and Practice

Third edition

Claire Mooney
Mary Briggs
Mike Fletcher
Alice Hansen
Judith McCulloch

LearningMatters

First published in 2001 by Learning Matters Ltd.
Second edition published in 2002.
Reprinted in 2002.
Reprinted in 2003.
Reprinted in 2004.
Reprinted in 2005 (twice).
Third edition published in 2007.

British Library Cataloguing in Publication Data
A CIP record for this book is available from the British Library.

ISBN 978 1 84445 099 2

The right of Claire Mooney, Mary Briggs, Mike Fletcher, Alice Hansen and Judith
McCulloch to be identified as the Authors of this Work has been asserted by them in
accordance with the Copyright, Design and Patents Act 1988.

Cover design by Topics – The Creative Partnership
Text design by Code 5 Design Associates Ltd
Project management by Deer Park Productions
Typeset by PDQ Typesetting Ltd
Printed and bound in Great Britain by Bell & Bain Ltd, Glasgow

Learning Matters
33 Southernhay East
Exeter EX1 1NX
Tel: 01392 215560
info@learningmatters.co.uk
www.learningmatters.co.uk

Contents

1
Introduction

About this book

This book has been written to satisfy the needs of all primary trainees on all courses of initial teacher training in England and other parts of the UK where a secure knowledge and understanding of how to teach mathematics is required for the award of Qualified Teacher Status (QTS) or its equivalent. This book will also be found useful by Newly Qualified Teachers (NQTs), mentors, curriculum co-ordinators and other professionals working in education who have identified aspects of their mathematics practice which require attention or who need a single resource to recommend to colleagues.

Features of this book include:

- **clear links with the Professional Standards for the award of QTS;**
- **chapter objectives;**
- **clear reference to Mathematics in the National Curriculum and the Primary National Strategy's Primary Framework for Literacy and Mathematics;**
- **pedagogical and professional knowledge and understanding for effective mathematics teaching and learning;**
- **research summaries;**
- **practical tasks;**
- **reflective tasks;**
- **summary of key points;**
- **moving on;**
- **further reading and references.**

Details of the Professional Standards for the award of QTS, Mathematics in the National Curriculum and the Primary National Strategy's: *The Primary Framework for Literacy and Mathematics* are provided later in this chapter.

Special note
In teaching mathematics, teachers (and trainees) are required to have due regard for inclusion (providing effective learning opportunities for all children). Certain aspects of inclusion (e.g. the educational needs of children in care, children with long-term medical conditions and children with physical and mental disabilities, significantly low attaining children, children for whom English is a second or additional language, travelling children and refugees) lie beyond the scope of this text.

What is primary mathematics and why is it taught?

Children need to develop a good mathematical understanding in order to function effectively as members of our society. The expression 'functional literacy' is frequently used when discussing children learning aspects of English language and literacy. However, we also need to consider 'functional numeracy', that which is required by children in order to operate and interact effectively within today's society. The number of occasions throughout the day when we all encounter mathematical concepts is manifold. An understanding of different aspects of number is required to find the correct house in the street, to call someone on the phone, to lay the table, … ; measures are used every day, either accurate or estimated, when shopping (mass, length, capacity, money), when driving a car, riding a bike or crossing the road (speed, distance, time), when telling the time or acknowledging the passing of time, … ; we live within a three-dimensional world, hence an understanding of spatial concepts is vital if we are to interact with and make sense of our physical environment; each day we encounter data, we evaluate data and we interpret data. All of this demonstrates just how important for children a clear knowledge and understanding of mathematics really is.

In order to achieve the aim of 'functional numeracy' children need to be able to think flexibly and to apply their knowledge to new situations, to solve practical problems, to experiment within mathematics itself, to develop the ability to reason mathematically and to communicate their reasoning to others. We cannot assume a child is 'functionally numerate' if they can only answer pages of questions. They need to be able to abstract and generalise from specific situations in order to demonstrate their mathematical thinking. These elements of generalising and communicating mathematical thinking need to be foremost in our teaching. However, we must also not lose sight of the awe and wonder of mathematics, the creativity and elegance that ensure the stimulation, challenge and enjoyment.

The Professional Standards for the award of QTS

The Professional Standards for the award of QTS found in *Professional Standards for Teachers* (TDA, 2007) are presented in three interrelated sections. Section 1 identifies the Professional Attributes required to be an effective teacher; section 2 the Professional Knowledge and Understanding and section 3 the Professional Skills. This book is written to support the development of the knowledge and skills that are required by teachers in order to demonstrate attainment in section 1, Professional Attributes, section 2, Professional Knowledge and Understanding and section 3, Professional Skills.

In order to demonstrate this attainment, it is important to know and understand certain things by the time a course of initial teacher training is completed. Within mathematics these include:

- **the key aspects of mathematics underpinning children's progress;**
- **methods of developing children's mathematical knowledge, understanding and skills;**
- **how to plan and pace mathematics lessons;**
- **the selection and use of mathematical resources;**
- **how to lead oral work and use interactive methods;**
- **recognising common mathematical errors and misconceptions and how to prevent and remedy them;**
- **assessing and evaluating mathematics teaching and learning;**
- **recognising standards of attainment in mathematics that should be expected of pupils;**
- **the importance of engaging pupils' interest in and enthusiasm for mathematics.**

Mathematics in the National Curriculum

Mathematics in the National Curriculum is organised on the basis of four Key Stages. Key Stage 1 for 5 to 7 year olds (Years 1 and 2) and Key Stage 2 for 7 to 11 year olds (Years 3 to 6) are for primary. The components of each Key Stage include Programmes of Study, which set out the mathematics that children should be taught; Attainment Targets, which set out the mathematical knowledge, skills and understanding that children should attain; and Level Descriptions, which describe the types and range of performance that children working at a particular level should be able to demonstrate within each Attainment Target. Mathematics in the National Curriculum is a minimum statutory requirement. Since its introduction in 1989 it has been significantly revised a number of times. The Programmes of Study for mathematics currently include:

- **Ma 1: Using and Applying Mathematics;**
- **Ma 2: Number and Algebra;**
- **Ma 3: Shape, Space and Measures;**
- **Ma 4: Handling Data (Key Stage 2).**

Mathematics in the National Curriculum also presents links to other subjects, and suggestions for the use of ICT.

The Primary Framework for Literacy and Mathematics

The National Numeracy Strategy (NNS) was introduced into primary schools throughout England in 1999. The NNS Framework for Teaching Mathematics (DfEE/QCA, 1999) was intended to supplement the NC Order and offer a sort of national 'scheme of work' for mathematics. The Secretary of State's publication of *Excellence and Enjoyment – A strategy for primary schools* in 2003 resulted in the establishment of the Primary National Strategy. This national strategy brought both the National Numeracy Strategy and the National Literacy Strategy together as the Primary Framework for literacy and mathematics. This Framework is designed to offer a flexible structure to meet the learning needs of all children.

FURTHER READING   FURTHER READING   FURTHER READING

Curriculum Guidance for the Foundation Stage (containing the *Early Learning Goals*). Available at:**http://www.qca.org.uk/5585.html.**

The National Curriculum for England. Available at: **http://www.nc.uk.net.**

The Primary Framework for Literacy and Mathematics. Available at: **http://www.standards.dfes. gov.uk/primary/.**

Professional Standards for Teachers. Available at: **http://www.tda.gov.uk.**

REFERENCES REFERENCES **REFERENCES** REFERENCES REFERENCES

DfEE. QCA (1999) *The National Numeracy Strategy Framework for Teaching Mathematics from Reception to Year 6.* London: DfEE.

DfES (2003) *Excellence and Enjoyment – A Strategy for primary schools.* London: DfES.

Curriculum Guidance for the Foundation Stage (containing the Early Learning Goals available at **http:// www.qca.org.uk/5585.html**

Professional Standards for Teachers available from **http://www.tda.gov.uk**

2
The daily mathematics lesson

Professional Standards for the award of QTS

This chapter will support you as you work towards evidencing attainment against the following Standards:

Q1, Q3, Q4, Q7, Q8, Q10, Q14, Q15, Q21, Q22, Q23, Q25, Q26, Q29, Q30, Q32

Chapter objectives

By the end of this chapter you should:

- **be able to describe the structure of the three-part daily mathematics lesson;**
- **understand the recent historical developments leading to the three-part daily mathematics lesson;**
- **be able to describe the purpose of each section of the three-part daily mathematics lesson;**
- **have considered some of the management and organisational issues associated with teaching within the three-part daily mathematics lesson structure.**

Introduction

This chapter will discuss the daily mathematics lesson, consider how its present form came about, what the recommendations are for its structure and the implications for, and management of, teaching mathematics in primary schools.

Background

The publication of the Cockcroft Report in 1982 marked the beginning of change in the way mathematics was taught in primary schools. Among its recommendations were:

- **the need to acquire mental strategies without moving too quickly into written calculations so encouraging children to develop their own calculation methods;**
- **the use of whole-class teaching;**
- **the integration of problem solving into the curriculum.**

The eventual outcome of the report was the content of the mathematics part of the National Curriculum (NC), introduced in 1991. The NC had the intention that all schools would have a nationally standardised syllabus content to follow, designed to develop knowledge, skills and understanding progressively. Schools were given guidance on the proportion of the teaching time in the week that was to be given to each subject, including mathematics, (Dearing, 1993), and from that the timetable for each day was determined.

The Cockroft Report included the statement: *The ability to solve problems is at the heart of mathematics* (Cockcroft, 1982: 249), which was taken as a recommendation for a necessary part of the NC entitled 'Using and Applying'. Initially this was written as a Programme of Study (POS) stated separately from the other POS. But the current edition of the NC (2000) (which came before the Primary National Strategy (PNS)) has incorporated the using and applying of mathematics into the Programmes of Study (PoS), although it still exists as an AT and has to be assessed. Dr Colin Sparrow states in NC (2000, p.61) that *mathematics is not just a collection of skills, it is a way of thinking*, and the change in the structure of the NC reflects this. Children often experience difficulties in transference, meaning that the more the curriculum is separated into discrete areas, the less likely it is that children will be able to transfer knowledge, skills and understanding from one area to another, both within and outside mathematically specific work. Consideration of integrating using and applying with the teaching of knowledge, skills and understanding should improve transference.

However, it became evident that while the NC gave clear directives on content and progression, there were weaknesses that needed to be addressed.

> *In particular, there were concerns about the level of basic calculation skills, including mental mathematics, overuse of commercial schemes that promoted standard calculation methods and teachers managing rather than teaching.* (Straker, cited in Thompson, 1999)

> *In addition, the emphasis on differentiation had resulted in a tendency for children to work individually through schemes with a consequent loss of cohesion through common strands.* (Brown, cited in Thompson, 1999)

The outcome of this was that too many children were not achieving the standard they possibly could. In 1996 the National Numeracy Project (NNP) was launched. From this arose the non-statutory National Numeracy Strategy (NNS), implemented in schools from September 1999, which gave a framework for teaching mathematics that promoted both equity and equality of teaching (Brown et al., 2000).

The recommendation from the NNP for a daily mathematics lesson was, in many schools, in place prior to the implementation of the NNS. For the preceding few years in local education authorities (LEAs), mathematics inspectors and advisory teachers were encouraging schools to ensure that mathematics was taught each day including using and applying through investigation and problem solving. There was, at this time, no nationally recommended structure to the daily mathematics lesson, but with the introduction of the National Literacy Strategy (NLS) in 1998, schools anticipated and so applied the advisory structure that would be given in the NNS.

With the advent of the PNS, the strategies for teaching literacy and numeracy were reviewed, with numeracy reverting to the title of mathematics. The renewed mathematics framework is different from the 1999 framework in the following ways.

- **It is an electronic version.**
- **It has a clearer structure.**
- **It has slimmed down objectives.**

> *'The renewal of the Primary Framework for... mathematics offers everyone involved in teaching children aged from 3 to 11 an opportunity to continue the progress made in raising standards by embedding the principles of both* Every Child Matters: change for children (2004) *and* Excellence and Enjoyment: learning and teaching in the primary years *into practice. (http://www.standards.dfes.gov.uk/primaryframeworks/)*

How the daily mathematics lesson is structured

The DfES recommended structure

The revised framework builds on the success of the NNS as a guide to inform teaching and planning in mathematics which addresses the mathematics curriculum in four 'senses':

- **content and balance;**
- **calculators and computers;**
- **sequencing;**
- **curricular differentiation (Brown et al., 1998: 366).**

Developing knowledge and use of the appropriate mathematical vocabulary is stressed throughout the framework, but it is up to you to decide how you manage this.

RESEARCH SUMMARY RESEARCH SUMMARY **RESEARCH SUMMARY**

The daily mathematics lesson (as stated in DfEE/NNS, 2000):

- **emphasises the role of language and the use of mathematical vocabulary; and**
- **provides opportunities for children to:**
  - **talk about the mathematics they are learning;**
  - **ask questions;**
  - **explain mathematical ideas.**

Mayow (2000: 17) states that *it is clearly important to introduce mathematical vocabulary as it is needed, but not to the point of obscuring the child's ability to understand*. She goes on to say that *meaning is crucial in bridging the gap in mathematical understanding, and therefore language and number are intrinsically linked*. Where bilingual approaches are employed, it is important that the first language is used not only when communication has broken down or just to interpret the occasional difficult word.

The PNS approach to teaching reflects the four key principles derived from the NNS, these being:

- **dedicated mathematics lessons every day;**
- **direct teaching and interactive oral work with the whole class and groups;**
- **an emphasis on mental calculation;**
- **controlled differentiation, with all pupils engaged in mathematics relating to a common theme.**

To encompass these key principles, including sufficient time for rehearsal, reinforcement and extension, you will need to plan to allow between three quarters of an hour and an hour for the daily mathematics lesson, depending on the age of the children. In addition, of course, it is important that you include mathematics in other subject areas, where appropriate, to further improve the children's transference skills and hence facility with the application of mathematics.

The PNS is non-statutory but the principles upon which it rests form a useful model for teaching mathematics, as shown in section 1 of the guidelines document. The rest of the Framework contains guidance on ways and means of implementing the content of the NC and the interpretation is therefore directed by the experience and mathematical confidence of each teacher, which includes you, within school policy guidelines.

RESEARCH SUMMARY RESEARCH SUMMARY **RESEARCH SUMMARY**

Askew et al. (1997) found that teachers of numeracy who were highly effective demonstrated a range of classroom organisation styles including whole class teaching, individual and group work, and this is reflected in the recommended structure of the daily mathematics lesson. The intention is to promote improvements in the teaching of mathematics (Ofsted, 2000); however, Brown (1999: 7) warns that *it's not whether it's whole class, group or individual teaching but rather what you teach and how you interact mathematically with children which seems to count.* Denvir and Askew (2001) observed that:

- **whilst children are willing to, wanting to and almost always taking part, many are frequently not engaged in mathematical thinking;**
- **children frequently copy from each other with some never doing the work for themselves, becoming adept at convincing the teachers they are good workers and thinkers. In general copying is not regarded by the children as being wrong.**

Mental mathematics

Despite the recommendations of the Cockcroft Report (1982) it was found by NNP that children (and teaching) were still too reliant on written or technological calculations, becoming too inflexible in their methods and thinking. As a result one of the most significant areas for attention became mental mathematics. The introduction of daily mental mathematics sessions is to redress this and encompasses children learning to:

- **remember and instantly recall number facts;**
- **use known facts to derive new facts;**
- **select and combine strategies to solve problems.**

The recommendation is that the first five to ten minutes of the daily mathematics lesson should be concerned with mental mathematics and, where possible, you should link the content to the subject being covered in the main lesson. This encourages your children to realise that mental mathematics is a desirable and often convenient way of approaching calculation. You should encourage children always to try to tackle a problem with mental methods before using any other approach (DfEE, 1999; DfEE/QCA, 2000). The integration of mental and written strategies for calculation and the development of making mental estimations of the answers to calculations (DfEE, 2000) will promote children's abilities to choose the most appropriate mathematics for their purposes. Therefore the mental and oral mathematics work you plan should i*nclude opportunities for pupils to explain the methods and strategies they use to reach an answer, to consider the efficiency of various methods and to apply their knowledge of number facts to 'real-life' problems* (Ofsted, 2000: p.9).

However, in the PNS training materials for teachers it is recognised that sometimes there is no directly related mental mathematics possible and, rather than force artificially created links, you should consider using discrete alternatives. These sessions may be taught at the beginning of the daily mathematics lesson, where they provide a valuable mental 'warm-up', or may be placed at a different time of the day if you consider this more appropriate or useful. For example, ten minutes before lunch could be used for working on some mental multiplication, or ten minutes after break might offer the opportunity for some mental work on equivalent fractions. And of course you can always use such times as registration or lining up for assembly for some number work related to dinner numbers or absent children.

Main teaching

Most of the rest of the time in the daily mathematics lesson is to be used for teaching and practice of the planned area of mathematics. You can decide each day the appropriate division of time between whole-class teaching and individual or group work.

For example, when introducing a new concept, you will need to spend time revisiting previously related concepts, ascertaining existing knowledge, skills and understanding, before the new (or developmental) concept is broached. You could manage this preliminary mathematics work through a variety of strategies including whole-class questioning, group tasks or individual assessment work. It may take ten minutes at the start of the lesson (including mental mathematics) or may take the whole lesson. The means by which you achieve this will depend on a variety of factors which will be unique to that particular situation, such as:

- **the age of the children;**
- **the ability of the children;**
- **the time since the concept was previously visited; and**
- **the complexity of the concept.**

From that stage, the introduction of the new concept may take up much of the teaching time for the first day with whole-class teaching, while a few days on your whole-class input may be minimal, serving merely to ensure that all are comfortable with the ongoing work before continuing with previous work in groups or individually.

Regardless of how the time is divided for this part of the lesson, what is important is that you, the teacher, are teaching throughout. The visual imagery that is developing through the mental and oral work needs concrete and visual models to help strengthen the pupils' understanding. The consequent improved flexibility of transference both within and outside mathematics lessons will in turn provide the basis and incentive for further expansion in both confidence and cognition. Whether you are teaching groups or individuals or even the whole class, you are required to give *clear explanations, illustrations and demonstrations of the mathematics* (Ofsted, 2000, p.14) and you will need to take time for planning the teaching materials, including resources to achieve this.

The integration of problem solving and investigations, previously noted as being weak, into this part of the lesson can build upon the mental and oral work done. Through this you will encourage your children to use and apply their knowledge and skills with reasoning and logical organisation and to learn and use the correct mathematical vocabulary to provide clarity to their explanations.

Your children's recording of progression through their work does not have to be written but it must be clear and evident. Talking through their work not only helps their peers but also helps your children themselves clarify their thoughts and therefore their processing and understanding of concepts.

Plenary/Review

Your lesson needs to be finished, not left. Even if the work is to be continued the following day, the plenary of five to ten minutes gives the opportunity for you to:

- **revisit daily and longer-term objectives so establishing progress;**
- **pick up on any errors and misconceptions;**
- **promote pupils' successes;**
- **allow pupils to practise communicating their thoughts and processes;**
- **note any areas that may need revisiting or reinforcing before moving on (possibly achieved in part by setting relevant homework). (NNS, 1999; Ofsted, 2000)**

It can be led by you or the children but you need to take care to ensure that it has a purpose related to the lesson and is therefore of value.

Aspects of the daily mathematics lesson

Some aspects of the daily mathematics lesson are mentioned here as an introduction and are covered in detail in other chapters.

Time of day

Most schools timetable the literacy lesson and the daily mathematics lesson for the morning, with what remains of the morning and the afternoon set aside for all other curriculum areas. However, Ofsted noted that *too many lessons are drifting well beyond the recommended time and this is having an adverse effect on the pattern of work in the mornings and on the time available to teach other subjects* (Ofsted, 2000). You should ensure that the daily mathematics lesson lasts for a maximum of an hour (and can be less) for the oldest pupils (Years 5 and 6) and for about 45 minutes for Key Stage 1, thus leaving time before lunch for other subjects to be taught.

It is not, of course, necessary to have the daily mathematics lesson in the morning and schools need to make their own decisions about how to organise the day. Neither is it necessary for you to have all three recommended parts of the daily mathematics lesson running concurrently (especially with the younger children), although a predominance of this structure during the week helps develop continuity and links between mental, oral and written mathematics. Opportunities for both planned and unplanned mathematics, especially to practise and develop mental strategies, can occur at any time during the day and you should be alert to possibilities.

Resources

See Chapter 11

With the inception of the NNS many commercial companies developed ranges of resources to meet the requirements of the daily mathematics lesson. Some of this was in response to recommendations within the NNS training materials, such as number lines, 100 squares and digit cards. Mathematics schemes were modified and cross-referenced to the NNS and specifically written supplements, new schemes and computer programs were written. These materials will still be valid following the reviewed PNS. Schools also embarked on producing their own resources. When planning, you need to decide:

- **which resources will enhance teaching and learning;**
- **when it is appropriate to use them;**

- how to progress learning through from concrete representations to abstract understanding;
- how to determine the appropriate application of concepts and so be discriminating in their use.

Differentiation

Throughout the daily mathematics lesson, differentiation is desirable, recommended and possible. This will be considered in more detail in Chapter 3 on teaching strategies; however, it is worth a brief look at this stage.

> **RESEARCH SUMMARY** RESEARCH SUMMARY **RESEARCH SUMMARY**
>
> In general, through the daily mathematics lesson, standards achieved by lowest performing pupils are getting better (Ofsted, 2000). The PNS view is that setting is not really desirable but that in mixed-ability classes pupils should not work at many different levels with a wide range of differentiated groups; rather there should be a *controlled degree of differentiation* (Brown, 1998; Brown et al., 2000: 464).

The best work for each child is that which provides both success and challenge, and this particular dilemma of providing effective differentiation in whole-class teaching exercises experienced teachers as well as student teachers. Therefore you need to plan specifically. Our own childhood memories of anticipating the possibility of being asked something we cannot answer and the subsequent humiliation (real or perceived) is sufficient evidence that the need for us as teachers to avoid this situation and promote self-esteem in our pupils is a high priority.

After all, as many children with high mathematical ability dread being wrong (often as expectations of them are high) as do average or lower ability children. Questioning that is differentiated and effectively directed can engage all at their own level and some ideas for questioning are given in the PNS vocabulary book. However, it is worth bearing in mind Davis' (1999, p.401) appeal for teachers to *interpret the exhortation to use 'open questions' not as a 'method that works' but as a guiding principle which they employ intelligently and flexibly with other principles.*

The use of teaching assistants for individuals or groups can provide you with valuable support throughout the daily mathematics lesson. The involvement of teaching assistants in planning and the preparation of resources, including ICT, helps to ensure that both teacher and assistants are working towards the same goals without any confusion that could arise through lack of communication.

While many schools have chosen to place children into sets for the daily mathematics lesson this does not absolve you of the need to differentiate. It is just the range that has narrowed and it is important to remember that differentiation is still necessary.

Reception/Early Years

See Chapter 3

The NC Foundation Stage is written to provide continuity for children in their first year of schooling. You can undertake planning for these children in very much the same way as for older children, from the basis of learning objectives. However, the three-part structure of the primary daily mathematics lesson needs to be interpreted to ensure the reception children are being taught in ways suited to their age and maturity. This may mean that you teach mathematics in much smaller time frames or in a form that integrates it with the rest of the day's work. A useful gauge is to work towards introducing the discrete mathematics lesson by the third term for most children, with perhaps just the very youngest not meeting it until the start of Year 1.

Mixed-age classes

Many schools, whether through choice or not, have more than one year group in each class. The daily mathematics lesson allows you to teach all children at their own level, taking account of social, emotional, cognitive and chronological development. The framework provided by the PNS has mathematical themes that progress through each year and the document can therefore be used for planning through direct alignment of objectives. Some mathematical topics can be taught to all children at the same time and others lend themselves better to separate taught sessions, but the development work can be planned in the same way as other differentiation.

Assessment

The inherent flexibility of the daily mathematics lesson, being objective led rather than task led, allows both for assessment to take place and for that assessment to directly influence the lessons which follow. While working with the whole class or with groups or individuals you have many opportunities to evaluate pupils' progress against the learning objectives.

See Chapter 5

Throughout the daily mathematics lesson you can monitor children's responses to the teaching either through general observations or through more specifically directed questions or tasks, built into the planning. Regular, formative assessment allows you to develop a comprehensive picture of the progress of the class and enables the adjustment of teaching to suit the requirements of each pupil. Early detection of errors, misconceptions or lack of understanding in the children, or of poorly determined differentiation through this routine assessment means you can maintain effective progress while avoiding frustration or boredom in your children.

In addition to the routine, everyday formative assessment, the daily mathematics lesson can be used, in whole or in part, for more formal, summative assessment. It has already been mentioned that it is usually a good idea at the start of a new area of mathematics to establish the current status of the pupils' knowledge, skills and understanding. Therefore, it is clearly valuable to ascertain how much has been added to this state during the course of the work. This assessment will then, in turn, inform the next stage of planning.

Information and Communication Technology (ICT)

ICT has a role to play in the effectiveness of the daily mathematics lesson. Our pupils are growing up in a technological society and schools need to both develop their technological expertise and to use technology to enhance learning. Much of the concerns expressed about the deskilling effect of the use of ICT results from inappropriate use to the detriment of effective learning. The phrase 'information and communication technology' encompasses many resources including video/DVD, audio tape/CD recorders, calculators, overhead projectors and computers. All of these can be used as useful resources for teaching but the main focus for developing effective skills in children is calculators and computers.

*See Chapter 3
page 33*

The NC recommends that the calculator is introduced at Key Stage 2. The PNS discusses the value of the calculator both as a teaching tool and as a resource for children to use to support well established mental and written calculation skills. Ruthven (1997, cited in Brown et al., 1998, p.367) argues that the evidence available at the time gave 'scant support' to the idea that the use of calculators was responsible for *disappointing mathematics performance*. Becta (2001) states that there is evidence that in schools where ICT is used effectively for teaching, Key Stage 2 SATS results were generally better than those schools in which ICT was poorly used.

The calculator provides a valuable resource for removing the unnecessary tedium of extensive or repetitive calculations. If a child understands the underlying mathematical concept of the calculation and is engaged in applying it to a problem or investigation, then the use of a calculator is appropriate. Of course, despite being relieved of the mechanics of calculation, the child needs to know how to use the calculator correctly and to be able to estimate the answer to each stage of the calculation so they are able to judge the reasonableness of the solution found. Teaching calculator skills is as important as teaching how to use any mathematical resource and should be integrated into planning.

Schools have generally one or both of two computer arrangements. Computers can be organised either into suites serving either all or some of the school, or can be sited in each classroom. Teachers have varying amounts of skills and confidence in the use of computers for teaching and learning but this is being addressed through training courses for qualified teachers and within ITT. Computers can be used for whole-class teaching as well as for group and individual work. It is important, however, that you choose software and internet access to complement the learning objectives and that children are taught how to use these programs. Effectively integrated computer work can help pupils practise and apply skills and knowledge through exciting, interactive adventure programs, pursue investigations using spreadsheets or expand understanding, use and application through internet challenges. The range of available, suitable material is expanding rapidly and the time you spend working through a program or website during the planning stages of the daily mathematics lesson is essential to ensure that the content matches the learning objectives and is appropriate for the age and abilities of the children who will use it.

Teachers' subject knowledge

If the daily mathematics lesson is to be of maximum benefit to the pupils, it is necessary for you to be fully competent and confident about your own mathematical subject knowledge, skills and understanding. Weaknesses in this area have long been identified as significant in the quality and effectiveness of mathematics teaching (Ofsted, 2000) and the instigation of the new Professional Standards for Teachers (TDA, 2006) and the Training and Development Agency for Schools (TDA) tests at the end of training are addressing this issue for new teachers. However, all teachers with weak subject knowledge, whatever their experience, need to address this.

Askew et al. (1997) found that less effective teachers tended to be more procedural than conceptual in their subject knowledge and understanding. This means that the resultant teaching can be limited and unimaginative with less flexibility in the breadth of application and explanations used. In managing their own insecurities, these teachers can resort to overreliance on non-discriminatory use of commercial texts and the predominance of 'safe' mathematics to the limiting or exclusion of more open problem solving and investigation.

However, a teacher who has had to work and think hard to overcome their own lack of understanding and mathematical self-esteem can often prove to be a more empathetic teacher than the teacher who has rarely had to question their own mathematical understanding. You have a professional obligation to be the best you can for your pupils and focus on direct, interactive teaching in the daily mathematics lesson has provided an impetus to improved subject knowledge.

Flexibility

The recommended structure of the daily mathematics lesson is not intended to be prescriptive and the non-statutory PNS document is deliberately entitled 'A framework'.

RESEARCH SUMMARY RESEARCH SUMMARY RESEARCH SUMMARY

Brown et al. (2000: 469) expressed concerns that *although it is too early to have any reliable evidence, the prescription of detail, while welcomed by many teachers, may cause additional stress for others in having to choose between literal interpretation and following their own professional judgement*. But good practice requires the use of this judgement and Askew (1999, p.5) states that *challenging tasks, teacher and pupils learning from each other, a variety of accessible tools and a supportive atmosphere – mathematics lessons that demonstrate these qualities may go beyond simply following the three-part structure*.

You need to exercise your professional skills to make constructive, creative use of the time while still adhering to the good practice principles of direct, interactive teaching in mental, oral and written mathematics. This allows you to plan for a variety of different approaches to teaching and learning mathematics determined by the nature of the particular aspect of mathematics being studied. After all, *mathematics is a creative discipline* (DfEE/QCA, 2000, p.60). For example, lessons can be prepared to meet objectives that might focus sharply on skills development or provide practice of varied strategies to improve depth and breadth of knowledge and understanding or to undertake extended investigations. If the daily mathematics lesson is to benefit children, it must engage, motivate, stimulate, excite, inspire, encourage, fulfil, challenge and satisfy.

A SUMMARY OF **KEY POINTS**

> The PNS Primary framework continues to advocate a three-part mathematics lesson.
> The role of language and the development of vocabulary are crucial aspects of teaching and learning mathematics within this structure.
> There should be limited differentiation around a theme common to the whole class.
> The structure designed to be implemented flexibly responding to the needs and experiences of the learners.
> The role of the teacher in direct teaching results in a clear requirement for confident and accurate mathematics subject knowledge.

Moving on

Since the introduction of the National Numeracy Strategy in schools, many resources have been produced to support the implementation of the three-part daily mathematics lesson. Consult your university tutors and/or ask colleagues in school, particularly the subject leader for mathematics, to access the appropriate training materials as you develop your pedagogical skills as a mathematics teacher.

REFERENCES REFERENCES **REFERENCES** REFERENCES REFERENCES

Askew, M. (1999) 'Teaching numeracy: will we ever learn?' *Mathematics Teaching*, vol. 168, pp. 3–5.

Askew, M., Brown, M., Rhodes, V., Wiliam, D. and Johnson, D. (1997) *Effective Teachers of Numeracy: Report of a Study Carried out for the Teacher Training Agency*. London: King's College, University of London.

Becta (2001) *Primary Schools of the Future – Achieving Today*. See: **http://www.becta.org.uk/ news/reports/primaryfuture/index.html**.

Brown, M. (1999) 'Is more whole class teaching the answer?' *Mathematics Teaching*, vol. 169, pp. 5–7.

Brown, M., Askew, M., Baker, D., Denvir, H. and Millett, A. (1998) 'Is the National Numeracy Strategy research-based?' *British Journal of Educational Studies*, vol. 46, no. 4, pp. 362–85.

Brown, M., Millett, A., Bibby, T. and Johnson, D (2000) 'Turning our attention from the what to the how: the National Numeracy Strategy'. *British Educational Research Journal*, vol. 26, no. 4, pp. 457–71.

Cockcroft, W. H. (1982) *Mathematics Counts*, 4/98. London: HMSO.

Davis, A. (1999) 'Prescribing teaching methods'. *Journal Philosophy of Education*, vol. 33, no. 3, pp. 387–401.

Dearing, R. (1993) *Interim Report on the National Curriculum and Its Assessments*. London: DfE.

Denvir, H. and Askew, M. (2001) 'Pupil participation in interactive whole class teaching'. Unpublished paper delivered at British Society for Research into Learning Mathematics day conference, 3 March.

DfEE (1998) *Teaching: High Status, High Standards – Requirements for Courses of Initial Teacher Training*. London: DfEE.

DfEE (1999) *The National Numeracy Strategy: Framework for Teaching Mathematics from Reception to Year 6*. London: DfEE.

DfEE/NNS (2000) *Supporting Pupils with English as an Additional Language*. London: DfEE.

DfEE/QCA (2000) *The National Curriculum: Key Stages 1 and 2*. London: HMSO.

Mayow, I. (2000) 'Teaching number: does the Numeracy Strategy hold the answers?' *Mathematics Teaching*, vol. 170, pp. 16–17.

Ofsted (2000) *The National Numeracy Strategy: the first year*. London: Ofsted.

TDA (2006) Professional Standards for Teachers. London: TDA.

Thompson, I. (Ed.) (1999) *Issues in Teaching Numeracy in Primary Schools*. Buckingham: Open University Press.

Useful websites

http://www.standards.dfes.gov.uk/primary/frameworks/mathematics/

3
Teaching strategies

Professional Standards for the award of QTS

This chapter will support you as you work towards evidencing attainment against the following Standards:

Q10, Q12, Q15, Q16, Q17, Q18, Q19, Q20, Q21, Q22, Q23, Q25, Q26, Q27

Chapter objectives

By the end of this chapter you will have:

- **considered the physical classroom organisation for teaching and learning mathematics;**
- **explored how to share objectives with pupils;**
- **considered the role of talk in the classroom;**
- **explored demonstrating and modelling;**
- **used creative and alternative starting points for teaching and considered how these can break down the barriers to learning;**
- **considered the use of the plenary in mathematics;**
- **classroom management in mathematics lessons;**
- **considered how to use display;**
- **considered the use of ICT in teaching mathematics.**

Introduction

The National Numeracy Strategy (NNS) required teachers to rethink their teaching and learning strategies for mathematics. The framework for the strategy resulted in raising the amount of time for teaching mathematics. It also raised the amount of direct teaching input by teachers during the daily lesson. This needs to be carefully planned and the teaching strategies carefully chosen for any lesson in order to make the most effective use of time and resources, especially the use of teachers and other adults working in the classroom. Mathematics can be enjoyable to teach and to learn, and fun for both the adults and the pupils. The most successful teachers of numeracy are those who make the links between aspects of mathematics. The following Research Summary shows the different teaching strategies identified in the research and how this relates to looking at learning theories as part of your training course.

RESEARCH SUMMARY RESEARCH SUMMARY **RESEARCH SUMMARY**

Askew et al. (1997) in their study of effective teachers of numeracy at King's College, London, have identified different teacher orientations and their effectiveness in teaching numeracy.

- *Transmission.* **The teachers with this orientation emphasise the role of the teacher as the source of mathematical knowledge and they impart the knowledge to pupils focusing on mathematics as a discrete set of rules and procedures. The pupils' role is subordinate to the teacher and receiver of knowledge.**

If you have looked at learning theories in your course you will recognise links with a behaviourist approach to teaching and learning.

- *Discovery*. **Teachers with this orientation emphasise the pupil at the centre of the learning process where the pupils construct or discover mathematical ideas for themselves. The teacher is the provider of activities, resources and support for the learners' discoveries. Mathematics is not seen as purely rules and procedures.**

Again the links here are with the constructivist approaches to learning, discovery rather than telling and potentially scaffolding the learning for pupils.

- *Connectionist*. **Teachers with this orientation emphasise sharing the work on the complexity of mathematics – pupils and teachers together. In their lessons they share their own strategies for doing mathematics. The teacher is not seen as the only source of mathematical knowledge. They value pupils' methods and explanations. They establish connections within the mathematics curriculum – for example, linking addition and multiplication. These teachers are considered to be the most effective in terms of learning in relation to a test of mathematics.**

This is considered the closest to the apprenticeship model of learning which you may have been introduced to, usually associated with Rogoff and Lave (1984) who focused on learning in quite different environments than the classroom and often with older learners.

REFLECTIVE TASK

Think about the teaching strategies you have experienced as a learner. How would you categorise the teachers in relation to Askew et al.'s (1997) orientations?

Consider the teachers you have observed teaching mathematics. How would you categorise them? Which teaching strategies were effective for which learners?

See Chapter 5 of Jacques and Hyland **Primary Professional Studies** *(2007) from Learning Matters and Chapter 2 in this book on the daily mathematics lesson.*

The physical organisation of the classroom for mathematics teaching

As a result of the three-part daily lesson, teachers reconsidered the arrangement of the furniture in their classroom. Increased whole-class teaching meant that all pupils needed a focus in the classroom at which they could all look for teacher demonstrations. This has continued to develop with the increased use of data projectors and interactive whiteboards (IWBs).

If a carpet area is used for whole-class teaching then there needs to be enough space around for the movement of pupils between the phases of the lesson while retaining sufficient space for all pupils to sit and work comfortably on the carpet and at tables. Some classes have spaces marked out on the carpet to ensure that pupils have their own area, and these can be allocated to pupils to avoid the potential for disruptive behaviour during the lesson. Pupils requiring the support of an additional adult during whole-class teaching can be positioned at the edge to enable the adult to sit next to them while not obscuring the rest of the class's view of the whiteboard or disturbing the attention of the rest of the class. Wherever the pupils are sitting they need to be able to see the overhead projector (OHP) or whiteboard without the sun streaming onto the screen and making it difficult for pupils to see the images used in teaching. This may sound a common sense issue but many older classrooms have limited options for the installation of whiteboards and so they are not always positioned in the most obviously logical place in the room. Problems with writing, cables and wall space have influenced the location of these resources. Check the organisation in relation to the windows and the lighting in the room when you are moving tables around (Levy, 2002; Smith, 2001).

Many classrooms do not have enough space to sit the whole class on the carpet and at tables without moving furniture during the lesson. The arrangement of tables and chairs must enable maximum flexibility while retaining a focal point. Horseshoes can provide the solution for this, particularly in upper Key Stage 2 where pupils may well feel unhappy about sitting on the carpet, seeing this as 'babyish', or where there is insufficient room for these larger pupils.

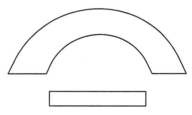

Within this arrangement or others used in whole class-teaching you will also need to consider where to place pupils who receive support from other adults or require additional resources to support their access to the content of the lesson. You will also need to organise the space so that you have easy access to all pupils to enable you to monitor and/or work with individuals, groups and the class. This should also include the pupils who are being supported by others during the lesson as you need to check that all pupils have the opportunity to achieve their potential.

One technique that has found favour recently is the need for 'brain gym' activities during the lesson. While there have been criticisms of the science behind this approach (see the Teacher Training Resource Bank, 'A Brain Gym Amnesty for Schools?' (**http://www.ttrb.ac.uk**) for the critique), pupils need focusing during the lesson to maintain their attention. Any physical orga-nisation of the furniture in the classroom needs to take account of the space required for activities such as the 'brain gym'. A direct criticism of all the pupils sitting at their tables for up to an hour without any movement is that this can result in a lack of motivation and concentration during the lesson. In Chapter 4 on planning you will be considering the need to plan linked activ-ities in focusing the learners' attention.

In this situation it is easy to monitor behaviour and attention to tasks, particularly during whole-class teaching. It does, however, have the disadvantage of potentially making it difficult to work with groups or for groups to work together in the main activity. Pupils who are being supported can be isolated at the edge of the class.

Tables facing in together can focus pupils on the task within a group and facilitate discussion while tables in lines or similar formations focus the pupil either on the whole-class task or on their own work.

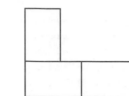

In choosing the layout of tables you also need to consider how easy each arrangement is for additional adults to work with individuals and/or groups.

Organising pupils on the carpet is equally important, to ensure everyone can see what is going on and to make it easy for you to monitor behaviour and focus on learning. You can also pick up on changes in posture and facial expression that can give you clues about pupils' understanding, which you can check through questioning. Small boards on the carpet can be better than working on a large chalkboard, whiteboard or IWB.

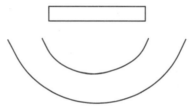

PRACTICAL TASK PRACTICAL TASK **PRACTICAL TASK** PRACTICAL TASK

Tables facing in together can focus pupils on the task within a group and facilitate discussion while tables in lines or similar formations focus the pupil either on the whole class task or on their own work. Try organising your classroom according to the type of work and evaluate the effect.

See Chapter 6 of Jacques and Hyland (2007) **Primary Professional Studies** *from Learning Matters and Chapter 2 in this book on the daily mathematics lesson.*

Objectives and how to share them

A key change with the introduction of the NNS was the need for teachers to be explicit about what they are teaching and what pupils are expected to learn. Before the introduction of the strategy many teachers did not share their expectations with pupils. You may have been into a classroom and seen the objectives/targets on the board or wall for numeracy lessons. Merely having them on display, however, is not sufficient. Since the objectives for the mental/oral and the main activity may be different we shall look at both phases of the lesson.

June, a leading mathematics teacher (LMT) in an infant school, described what she does:

> *I have a clear child-friendly written objective for each part of the lesson. Right at the beginning I get the class, or sometimes an individual, to read the objective with me and say what we are going to do, e.g. to improve our counting in tens and fives from any number and back again.*

She then counts with her class using a counting stick as a prompt. When the counting has finished and all the questions have been asked June then reviews the mental/oral phase with her class, asking them if they think they have improved and specifically praising particular pupils who have worked hard. She then moves on to the main activity part of the lesson, again asking the class or an individual to read the objective, and questions their understanding of what the objective actually means. During the plenary she returns to the main activity objective and each part is reviewed. In this way the teaching and learning for all parts of the lesson is made explicit to all learners.

Once objectives have been shared with pupils they should be displayed on the board or somewhere prominent in the classroom so that the teacher or the pupils can refer to them at any point in the lesson. This emphasises exactly what you are all working towards.

Many teachers use projected PowerPoint presentations as part of their teaching. In relation to the objectives this has a significant advantage as the objectives can be shared on a slide with the class and can be left on display during their work. Some teachers find it useful to copy the slide with the objectives on and add this to the end of their presentation, ensuring that they return to the objectives in the plenary when reviewing the learning that has taken place. These could even be annotated using the IWB facilities to assist with evaluation and assessment.

Sharing the objectives with pupils remains an issue in observed lessons as it is clear from the following comment in the 2005 evaluation of the Primary National Strategy: 'Objectives are not always clear or discussed fully so that pupils are left wondering where the lesson is heading (HMI/Ofsted, 2005). For trainees it is often the first thing to be forgotten when they are being observed so this is an important teaching strategy that needs to be embedded into your practice.

The role of talk in the classroom

As part of the Primary National Strategy (PNS) the role of speaking and listening has been given a high priority. We tend not to think of mathematics as a subject that promotes discussion and the development of language skills yet there is a wealth of opportunities for talk in the mathematics lesson. The first area that will be explored here is questioning.

Questioning pupils is a key teaching strategy in the PNS. It can be used to:

- **assess pupils' understanding;**
- **assess errors and misconceptions;**
- **unpack pupils' methods;**
- **focus discussion by using pupils' ideas;**
- **elicit concrete examples of principles or concepts;**
- **explore language and vocabulary;**
- **encourage reflection.**

See Chapter 8 for Jacques and Hyland (2007) **Primary Professional Studies** *from Learning Matters.*

There are two main types of questions that you will use in teaching, closed and open. Closed questions usually require one-word or brief responses whereas open questions require more extensive responses.

There are different times in the three-part lesson when you will want to use these types of questions. In the mental/oral phase most of the questions are likely to be closed as you will be keeping the pace brisk and therefore you won't want extended explanations from pupils. The questions are likely to be:

- **How many?**
- **How much?**
- **What would...?**
- **What are...?**

In the main activity you will want to find out more about pupils' understanding and to use pupils' ideas to focus discussion about concepts. The questions are likely to be:

- **How did you work that out?**
- **Tell me how you decided to work it out that way.**
- **What does this mean and can you give me an example?**
- **Can you explain how you did that?**

Brown and Wragg (1993, p. 18) describe the common errors in questioning:

- **asking too many questions;**
- **asking a question and answering it yourself;**
- **asking questions only of the brightest or most likeable;**
- **asking a really difficult question too early;**
- **asking irrelevant questions;**
- **asking the same types of questions;**
- **asking questions in a threatening way;**
- **not indicating a change in the type of question;**
- **not using probing questions;**
- **not giving pupils the time to think;**
- **not correcting wrong answers;**
- **failing to see the implications of answers;**
- **failing to build on answers.**

Some of the issues raised by Brown and Wragg have implications for different parts of the PNS lesson. Not giving pupils time to answer can be difficult in the mental/oral phase as if pupils are given too long the pace drops and pupils lose the brisk start to their lesson. The match of pupil to question is also crucial to allow pupils to be able to answer while providing the right level of challenge.

A strategy to avoid this occurring that can be employed is to give a pupil a question and give them time to think about an answer and, while they are doing that perhaps supported by an additional adult, you can ask several further questions of others in the class. You then return to the pupil who has been given time for a response which enables you to keep the pace high and helps everyone reach their potential. It also assists with classroom management as the majority of the class are not losing their attention on the tasks given. An alternative strategy can be to use talk partners where pupils talk to a partner rehearsing their responses to questions. Everyone is involved and everyone has time to consider their response. Talk partners can be used to solve questions where they share a small whiteboard to jot down their ideas and any notes required to assist them. These ideas for extending the strategies used link to the following Research Summary from the area of assessment.

RESEARCH SUMMARY RESEARCH SUMMARY RESEARCH SUMMARY

Asking the right questions in the right way

From work on formative assessment or assessment for learning Black and Wiliam (1998) discuss the issue of asking questions in the right way. Questioning can be an effective means of finding out what pupils have understood. All too often, as research has shown, teachers unconsciously inhibited learning by:

- **trying to direct the pupil towards giving the expected answer;**
- **not providing enough quiet time for pupils to think out the answer;**
- **asking mainly questions of fact.**

Black and Wiliam suggest that teachers can break this cycle when they give pupils:

- **time to respond;**
- **opportunities to discuss their thinking in small groups;**
- **a choice between several possible answers and the chance to vote on the options;**
- **opportunities to write down their answers from which teachers then read out a few.**

All these strategies can be used in all phases of the daily mathematics lesson.

REFLECTIVE TASK
REFLECTIVE TASK

Review the last mathematics lesson you observed or taught. Using the suggestions from Black and Wiliam did the lesson allow pupils any of these opportunities? How could you alter the next lesson in order to allow these suggestions to be incorporated into your lesson?

'Follow-me' cards can be helpful here as giving the answer – for example, the doubles of numbers can give pupils an opportunity to work out which question they should be listening for. What can also help pupils with the pace of the mental/oral phase is to tell them what kinds of question you are going to ask and when you are going to change the format of the questions. This will particularly support the less able pupils in any class.

In the main activity and plenary phases the type of questions will probe pupils understanding. In these phases you will be able to allow pupils longer to answer questions and to explore their ideas and those of others.

For more detail on probing questions see p. 80, Chapter 5.

Not seeing the implications of the answers to questions is more difficult to address and relies upon your own understanding of the connections between areas of mathematics. An example of this might be the able pupil who is able to see connections and also flaunts the rules by moving the decimal point when dividing and multiplying by ten. While this is all right for the pupil who has a clear understanding of the underlying principles involved there are problems with this type of explanation being articulated in the classroom for all to hear. The decimal point doesn't actually move – it is the digits that move places and change their value, and pupils who do not have a clear understanding of place value could potentially increase their misconceptions if you do not intervene after a response such as this. The pupil who offered this explanation should be thanked and a clear model should be provided for the whole class. The same applies to short cuts that are not generalisable, such as adding a zero when you multiply by ten, which does not make any difference with decimals.

It is very easy to fall into the trap of asking questions of pupils, which merely elicit information about what they already know and do not assist in the progression of their learning. Across the daily lesson there must be a balance of asking and telling through demonstration and modelling.

Girls and boys

One issue in relation to talk in mathematics is gender. If you are asking questions, who are you asking? Do you ask as many girls as boys? This is a difficult question if the class you are working with has a disproportionate number of one or the other gender but it is an important question to ask. Groups can dominate questioning sessions as they want to get noticed, or you may be using a question to refocus a pupil's attention on the lesson putting them on the spot to check if they have been paying attention.

PRACTICAL TASK PRACTICAL TASK PRACTICAL TASK PRACTICAL TASK

Record yourself during a mathematics lesson and then listen for the type of questions you use. Do you use some types of questions more than others? Are these types of questions used at particular times during the lesson? How could you increase the range of questions you use? Try writing down the starts of questions to use in your lessons. You might also find that particular groups of pupils are asked more questions than others. What kind of questions assist you in helping pupils to make connections between areas of mathematics? After you have worked on this aspect of your teaching you might suggest that it is an agreed focus for observation by your tutor or teacher.

Introducing and using vocabulary

Among the training materials for schools is a CD-ROM containing a bank of all the words from the vocabulary book sectioned in key stages and topic areas. Small labels can be printed out on A4 paper for display or for use with a group. Larger size labels for whole class can be made either by altering the type size of the original labels or by using a program like Publisher to produce banners.

Once you have the vocabulary that you need for a specific topic then you need to think about how you will introduce this to the class. Try to look for words that go together rather than just going through the vocabulary associated with a topic in the first lesson and assuming that the pupils will be able to use the appropriate language when required. Pupils need to be introduced to the words to know what they mean, have their use modelled for them in lessons and have opportunities for practising their use in the appropriate contexts. As each new word is introduced try to give an example of what it means, such as 'factor, one of two numbers which when multiplied together give another number – for example, two factors of 12 are 2 and 6.' Over a number of lessons using the same vocabulary different examples could be added each day. Single examples can lead pupils to think that the vocabulary applies only for specific cases rather than generalisable items. This links to the discussion earlier in the chapter about questioning and how this can help pupils make connections.

You could also select a number of words and ask the class if they are associated with the topic or not. If they are you can ask pupils to give you an example of the connection between the vocabulary and the topic. An example of this would be 'how many?' This is an interesting example as it can apply to a number of topics: 'How many would I have if I multiplied 3 by 4?', 'How many would I have if I added 4 to 2?', 'How many is 16 divided by 4?' Other vocabulary is more specific such as the terms 'product' or 'parallel'.

Demonstrating and modelling

In relation to teaching strategies, demonstrating and modelling is of key importance to delivering an effective lesson. In 2005 an evaluation of the Primary National Strategy teaching still remained no better than satisfactory in one in three lessons. A key aspect of successful and effective lessons is the way that the teacher demonstrates and models for the pupils during all phases of the lesson.

Mental methods

There is considerable debate about whether it is actually possible to teach mental methods. It is possible to teach a range of strategies from which pupils can choose the most appropriate for the particular question.

RESEARCH SUMMARY RESEARCH SUMMARY **RESEARCH SUMMARY**

Tall et al. (2001) have discussed many of the key issues relating to procedural and conceptual thinking. They focus on the pupils' attention during actions on objects when calculating. Often 5 + 3 can be seen as arrays of objects which pupils imagine in order to combine the quantities. For some pupils seeing arithmetic in terms of mental images of objects persists and this prevents them from moving into the higher realms of mathematics. These pupils rely heavily on counting strategies, which increase the possibilities for errors with increasing number size. The higher achievers seem to focus more on the symbolism itself. They utilise known facts and move away from counting strategies more quickly, seeing the relationships between numbers.

The reason for highlighting the recent but ongoing research above is that it has an important message for teachers. Counting methods are fine as a starting point but pupils can't continue to rely upon them if they are to be successful with mathematics. When you teach mental methods you will need to emphasise the relationship between counting activities and move towards known facts. If counting in 3s, for example, the links should be made to the 3 times table if counting starts at 0. Showing pupils that it is easier to count on from the larger of two numbers than to continue to 'count all' is important before pupils begin to work with larger numbers. An example reported by a student involved a pupil counting out 62 Multilink cubes in order to add on another two-digit number. The potential for errors using this method is great. The counting strategy here is not appropriate.

Encouraging pupils to hold numbers in their head during calculation can be assisted by using arrow or number cards to act as a store and provide a visual reminder of the number to be held. Holding numbers in your head requires practice and will not come easily to all pupils. Different pupils will need differing kinds of support. Some will find the visual support helpful; others will find listening to the sound of the numbers easier to work with.

Mental strategies will be taught in the introduction to the main activity to the whole class. The pace of the teaching will be slower than the mental/oral phase where the emphasis is on rapid recall and rehearsal of skills. The main activity is where the clear demonstration and modelling occurs.

One concern over the emphasis on mental methods in the PNS is that these will become the 'new algorithms' and the only ways of working. The important issue with mental methods is that to work effectively they need to be generalisable, that is work for a range of situations, not just one specific case. A good strategy is to show pupils different ways that you might have worked out a calculation mentally. The reason for this is that if you are teaching strategies to pupils then they tend to apply the strategies you have taught or use those that they have confidence with. The latter are likely to be earlier strategies that pupils revert to if not clear about new ways of working. Your demonstrations offer pupils the opportunity to see different ways of thinking.

You can also model your own use of known facts to show pupils how you can explain what you did without just saying 'I knew it'. For example, to double 60 you might say you know that 'double' is the same as ×2, that 2×6 is 12 and that 60 is ten times bigger than 6. So the answer will also be ten times bigger, or 120. Developing number facts can be emphasised by looking at 'turn arounds' or commutativity, i.e. for addition and multiplication the order of the calculation doesn't matter: $2 \times 3 = 6$ and $3 \times 2 = 6$ or $6 + 3 = 9$ and $3 + 6 = 9$. If we know one of each pair of known facts we automatically know the other in the case of addition and multiplication.

Other ways of encouraging mental mathematics are as follows.

- **Place a number on the back of a pupil or on a headband and either they can ask questions of the rest of the class or the class can make statements to assist them in guessing what the number is.**
- **The same activity can be used with a shape displayed on the pupil.**
- **The same kind of activity can be undertaken except that the pupil out at the front has the number or shape and the rest of the class have to ask questions of the individual in order to find out what it is. This strategy can be problematic with younger or less able pupils and so the number, a picture of a shape or the shape itself can assist the pupils to remember the item chosen.**
- **Pupils can do this activity in pairs where they write a number to attach to each other's headband and then have to ask each other questions to find out what they have.**
- **Quick draw tables – the class is in two teams; each select a player and when a question is asked the pupil who answers first gains a point for their team. You need to make sure that the teams are reasonably evenly matched.**

The empty number line

RESEARCH SUMMARY RESEARCH SUMMARY **RESEARCH SUMMARY**

Meindert Beishuizen (1999) describes the use of an empty number line for teaching calculating strategies in Holland, which developed out of experiences with the new 'realistic' textbooks during the 1980s. Research at Leiden University led to a new project with the empty number line between 1992 and 1996 from an idea by Treffers and De Moor (1990). The empty number line combines the partitioning of numbers with mental methods of calculating. Beishuizen gives four arguments for the empty number line:

1. a higher level of mental activation in providing learning support;
2. a more natural and transparent model for number operations;
3. a model open to informal strategies which also provides support for pupils to develop more formal and efficient strategies;
4. a model enhancing the flexibility of mental strategies, in particular variations of N10.

(Adapted from Beishuizen, 1999)

The empty number line can be seen demonstrated several times in the PNS training materials which show Ian Sugarman working with several Key Stage 2 pupils with different addition and subtraction calculations. The video material shows how the strategy helps a pupil called Cheryl who is having difficulties with subtraction using decomposition. She appears to have little idea of how close numbers are to judge if her answer is correct. She ends up by taking the largest digit from the smallest regardless of its position in the calculation. Ian Sugarman then introduces her to using the empty number line and she is able to use this to solve the calculations.

Below are two examples which, though not specifically taken from the video material, show how a pupil can use this strategy to add and subtract:

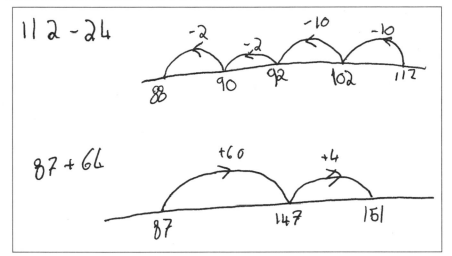

Demonstrating the empty number line

This is one informal calculating method on route towards the use of formal written algorithms based upon understanding. It must be stressed that this is not the only strategy that you will teach pupils but it is a natural progression from mental methods and informal written strategies.

The strategy described here is for subtraction but it can be clearly be used for different kinds of calculation. To begin with, you would demonstrate subtracting multiples of 10, first singly then as multiples:

For more on using an empty number line see pp. 128–129, Chapter 8.

64 – 30

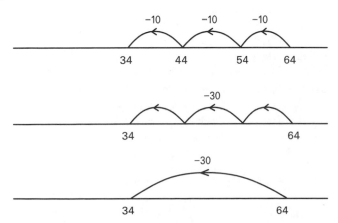

Then partition the number, which could be achieved by counting back to find the answer:

64 − 33

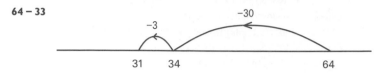

Or focus on the difference and count up from the number to be subtracted:

64 − 33

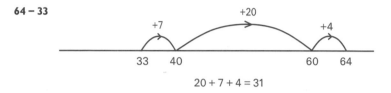

$$20 + 7 + 4 = 31$$

The choice between these two ways of using the number line depends upon the mental methods that you are emphasising. Pupils are also likely to adapt these methods to link them with their own mental strategies. This method can be seen as a bridge between mental strategies and written algorithms. Once you have decided how you will demonstrate the use of the empty number line you will need to ask pupils to also demonstrate this strategy. It can be a particularly useful method to reinforce the proximity of numbers:

For more on the progression of written strategies see p. 127, Chapter 8.

101 − 97

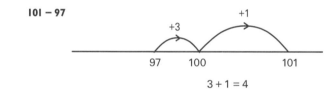

$$3 + 1 = 4$$

When larger numbers are introduced pupils can often think that it means the answers are going to be large. They are not looking at the relative size of both numbers.

Creative and alternative starting points for teaching

One of the newer areas for development within the PNS is that of creativity. In this chapter we will look briefly at creative teaching strategies and we will return to planning these in the following chapter. One criticism of the PNS has been the effect that it has had on teacher's creativity in their approaches to teaching mathematics. All mathematics lessons look very similar with the three-part structure. Using pupils to physically model mathematics gives an alternative approach and makes the learning memorable for the learners. Starting with sales advertisements from magazines and newspapers to begin a lesson on percentages gives you a teaching strategy that can link with setting an appropriate homework task. Every Child Matters (ECM) focuses on the need to break down the barriers to children's learning. Since children do not all learn in the same way it is important to offer different approaches to teaching and learning. The following example illustrates using a book as a starting point for a lesson.

Using a book as a starting point

English is not the only the subject for which books can be used as part of the teaching strategy. Many commercial mathematics schemes include large textbooks to introduce topics either through text, which includes worked examples of calculation strategies, for example, or stories which are used to introduce concepts like subtraction. Ordinary storybooks can also provide a different way to start the main activity.

CLASSROOM STORY

In order to introduce multiplication ×2 to a class of Year 1 Sue started by telling a short version of the story of Noah's ark where the animals were entering the ark two by two. Sue had prepared a display of an ark with a ramp to the door, which she then used to allow pairs of animals to enter the ark, counting in twos with the class. The differentiated worksheets she gave the class were all about the animals entering the ark.

Although this could be seen as creating an artificial context for the mathematics the teacher wanted to make the lesson interesting and offer images that might assist the pupils in remembering multiples of two. It also provided interest and a different approach for the class so adding the notion of novelty.

It can be helpful in focusing pupils' attention if you sometimes present things in different and novel ways. The important issue for teaching like this is that the mathematics must be explicit regardless of the context.

Below is part of the lesson plan to show how Sue planned to use the story as a starting point.

NC ref. 2a, 3b NNS Year 1 number and number system 4	Learning objectives *By the end of the lesson most pupils will be able to recognise even numbers.* *By the end of the lesson most pupils will be able to count in twos.*
Vocabulary *Even, lots of, how many?, altogether, more, counted.*	
Resources *Where next Mr Noah?* *Differentiated worksheets*	Assessment criteria *Pupils can give examples of even numbers.* *Pupils can count in twos – note how far.*
Use of story *This story is familiar to the class but I have not used this for mathematics. I want to offer a different image for pupils to assist them in recalling multiples of two. Provides a varied main activity and should motivate pupils to take part.*	Use of display *Before lesson prepared a display board with an ark and cut-outs of pairs of animals. Later I plan for the pupils to add pairs of animals to the display.*

PRACTICAL TASK PRACTICAL TASK PRACTICAL TASK PRACTICAL TASK

Try to find a book that you could use as the starting point for introducing vocabulary, a specific concept or investigation for a class. The PNS training materials also has a useful list of books as a starting point for your search. Think about how the book would assist the pupils' visualisation, concept definition or concept image.

The use of the review (plenary) in mathematics

The plenary session, which is unsatisfactory in one in six lessons, is still the least successful part of the daily mathematics lesson. (Ofsted, 2001)

The plenary is the most challenging part of the numeracy lesson and is often swallowed up by tidying up or becomes a reporting-back session for the groups/individuals that the teacher has not worked with. In an effort to raise the profile of this part of the lesson we suggest thinking about setting up challenges during the main activity teaching time to return to in the plenary. Some examples of this would be to use one of the wipe-off sheets that are now more widely available which have scales, rulers or other measures on. On one of these sheets add the appropriate objects to be weighed and the scale. Ask specific groups or the whole class to think about how they might solve the challenge for the plenary and ask them to think about it as they are working during the main activity. Alternatively a question could be raised, again to be solved during the plenary, and put on a board for reference during the main activity working time. Or you could set a practical task, say a bag of different length snakes that you want the pupils to sort by length from longest to shortest. This task would give you another opportunity to use the appropriate vocabulary of shorter, longer, longest, shortest or shorter than, etc.

> **PRACTICAL TASK** PRACTICAL TASK **PRACTICAL TASK** PRACTICAL TASK
>
> Design three challenges that you might use in a plenary for a lesson on measures.

Classroom management in mathematics lessons

Classroom management can support an effective mathematics lesson. One area that you can develop is setting the time and expectations for pupils, especially when they are given more independent work.

When you move from whole-class work during the introduction of the main activity to group/paired/individual work, the pace of work will inevitably fall. Even though the pace will be different it is your job as teacher to keep the pupils focused on their task. Before pupils move to their tables or begin to work more independently they need you to tell them what you expect in terms of the amount of work to be completed during this part of the lesson.

One strategy used by a Year 3 teacher involves setting the clock hands. One of the pupils then draws what the clock will look like when the time is up and the class knows at that point they need to stop work and return to the carpet for the plenary. This reinforces work on the concept of time, which is one of the hardest in mathematics, as well as the expectations of the pupils, particularly those not working with the teacher. When seen in action, the pupils in this class are obviously used to this way of working. It is a strategy you would have to introduce gradually before the class are able to look at the work, look at the clock and stop on time.

See Chapter 7 of Jacques and Hyland (2007) **Primary Professional Studies** *from Learning Matters.*

Working with a group

When working with a group the first thing is to ensure that the rest of the class are settled, so you might give your chosen group time to write the date and the objective while you check on everyone else. You could give them a reinforcing activity with a time limit, e.g. how many number sentences they can answer in 5 minutes. Once you know everyone is settled, you can sit with the group. Make sure that you position yourself where you can see the whole class by looking up even though you are predominantly focusing on one group.

This is an important teaching and management strategy since, as the teacher, you are responsible for the whole class, regardless of who else is working in the class. You can't assume that a group will be all right if they have adult support. The adult might want your support as well as the pupils during the lesson.

Another good teaching strategy is, where possible, to have the group near to a board on which everyone can record words, ways of working, questions and answers. This can be quite difficult for every group in the class and can mean that some groups spend a lot of the lesson on the carpet when during the main activity you might want them to record or work with equipment. An alternative is to take a small board to the group to use with them; if one is not available then a small easel with paper attached is a good substitute.

Transitions and how to manage them

Transitions between the phases of the three-part lesson can be one of the most difficult areas for the trainee teacher. It is the time when pupils have more opportunity to talk and interact with each other and consequently the noise level often rises. Time is often lost from the numeracy lesson as a result of pupils not settling to the next part of the lesson. Below are a few ways which you might consider to manage these transitions.

- **Keep pupils at their tables during the whole lesson – this has the disadvantage of not providing a slight break for pupils so they can refocus their attention but it does cut down the movement around the class.**
- **Move groups one at a time, so from the mental/oral and introduction of the main activity send one group at a time to settle to the main activity in groups/pairs or individually. This way you can see the group settle before sending the others. It might be useful to keep the group you are going to work with until last when the rest of the class are settled and you can move with this last group and be able to start work with them. The disadvantage is the amount of time this might take at least to begin with until the class is used to settling quickly. You could either have equipment out on the tables ready or have specific pupils responsible for collecting materials for class.**
- **Don't clear up at the end of the main activity before the plenary. The plenary can often be swallowed up by the tidying up time. Do the plenary first, then send all pupils or one per table back to tidy quickly before moving on to the next lesson or a break. Before a break pupils are definitely quicker to tidy.**
- **Use the time and expectations to trigger pupils moving to the plenary.**
- **You may also use the transitions to introduce a 'brain gym' activity which will allow pupils some movement before refocusing on their work.**

See p. 18, this chapter.

Practical mathematics and how to organise

See Chapter 7 of Jacques and Hyland **Primary Professional Studies** *from Learning Matters.*

The practical aspects of mathematics concern many teachers because of the organisational issues. The idea of having 30 pupils all working with water at the same time is clearly the stuff of nightmares! Doing some aspects of practical mathematics as a whole class is a non-starter unless you have a lot of assistance in the class. There are also the obvious considerations of the amount of equipment needed for a whole class to undertake practical work at the same time. If you haven't got assistance in the classroom then many pupils may make significant errors or continue to hold misconceptions about weight, for example, if you or another adult are not there to check and to interact with them. Nor will you be in a position to assess pupils' understanding accurately without observation.

So how can you organise so that you can see what pupils are doing? You need to consider what some pupils can do by themselves while you work with another group or two. It may be possible to consider a more limited differentiation for these lessons, at least to begin with. You might decide to work with half the class while the other half are working on reinforcing their number skills in a measures context, e.g. adding and subtracting weights. Working with half the class means that you have the opportunity directly to teach pupils how to use a bucket balance or scales before they have an opportunity to practise these skills. In the next lesson the halves of the class would swap over. If you work with just one group you would possibly be looking at three lessons to fit in each of the levels of differentiation.

The first thing that you need to make sure is that the level of the work given to pupils who will work on their own is right. The match between pupils and task is crucial in enabling pupils to get on by themselves practising a skill or using a strategy you have demonstrated in the introduction to the main activity.

In all situations where you are working with a group pupils need to be 'trained' to know when it is appropriate to interrupt you. You could give them a set of ideas to follow before coming to you. A suggested list might be as follows.

- **Read through any instructions carefully.**
- **Ask a friend.**
- **Read through your work to check answers.**
- **Make sure that you have not got any other work that you can do first before going to your teacher.**
- **Use a calculator to check answers.**

You also need to plan times to monitor the rest of the class during the main activity and pick up on pupils who might be off task.

Many texts for teaching measures ask pupils to estimate and then measure. One of the difficulties that pupils have is they can find the estimating difficult. A misconception many pupils hold is that the estimate has to be accurate. In order to move pupils away from this view of measures and, particularly, estimating, first give them plenty of opportunity to measure items. Once pupils have had experience of measuring they can then make sensible estimates for items. Thinking about estimating to the nearest 100 g or nearest 10 cm, depending on the item to be measured, can give pupils a clearer idea of how they might begin to estimate. Activities like 'show me 1 cm or 10 cm' and 'how far can you hold your fingers apart' in a mental/oral phase of a lesson can also assist pupils in visualising measures.

Using displays

Displays of mathematics in many classrooms have been limited to tesselation and data handling. Mathematics displayed around the classroom gives a different view of mathematics which pupils might otherwise only associate with the images in their books.

Displays can form part of your teaching strategies for mathematics as they can offer pupils different images of mathematics to assist them in making the connections between the various aspects of the subject. For example, displays of calculation strategies used in previous lessons can be referred to during future lessons to remind pupils about the strategies you have already introduced and/or how these link to new strategies.

Number lines and number squares might be part of a semi-permanent display but can also be used to emphasise specific issues such as 'difference'.

Some other suggestions of how you could use displays as part of your teaching strategies are as follows:

- details of the controls for a computer program/interactive whiteboard program that you are going to use with your class;
- vocabulary and the pupils' explanations of the terms;
- problems to be solved, which can act as extension/homework tasks associated with the series of lessons being taught (this will need to be changed as the topic changes);
- examples of strategies being taught;
- a record of an activity – for example, pupils in a reception class had to walk along a tree on the floor which had two branches, to decide if they liked apples or not and place their name on an apple on the appropriate branch of the tree. This work was later displayed on the wall and referred back to by the teacher;
- examples of practical applications of topics, particularly measure;
- examples of practical applications of number e.g. percentage reductions and the language that is used to describe this in shops;
- how to use a calculator and its function keys;
- number or shape of the day/week as a focus of a collection of items for younger pupils to add to;
- display of storybooks associated with a topic, e.g. size – *'You'll soon grow into them, Titch'*;
- display of non-fiction books about numbers, shapes, measures, encouraging pupils to read mathematics books.

PRACTICAL TASK PRACTICAL TASK **PRACTICAL TASK** PRACTICAL TASK

Make a note of the displays in classrooms you visit and any ways in which the teachers use the displays in their teaching.

The use of ICT in teaching mathematics

Information communication technology covers a wide range of resources to support the teaching and learning of mathematics in the primary classroom.

Using an overhead projector as a teaching strategy

The overhead projector can be used in a variety of ways to enhance teaching strategies. The following is a starting point for thinking about how you might use this piece of equipment in teaching mathematics.

Focusing on visual scanning

By putting number sequences or patterns on the overhead with items missing or pieces added you can use questions such as 'What is missing?', 'What has changed?', 'What is the pattern?' The following list provides some examples.

- **For Reception a number sequence could read '1, 2, 3, □, 5'.**
  The question would be 'What number is missing?' You could either ask the pupils as a group to show you what is missing or you could ask an individual to come out and write the missing number in the gap.
- **For Year 2 the sequence could be '85, □, 91, □, 102'.**
  As before, you could either ask the group as a whole to fill in the gaps or get an individual pupil to write in what is missing.
- **For Year 5 you could use a similar technique with the sequence '–9, □, –5, □, –1'.**

Focusing on predicting

- **Using a shape under a piece of paper –**
  What is the shape, does your prediction change as you gain more information?
- **Unfinished shape drawn just with lines or maybe using co-ordinates –**
  At what point can you decide what the shape is?
- **Using pupils as a function machine where they record the number they are given by another pupil and the result after they have performed an operation on the number. After more recording does the prediction change? Which numbers are useful to try in order to work out what has happened to the number? Does the same apply if there are two operations used?**
- **For Year 2 as an example on a number line placing in the halves from 0-5, □ , $1\frac{1}{2}$, etc.**

Focusing on checking procedures

Here the overhead is clearly a useful means of checking the accuracy of pupils working with other technology such as a calculator or with specific mathematical methods:

- **Using an overhead calculator to check correct strategies for using a calculator.**
- **Pupils explaining written methods e.g. informal, empty number line or towards formal algorithms, grid method for multiplication.**

You could also allow the pupils to ask the questions. With any of the above suggestions the pupils could be in control of setting the questions to other members of the class.

The interactive whiteboard

Many of the features in the activities using an overhead projector can be exploited using an interactive whiteboard (IWB) in more and more classrooms. These are usually connected to a tablet or individual laptop or PC enabling access to a wide range of resources on the web. Here are two examples:

Big talking calculator

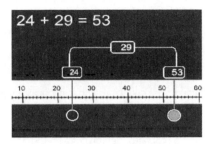

Number lines

This type of equipment means that you don't have to reinvent the resources to use with an overhead projector or other devices. You can use the programs directly from the web. Many exploit the interactive functions of the boards so that pupils can touch the screen and move items around to write on the board with the special pens. IWBs can enhance mathematical modelling and improve the quality of interactions during whole-class teaching. Using an IWB enables the teacher to increase the pace of the lesson when appropriate and can help redress the balance in making resources and planning for teaching.

It is important to note that although an IWB can be used effectively to support interactive whole-class teaching it should only be used when it contributes to the specific development of mathematics objectives. An IWB should be used to complement alternative teaching and learning strategies such as the use of practical apparatus, digit cards, number fans, counters and dice. Showing images on the IWB will support visual learners in particular but those who are kinaesthetic learners will be supported by the use of practical equipment so it is important to balance the use of different kinds of resources.

Using a computer

In Chapter 4 a way is suggested way of organising the daily maths lesson in a computer suite. In terms of teaching strategies we will look here at a situation where there is one computer for the class during a maths lesson.

Look carefully at the objectives for the lesson. How might they be enhanced by the use of ICT?

The following examples are brief descriptions of lessons which incorporate ICT. The plans are not given in detail but are designed to give you an outline of how you might think about the situation in different ways.

Key Stage 2 Year 6

Key objective
Make turns; estimate, draw and measure angles.

Mental/oral

Activities focusing on the degrees needed to add to numbers to make a right angle (90°) or straight line (180°), or how many more degrees than a right angle and a straight line. Rapid recall of facts. Then each pupil has a set of cards with the following words on: acute, right angle, obtuse, reflex, and they are asked to choose an appropriate card when the teacher says a number of degrees.

Main activity

Recap on the definitions and vocabulary and ways of remembering acute and obtuse: *a* before *o* in the alphabet, *A* looks like an acute angle. Draw upon ideas from the class.

Using a protractor demonstrate on the board how to measure. Get pupils to come out and try with a board-size protractor or one on an overhead projector.

Group activities

1. *Higher attainers*. Challenge to draw triangles with acute, obtuse, right angles and combinations. Which can you draw, which can't you draw and why?
   Draw several different triangles and rearrange the angles to show the sum of internal angles in a triangle.
2. *Average attainers*. Worksheet with angles to estimate and then measure. This group will then draw angles for each other.
3. *Lower attainers*. Worksheet and pairs on the computer. The program on the ICT and mathematics package from NNS offers opportunities to estimate angles of different sizes and gain instant feedback of the accuracy of the estimates. You can start with estimates to the nearest 10°.

Teacher to work with groups 2 and 3, paying particular attention to the measuring of angles and the use of the protractor which need to be checked individually.

Plenary/Review

Brief feedback on the computer program from those working on this during the lesson. Over a series of lessons more pupils will work on the computer. Split class into half: one half to ask questions of the other about the types of angles and/or questions such as 'give an example of an acute angle'.

Key Stage 1 Year 1

Key objective

Know by heart addition and subtraction facts – for all numbers up to and including 5 and pairs of numbers that total 10.

Mental/oral

Using paddles rapid recall of +/− facts up to 20 to cover range of ability.

Main activity

Focus on increasing known facts and modelling number sentences from the same three numbers, for example:

$$4 + 5 = 9 \quad 5 + 4 = 9 \quad 9 - 5 = 4 \quad \text{and} \quad 9 - 4 = 5$$

Group activities

1. *Higher attainers*. Box of numbers from which group chooses two different numbers to form as many sentences as they can as in the introduction of the main activity. Record favourite set of different numbers for display. Teacher to work with this group.
2. *Average attainers*. Developing number software complement of numbers to 10. Pupils to work in pairs with a classroom assistant to practise number bonds. Others to practise number bonds to 10, addition and subtraction. The classroom assistant will need to know what kinds of questions to ask pupils and the kinds of interventions that would be appropriate.
3. *Lower attainers*. Number facts to 5. This group to use stamps of objects to record their sentences and/or stamps of numbers to record sentences. Large strip of card on which to record their favourite sentences for display.

Plenary/review

Using the activity that the higher attainers have been working on focus on introducing the idea of the missing number in a sentence and how pupils can use known facts to solve these problems. More work on this in the next lesson.

Alternative strategies using ICT

1. Alternative strategies for using a computer would be to teach the use of a specific program to an individual, pair or small group and then get the pupils to teach others in the class how to use the same program. This is the cascade model.
2. Not all pupils need to use the same program as programs meet pupils' needs in different ways. It is not always necessary to use ICT with all pupils. Sometimes you may find yourself under pressure to ensure that everyone in the class has had a turn, particularly with regard to the use of the computer. Doing so may mean not so much focusing on the objectives for teaching mathematics but rather focusing on the need to increase ICT skills. These are not the same things and in mathematics teaching it is the mathematics objectives that are important.
3. You could demonstrate with ICT to the whole class if you have projection facilities, or perhaps onto an interactive white board.
4. You might use a program for checking specific cases if pupils are working on an investigative task. An example of this for Reception/Year 1 is the river crossing problem where you have two girls and two women to get across a river. The boat will only take one woman or two girls and all have to travel across the river. Pupils can work on the problem away from the computer but then check their solutions on the computer at different points in their investigation. For Year 5/6 you might have the class working on the handshakes problem where people are introduced and must shake hands once with each other. The number of people increases and hence the number of handshakes. How many handshakes for 10 people? For 20 more? You could use a program like Mystic Rose to enable pupils to check answers to specific cases as they work towards generalisation.

A SUMMARY OF **KEY POINTS**

> **Teaching strategies should encourage pupils to make connections between aspects of mathematics that will assist progression in learning.**
> **Effective teaching strategies include sharing the learning objectives with the pupils.**
> **Effective teaching strategies include using a variety of stimuli to aid pupils' mathematical thinking.**

> Effective teaching strategies make full use of the time available for teaching and learning.
> Effective teaching strategies make use of a range of questions with an awareness of the implications of your choice of questions on teaching and learning.
> Effective teaching strategies make appropriate use of ICT when it supports the progress of learning against the objectives for the lesson or series of lessons.
> Pupils need to be set clear targets for the amount of work to be completed, particularly in the main activity.
> There is a variety of strategies for effective classroom organisation.
> There is a variety of strategies for effective teacher demonstration and modelling.
> There is a variety of strategies for the use of resources in the teaching and learning of mathematics.

Moving on

In order to develop your teaching strategies during your NQT year you may consider arranging to observe colleagues teach in your school and/or arrange to observe leading mathematics teachers or advanced skills teachers in other local schools. You will also gain feedback from observations of your teaching during this year and you and your mentor will discuss supporting the development aspects of teaching mathematics.

REFERENCES REFERENCES **REFERENCES** REFERENCES REFERENCES

Askew, M., Brown, M., Rhodes, V., Wiliam, D. and Johnson, D. (1997) *Effective Teachers of Numeracy: Report of a Study Carried out for the Teacher Training Agency*. London: King's College, University of London.

Beishuizen, M. (1999) 'The empty number line as a new model', in Thompson, I. (ed.), *Issues in Teaching Numeracy in Primary Schools*. Buckingham: Open University Press.

Black, P. and Wiliam, D. (1998) *Inside the Black Box*. London: King's College.

Brown, G. and Wragg, E. C. (1993) *Questioning*. London: Routledge.

Levy, P. (2002) *Interactive Whiteboards in Learning and Teaching in Two Sheffield Schools: A Developmental Study*. Sheffield: Department of Information Studies, University of Sheffield.

Ofsted (2001) *The National Numeracy Strategy: The Second Year*. London: Ofsted.

Ofsted (2005) *Primary National Strategy: an evaluation of its impact in primary schools 2004/05*. London: Ofsted. See **http://www.ofsted.gov.uk/publications/index/cfm?fuseaction= pubs.displayfile&id=4117&type=doc**.

Qualifications and Curriculum Authority (QCA) (1999) *Teaching Written Calculation Strategies: Guidance for Teachers at Key Stage 1 and 2*. Sudbury: QCA.

Rogoff, B. and Lave, J. (eds) (1984) *Everyday Cognition: Its Development in a Social Context*. Cambridge, MA: Harvard University Press.

Smith, H. (2001) SmartBoard Evaluation: Final Report. Kent NGfL. See: **http://www.kented.org.uk/ ngfl/whiteboards/report.html**.

Tall, D., Gray, E., Bin Ali, M., Crowley, L., DeMarois, P., McGowen, M., Pitta, D., Pinto, M., Thomas, M. and Yusof, Y. (2001) 'Symbols and the bifurcation between procedural and conceptual thinking'. *Canadian Journal of Mathematics and Technology Education*, pp. 81–104, vol. 1, no. 1.

Treffers, A. and De Moor, E. (1990) *Specimen of a National Program for Primary Mathematics Teaching. Part 2: Basic Mental Skills and Written Algorithms*. Tilsburg: Zwijsen.

FURTHER READING   FURTHER READING   FURTHER READING

Anghileri, J. (ed.) (2001) *Principles and Practices in Arithmetic Teaching: Innovative Approaches for the Primary Classroom*. Buckingham: Open University Press.

Briggs, M. and Pritchard, A. (2002) *Using ICT in Primary Mathematics Teaching*. Exeter: Learning Matters.

Cockburn, A. (1999) *Teaching Mathematics with Insight: The Identification, Diagnosis and Remediation of Young Children's Mathematical Errors*. London: Falmer.

Dunne, E. and Bennett, N. (1990) *Talking and Learning in Groups: Activity Based In-service and Pre-service Materials*. London: Macmillan.

Fox, B., Montague-Smith, A. and Wilkes, S. (2000) *Using ICT in Primary Mathematics: Practice and Possibilities*. London: David Fulton.

Frobisher, L., Monaghan, J., Orton, A., Orton, J., Roper, T. and Threlfall, J. (1999) *Learning to Teach Number: A Handbook for Students and Teachers in the Primary School*. Cheltenham: Stanley Thornes.

Harries, T. and Spooner, M. (2000) *Mental Mathematics for the Numeracy Hour*. London: David Fulton.

Jacques, K. and Hyland, R. (eds) (2007) *Professional Studies: Primary Phase*. Exeter: Learning Matters.

Qualifications and Curriculum Authority (QCA) (1999) *Teaching Mental Calculation Strategies: Guidance for Teachers at Key Stage 1 and 2*. Sudbury: QCA.

Allen, J., Potter, J., Sharp, J., and Turvey, K. (2007) *Primary ICT Knowledge, Understanding and Practice*. Exeter: Learning Matters.

Thompson, I. (Ed.) (1997) *Teaching and Learning Early Number*. Buckingham: Open University Press.

Thompson, I. (Ed.) (1999) *Issues in Teaching Numeracy in Primary Schools*. Buckingham: Open University Press.

Wragg, E. C. and Brown, G. (1993) *Explaining*. London: Routledge.

Useful websites

http://www.coxhoe/durham.sch.uk/curriculum/Numeracy.htm#Links%20to%20Useful%20Sites

http://www.newdealedzone.com/whiteboardres.html

http://www.nwnet.org./uk/pages/maths/yr12/yr12.html

4
Planning

Professional Standards for the award of QTS

This chapter will support you as you work towards evidencing attainment against the following Standards:

Q15, Q19, Q20, Q24, Q27, Q28

Chapter objectives

By the end of this chapter you will have:

- **considered the different levels of planning in relation to the teaching and learning of mathematics;**
- **explored general issues about lesson planning;**
- **considered the planning required for any additional adults;**
- **considered the need for progression in pupils' learning;**
- **considered how to differentiate the activities and approaches within any given lesson;**
- **considered the use of resources;**
- **considered planning for the use of ICT by the teacher and by pupils;**
- **considered how to evaluate the lesson and how this information feeds forward into planning for the next lesson;**
- **considered setting targets for the future in relation to teaching and learning.**

Introduction

Planning is the area that can often be a source of conflict between trainees and their ITT institutions. One reason for this is that the model that some trainees see of teachers' planning in schools can be less detailed than that required of trainees. There are several reasons for this. The teacher in school is firstly not being assessed against the Standards. More importantly the teachers in school fully participate in discussions about planning at the different levels in school and therefore have ownership of the ideas and procedures. They also have experience and therefore do not always need to write down all the details in their plan. They have assimilated aspects of their professional knowledge so that it becomes second nature.

For more on general planning see Chapter 2 of Jacques and Hyland (2007) **Primary Professional Studies** *from Learning Matters.*

When thinking about this it is helpful to consider an example of something else that you may have learnt to do, such as drive a car. When you first start there appear to be many things to remember to do and all at the same time. With practice many aspects of driving become automatic. The same is true of planning and preparation for teaching.

Another key reason for planning lessons is that you do then have a plan to follow. It is easy, when you first start teaching, to become concerned about control and classroom management. If your planning is clear and detailed you will be able to pick up the threads of a lesson even after dealing with pupils in the classroom. With a mentor and/or class teacher it can be the focus of discussion for setting targets for you and the pupils. Effective planning should be seen as a support to enhance the teaching and learning, not purely as a chore. It will also enable you to stay closer to your objectives rather than be drawn into discussions about other areas of mathematics.

Levels of planning in school

There are three levels of planning in school – long-term, medium-term and short-term – although, including the weekly and daily sheets which most schools now use, there can be up to four levels. With the PNS the long- and medium-term plans are often merged. There are also unit plans available to support teachers' planning in mathematics.

Long-term planning

This planning is usually the focus for the whole school and is designed to ensure continuity and progression throughout the age range of the school for pupils in a subject area. In terms of coverage this level of planning should ensure that the requirements for the programmes of study in the National Curriculum are met for all pupils in the school. Some schools are using the medium-term plans from the first set of training materials for the implementation of NNS for their long/medium-term plans.

As a trainee the long- and medium-term planning is probably the level that you are likely to be given by the school, though you are unlikely to have access to staff discussion about this level of planning while you are on placement. If you do have the opportunity it is good experience to join in the discussions even if you will mainly be listening to the other teachers. It would also be worthwhile talking to teachers about how this plan was developed so that you can gain a sense of the process. However, this level of planning you will have to accept from the school.

Medium-term planning

Medium-term planning is in greater detail than the long-term planning and usually comprises half-term to termly blocks. As a trainee you may find yourself being given a school's existing medium-term plan or scheme of work. It can be difficult to work from someone else's plans as you may not have been part of the discussion about the order of topics or the amount of time to be given for teaching those topics. For the trainee it is worth making these plans your own by looking at the medium-term plan as the length of time for the placement in school and adding in appropriate detail to support your work and to address the specific standards related to planning in mathematics.

It can be particularly important to gain an overview of what is to be taught when dealing with a mixed year group class. You will need to ensure that the areas of mathematics to be covered by both years (if, say, a Year 1/2 class) coincide so that the same areas are being taught to the two year groups at the same time. This will make it easier to plan in the short term and for you to offer a coherent approach to all pupils regardless of year group.

Martin Skelton, writing for *Primary File* (1995, p. 35), suggests that a scheme of work should set out to ensure that:

- **what pupils are learning is appropriate;**
- **teachers are using the most appropriate ways of enabling pupils to learn;**
- **the school is able to deliver what it has planned;**
- **there is a degree of consistency in the experiences that teachers provide for pupils.**

Here is a suggested list of headings for a scheme of work or medium-term plan that you could use to add to a plan from a school or use for planning from scratch for the length of your placement.

NC ref/ PNS objs	Time scale	Previous knowledge	Teaching and learning objectives	Vocabulary, terms, definitions	Resources for mental/ oral and plenary	Resources for main activity

Organisation	Activities/ tasks	Assessment opportunities	Assessment criteria	Different-iation and challenge ref. to IEPs	H/w	Adult support for specific activities

In this level of planning the important issue to consider is the progression in learning expected of the pupils over the period of time the plan covers. It should take account of the pupils' prior knowledge and understanding and enable them to progress through the activities planned. This level of planning then acts as the guide to the short-term planning.

Learning objectives should appear in both medium- and short-term planning. In the medium-term plans these will be broad; for example, pupils will be taught to derive near doubles. In the short-term plans they will be more specific showing what you will be looking for in terms of a learning outcome; for example, pupils will give examples of known facts of doubles and explain how they will use these to derive near doubles. These need to be clearly defined and written in such a way that you will be able to collect evidence of whether or not pupils have achieved the objectives set. As an example of this, an objective could be stated as 'pupils will be able to describe the features of a triangle', or 'pupils will be able to explain orally their methods of calculating using short division'. If you state the objectives in terms of what pupils will know or understand, how will you be able to collect evidence of knowledge and/or understanding? When writing objectives the following words could be used to phrase an objective in order to make it easier for you to collect evidence of achievement:

state	**describe**	**give examples**
suggest reasons	**explain**	**evaluate**
pick out	**distinguish between**	**analyse**
carry out	**summarise**	**show diagrammatically**
compare	**demonstrate**	

This is not an extensive list but does give you some examples. If you use one of these starting points it is possible to include knowledge and understanding, for example 'pupils will be able to demonstrate their knowledge and understanding of multiplication by explaining orally their methods of calculating a two-digit by one-digit multiplication'. How do you know if you have worded the objectives for the lesson in an appropriate way? If you can see or hear a response to the statement then you have worded your objective to make initial assessment easier. Making judgements about whether or not pupils have achieved the objectives set for a lesson is part of the assessment process.

See Evaluations, p. 63, and Recording, Chapter 5.

Assessment should be an integral part of the medium- and short-term planning, it should not be seen as a bolt-on extra. In the current versions of the PNS medium-term plans there are a number of days allocated to assessment. It is worth finding out how schools are using this time – whether they are using specific assessment tools perhaps from a commercial scheme or developing their own assessment and review materials.

Short-term planning

Weekly planning

For the PNS this comes in two additional levels. The first level is the weekly planner with an overview of the week's lessons and including an evaluation of the week's work in order to inform the following week's plans for teaching and learning. This is the beginning of translating the long- and medium-term plans into actual teaching and learning for the pupils in your class. This plan will enable you to ensure a variety of teaching strategies is employed throughout the week to enhance pupil participation and motivation for learning.

	Mental/oral			Main activity								Plenary/Review
	Objectives	Activity	Key vocabulary	Objectives	Assessment	Resources adults	Key questions	Low attainers	Middle attainers	High attainers		Focus
Mon												
Tues												
Wed												
Thur												
Fri												

Outline headings for weekly planning

After using this plan, one of the comments from teachers and trainees was that the key vocabulary might need to be different in the mental/oral phase from the main activity. In the mental/oral phase one of the reasons for listing the vocabulary is to remind you, as the teacher, of the emphasis on the language you will use for phrasing the questions. In the main activity the emphasis will be on reinforcing known vocabulary and introducing the new.

A tip at this stage of your planning would be to look at the mathematics vocabulary in the PNS online and the list for the year group(s) you will be teaching. Then ask either your placement school or your training establishment if you can access the lists on the training material CD-ROM. On this you will find the lists for each key stage which can be printed out on A4 sheets to use as flash cards. Alternatively you can download, save and then alter the size of the cards for use with the whole class or you could enlarge them with a photocopier. Once you have made a set of these laminating or covering them will enable you to keep them as a ready resource for teaching.

Unit plans

Planning is a time-consuming business to get right. As a result of the workload issues for teachers unit plans were drawn up to address the amount of time teachers spent on planning. Unit plans are now available to support teachers' planning and provide a direct link between planning from the Framework for teaching mathematics and the medium-term plans. They also assist teachers in planning the appropriate content, pace and pitch of the lessons. In mathematics they take the form of five daily lessons linked to the appropriate key objectives. Key questions are highlighted to guide teaching, provide assessment and information and to structure the plenary. Each lesson provides a focused plenary with guiding outcomes to the Supplements of Examples. Weekly homework is included in each unit plan.

However, unit plans are designed to guide teaching – it is essential that the plans are adapted to meet the needs of the specific class within the teacher's medium-term plan. They can only be a guide as each class is different. What is very useful for you starting out as a teacher is that it gives you a very clear guide about the expectations for specific topics with specific year groups. It may be that the class you are working with are not ready to work at this level but you will have a clear idea about what to aim for, especially for the more able in any class. What is important to recognise here is the teacher's responsibility under *Every Child Matters* (ECM) to break down any barriers to learning and so teachers must be aware of how their planning of lessons will allow access for all children to the mathematics curriculum.

Annotating a unit plan is an appropriate process for tailoring the unit plans to the needs of your own class. Under the current guidance there is also more flexibility with the suggested time that topics will take with classes. The teacher may take two or three weeks to consolidate a specific topic with some learners whereas for others only a week is needed. You may therefore need to take the content of unit plans and break them down into more individual lessons for your class. Whether you are using the unit plans as they are or adapting them you will need to consider how to maintain the pace of learning throughout the lesson. How will you intervene to monitor progress, inform and redirect learning when necessary? You must remember to keep mental oral starters to between 5 and 10 minutes and don't let them either become too short or too long. You will also need to maintain the focus on the learning objectives throughout the main part of the lesson whether you are using the suggested activities or activities of your own.

PRACTICAL TASK PRACTICAL TASK PRACTICAL TASK PRACTICAL TASK

For the year group you know you will be teaching next find the appropriate unit plans on: **http://www.standards.dfes.gov.uk/primary/mathematics/**.

You will find it helpful to consider the following bullet points from the site:

- **Read through the whole unit plan before using it.**
- **Adapt plans to take account of the least and most able children.**
- **Provide further key questions to prompt, probe and promote children's learning.**
- **Develop additional problem-solving skills by asking extension questions and encouraging children to ask questions of their own.**
- **When supplementing or replacing activities ensure any new activities are directed by the learning objectives.**
- **Identify the role of any teaching assistants or additional adults.**
- **Use the school's own materials if the suggested resources are not available.**
- **How the Interactive Teaching Programs (available at the Publications area of this website) or other software can be incorporated into lessons.**

Daily or lesson planning

The second level of short-term planning is lesson planning. Some teachers use their weekly planners as the main short-term planning rather than working on individual lessons, though you will find schools where teachers do plan lessons or perhaps use one of the many schemes that include ready-made plans for each day. These still need to take account of the needs of the pupils in specific classes and matching the content with their prior knowledge. However, as trainees you will need to plan individual lessons in order to satisfy a number of the standards for QTS.

National
Numeracy *Strategy*

Unit 8
Angles, 2D and 3D shapes, perimeter and area

Year 6
Spring term

Five daily lessons

This Unit Plan is designed to guide your teaching.

You will need to adapt it to meet the needs of your class.

Resources needed to teach this unit:

- Resource sheet 8.1
- Resource sheet 8.2
- Activity sheet 8.1
- Activity sheet 8.2
- Activity sheet 8.3
- Activity sheet 8.4
- OHT 8.1
- OHT 8.2
- OHT 8.3
- OHT 8.4
- OHT 8.5
- CD from Using ICT to Support Numeracy pack
- Protractors
- OHP protractor
- Arrow cards
- Whiteboards
- Centimetre squared paper
- Interlocking cubes
- Cardboard box
- Models of prisms and pyramids
- Related Key Stage 2 national test questions

department for
education and skills

Unit Objectives

Year 6

- Recognise and estimate angles. — Page 111
- **Use a protractor to measure and draw acute and obtuse angles to the nearest degree.**
- Check that the sum of the angles in a triangle is 180 degrees. — Pages 103, 109
- Calculate angles in a triangle or around a point.
- Describe and visualise properties of solid shapes such as parallel or perpendicular faces or edges. — Page 105
- Visualise 3D shapes from 2D drawings and identify different nets for a closed cube.
- **Calculate the perimeter and area of simple compound shapes that can be split into rectangles.** — Page 97

Link Objectives

Year 5

- Use a protractor to measure and draw acute and obtuse angles to the nearest 5 degrees.
- Identify, estimate and order acute and obtuse angles.
- Calculate angles in a straight line.
- Make shapes with increasing accuracy.
- Visualise 3D shapes from 2D drawings and identify different nets for an open cube.
- **Understand area measured in square centimetres (cm²). Understand and use the formula in words 'length times breadth' for the area of a rectangle.**

Year 7

- **Know the sum of angles at a point, on a straight line and in a triangle** and recognise vertically opposite angles.
- Use angle measure; distinguish between and estimate the size of acute, obtuse and reflex angles.
- Use a ruler and protractor to measure and draw lines to the nearest millimetre and angles to the nearest degree.
- Use 2D representations to visualise 3D shapes.
- Begin to identify and use angle, side and symmetry properties of triangles and quadrilaterals; solve geometrical problems involving these properties, using step by step deduction and explaining reasoning with diagrams and text.
- Know and use the formula for the area of a rectangle; calculate the perimeter and area of shapes made from rectangles.

(Key objectives in bold)

NNS Unit Plans

Planning sheet	Day One	Unit 8	Angles, 2D and 3D shapes, perimeter and area	Term: *Spring*	Year Group: 6

Oral and Mental

Objectives and Vocabulary

Recall multiplication and division facts up to 10 × 10. Recall squares.

VOCABULARY
square numbers

RESOURCES
Whiteboards

Teaching Activities

- Give the children 'quick-fire' questions. Children to show their answers on whiteboards.

  Q What is 7 × 9?
  Q What is 48 ÷ 8?

  Ask questions that highlight the link between multiplication and division, e.g. 5 × 6 and 30 ÷ 6 etc.

- Remind children of square numbers. Get the children to chant the square numbers starting with:

  '1 squared is 1'
  to '10 squared is 100'.

- On their whiteboards children show their answers to questions involving square numbers.

  Q What is 6 squared minus 3 squared?
  Q What is 4 squared add 10?
  Q What is the difference between 5 squared and 4 squared?

Main Teaching

Objectives and Vocabulary

Recognise and estimate angles. Use a protractor to measure and draw acute and obtuse angles to within one degree.

VOCABULARY
acute
obtuse
right angle

RESOURCES
CD from using ICT to Support Numeracy pack
Protractors
OHP protractor
Activity sheet 8.1

Teaching Activities

- Use the 'What's my angle?' program on the CD from the Using ICT to Support Numeracy pack. Run the introduction and set the program to the 'Make and measure' section. Construct angles on the screen and invite children to estimate the angle. Emphasise that an angle describes a turn about a point.

  Invite children to use the 'on-screen' protractor to measure the angles. Invite children to 'draw' an acute angle, a right angle and an obtuse angle on the computer.

  Q How do we describe an acute and obtuse angle?

  Establish that acute angles lie between 0° and 90°, obtuse angles between 90° and 180°.

- Using an OHP protractor demonstrate how to draw angles of given size, emphasising the need to place the protractor in the right position on the line. Ensure not all lines are horizontal.

- Give out Activity Sheet 8.1, protractors and sheets of paper. Children to work in pairs, on Question 1. One child draws the angles under A, the other child draws the angles under B. After they have finished, they swap their answer papers to measure and check their partner's angles.

  Q Which two angles, one from A and one from B, will fit together to make a right angle?

  Confirm that 35° and 55°, 66° and 24° will do so. Get the children to put the pairs of angles side by side to check. Use tracing paper if necessary.

(Plenary – continued main teaching)

- Q Which angles will fit together to make a straight line?

  Establish there are 180° in a straight line and confirm that:

  47° and 133°, 161° and 19°, 52° and 128° will do so. Put them together to check.

- Q Which two angles are left? What do they add up to? What is special about this angle?

  Get the children to put the two angles together. Confirm that they give 270°, three-quarters of a complete turn and the angle needed to make the complete turn is 90°.

- Q What four angles add together to give a complete turn?

  Collect children's responses and confirm the totals are 360°.

  Ask children to answer Question 2 and to measure the angles, working in pairs as before. Remind them they can turn the paper around if it helps them. Get them to swap papers and check one another's answers.

Plenary

Teaching Activities / Focus Questions

- Q What shapes can you think of with just acute angles?
- Children discuss in pairs.
- Q What shapes can you think of that have only obtuse angles?
- Children discuss in pairs.
- Q What shapes have combinations of acute and obtuse angles?

  Invite children out to draw shapes on the board that fit each of the three conditions.

By the end of the lesson children should be able to:

- **Identify, estimate, measure and calculate acute and obtuse angles;**
- **Use a protractor to draw angles to the nearest degree.**

(Refer to supplement of examples, section 6, page 111.)

Page 44 shows an example of a format for lesson planning. Templates that can be photocopied can restrict you if there are set size boxes for specific aspects. What is important is that your plans include the key elements that are required to ensure a clear and effective plan that will support the teaching and learning in the classroom.

This lesson plan is clearly intended for planning lessons according to the features of the NNS three-part lesson.

For more on the three-part lesson see Chapter 2.

Foundation stage

When teaching in the Foundation Stage this plan is not as appropriate as there may not be a clear numeracy lesson identified. The critical aspects for planning in the foundation stage are that the objectives are identified clearly and mental/oral activities are planned for the whole class/ groups as are activities that ensure that pupils have opportunities to practise skills learnt. Vocabulary and the use of mathematical language are crucial with young pupils as this forms the basis of work in Key Stages 1 and 2. Plenaries may not be as important in the foundation stage but may be combined with the next day's mental/oral. Preparation of resources and the activities, however, will be even more critical for the youngest learners along with guidance for other adults working with the pupils.

For more on Early Years mathematics see Chapter 6.

The template on p. 47 is an example of how you might start to think about planning mathematics activities in the Foundation Stage. Some schools have mathematics days in which case you would need to consider more activities. Other schools organise more of an integrated day where subjects do not have clearly separate times. Many schools, however, move to a numeracy lesson during the latter part of the summer term in reception to give pupils a gentle introduction before moving to Year 1. In this case the planning format for KS1/2 would probably be more appro-priate.

The activities are going to be different ones focusing on the same objectives to provide a range of differing experiences for reinforcement for basic concepts such as counting. The activities are likely to be shorter than in the numeracy lesson and will include using puzzles, sand and water, construction toys, play dough, cutting and sticking, and games linked to the objectives.

General issues about lesson planning

Lesson plans provide the structure of the lesson in detail so that as a trainee you know what you will need to prepare in order to teach the lesson and that anyone observing will know what is intended to happen during the lesson. The plan can also act as a prompt as you are teaching so that you remember key vocabulary, for example, what you will be introducing and how you will be explaining definitions and use of terms.

If you have other adults working in the classroom they will also need copies of the plan of the overall lesson structure including timings and then specific details of what is expected of them and the pupils with whom they will be working. It is also useful to indicate the kinds of questions you would use to elicit responses from pupils as an aid for these people. Clearly the amount of guidance you provide is dependent upon the adults' experience with the pupils and whether or not you have time to sit down with them and go through the lesson plan. The latter is not always possible with adults who come in for short periods of time during a week. It is, though, your responsibility as the teacher to plan, guide the adults and monitor the teaching and learning for any groups working with other adults. Alternatively you may use a focus and assessment sheet (see p. 50) prepared for the adult.

Date	Class/year group or set

Notes from previous lesson from assessment including errors and misconceptions that need to be addressed in this lesson.

Learning objectives: NC, ELG and PNS references including, where appropriate, level descriptors
(you might also wish to include standards that you are addressing particularly if you are being observed during this lesson)

Cross-curriculum focus: *Spiritual, social, cutural, moral*
Learning Style: VAK
ECM outcomes

Resources including ICT: *Mental/oral:* *Main activity:* *Plenary:*	**Mathematical language:**
Mental/oral starter: *Activity and questions to ask:* Can the pupils...?	**Assessment:**

Introduction to the main activity *Teacher*	*Pupils*

Main activity: *Phase:* **Assessment:** Can the pupils...?	*Less confident:* *Extension/challenge:*	*Average:* *Extension/challenge:*	*More confident:* *Extension/challenge:*

Teacher's role during the main activity:

Differentiation/target setting including IEPs where appropriate:	**Use of in-class support, including guidance for supporting adult** (though this may require additional written guidance for the individual adults):

Plenary/Review:
Key questions to ask/areas to discuss:

Introduce homework where appropriate.

Note any errors/misconceptions to focus on in the next lesson on this area.

Mental/oral activities:	Objectives and ELG refs:		Vocabulary: Rhymes/stories:		Resources:	
Whole-class/larger group teaching time:	Objectives and ELG refs:		Vocabulary:		Resources:	
Group/pairs/individuals Activities:	1.	2.	3.	4.	5.	6.
Objectives and ELG refs:						
Vocabulary:						
Time for activity and/or when during the day:						
Resources:						
Adult involvement:						
Questions to ask:						
Assessment:						
Possible extension:						
Plenary/Review opportunities: Assessment issues to note for future planning in terms of learning and in terms of evaluation of activities:						

Template for the lesson plan at the Foundation Stage

You cannot make assumptions about the quality of the experience that a group of learners will have without monitoring during and after the lesson. With experienced and qualified teaching assistants the partnership will be different and as a trainee you can often learn a lot from them about the pupils and how to organise and interact with them.

PRACTICAL TASK PRACTICAL TASK PRACTICAL TASK PRACTICAL TASK

Read the curriculum guidance for the Foundation Stage document, National Curriculum for mathematics in Key Stages 1 and 2, DfEE/QCA (1999) and Primary Framework for Literacy and Mathematics. Choose a year group and a topic in number and think about what kinds of evidence you would want in order to be able to judge if a pupil had achieved the objective. Try to word the objective in such a way that your task is as easy as possible.

Planning for mathematics

With all the levels of planning described here the initial starting point has to be the previous experiences and knowledge of the pupils you will be working with. You will need to match their experiences and knowledge to the progression in learning objectives outlined in the PNS. The school you will be working in may also use a commercial scheme that you can consult for ideas and for the structuring of the lesson and the specific activities. You will also need to look closely at the actual mathematics. For example, if you are going to be teaching subtraction look at the progression in skills, knowledge and understanding required. What do you know about common areas of errors and misconceptions that will inform the planning of specific activities and focus your teaching? Then match this to the age group and experience of the pupils you are planning for and decide over the number of lessons for this topic what you want the pupils to learn. At this point you can begin to look for activities that will assist you in teaching your key focus, rather than deciding on the activities and then fitting the lesson around them as this may or may not assist in teaching or enable practice of the key ideas.

Since there are increasing numbers of 'off-the-shelf' plans available which as a trainee you might regard will cut down your workload try the following task:

Though a source of good ideas particularly for the style of activities for each of the phases of the lesson, 'off-the-shelf' plans do not always match with classes/individuals and need to be used carefully by trainees. However, as you develop experience with planning, teaching and assessing you will be able to make more effective use of all resources available to you.

Now you are ready to try a practical task unpicking an experienced teacher's planning.

REFLECTIVE TASK

Observe a numeracy lesson (if you can, one led by a Leading Mathematics Teacher (LMT)) and write down what you would need to have planned in order to have taught the lesson. This will give you an idea of how important the planning of each lesson is. If you can, talk to the teacher afterwards and ask them to talk you through their thinking process while planning.

NNS	NC/ELG	Key concepts	Example Activities	Level of Attainment
Reception 7. Counting	ELG and KS 1, Ma 2.2b	Counting In 2's and 10's	Recite the sequence ten, twenty, thirty … say backwards. Rhymes like 2, 4, 6, 8 who do we appreciate.	Working towards level 1.
Year 1 Continuation of reception				Level 1 and start on level 2.
Year 2 46–51 Calculations	KS 1, Ma 2.3c	Understand × as repeated addition. Understand the effects of doubling. Be able to record × sentences.	Arrays Mentally doubling numbers. $2 \times 5 = 10$	Consolidation of level 2 and start on level 3.
Year 3 47–57 Calculations	KS 2, Ma 2.3j	Recognise the use of symbols to stand for an unknown. Derive and recall facts for 2, 3, 4, 5, 6 and 10 times table. Multiply 1 digit and 2 digit numbers by 10 or 100 and describe the effect. Use practical and informal written methods to multiply 2 digit numbers.	$\square \times 6 =$ $\square \times \square = 30$ 13×5	Revision of level 2 but mainly level 3. From level descriptors level 3. They use mental recall of 2,3,4,5, 6 and 10 tables.
Year 4 52–69 Calculations	KS 2, Ma 2.3j	Use, read and write times, multiply, multiply by, product, multiple and the × sign. Derive and recall multiplication facts up to 10 x 10 and multiples of numbers to 10 up to the tenth multiple. Develop and use written methods to record, support and explain multiplication of 2 digit numbers by a 1 digit number	Writing sentences using vocabulary. Completing multiplication squares. Use grid method. 15×6 $15 \times 3 = 45$ $45 \times 2 = 90$	Consolidation of level 3 and start on level 4.
Year 5 52–69 Calculations	KS 2, Ma 2.3j	Recall quickly common multiples and multiplication facts up to 10 × 10. Use of factors. Grid method extended to a 2 × 2 grid and start column multiplication.	72×38	Revision of level 3 but mainly level 4. From level descriptors level 4. Pupils use their understanding of place value to multiply by 10 or 100. Know × facts to 10 × 10.
Year 6 52–69 Calculations	KS 2, Ma 2.3j	Use knowledge of place value and multiplication facts to 10 x 10 to derive related multiplication facts involving decimals. Use knowledge of multiplication facts quickly to derive squares of numbers to 12 x 12 and corresponding squares of multiples to 10. Recognise prime numbers and identify primes fewer than 100. Find prime factors of 2 digit numbers. Calculate mentally with integers and decimals. Use efficient written methods for multiplication.	20^2	Consolidation of level 4 and start on level 5. From level descriptors level 5. Pupils use their understanding of place value to multiply whole numbers and decimals by 10, 100 and 1000.

Outline progression plan for multiplication

For adult support in the classroom during the numeracy lesson.

Teaching focus and assessment sheet

Teacher: .... Class:...

Date: .... Focus for the lesson:.............................

Name of classroom assistant/additional adult: ....

Activity: Brief account of the activity and focus for additional support.

Equipment needed for group:

Vocabulary: *Key vocabulary to be used by adult and introduced to pupils.*

Questions: *Key questions to be used.*

Learning objectives: *These are from the main objectives but likely to be broken down into smaller and more manageable steps.*

1.
2.
3.

For the adult to complete.

Pupils' names		Can do	Needs help	Note: difficulties/issues for teacher to plan next lesson/support
	1			
	2			
	3			
	1			
	2			
	3			
	1			
	2			
	3			
	1			
	2			
	3			
	1			
	2			
	3			

Lesson: Addition using counting on and counting all strategies	Date: N/A
Year group/class: Reception (mixed ability)	Size of class: 30

Children's previous experience:
Children have spent several lessons on addition of numerals 1–10 using methods of counting on and counting all – including both written and practical work. Also have experience of counting up to 10 objects and chanting numbers 1–20.

Notes from previous lesson's assessment including errors and misconceptions that need to be addressed:
Some children find it difficult to 'add one' to numbers 1–10 because they are uncertain of the number sequence 1-10 (lower ability group) - need to improve their counting accuracy. Other children have difficulty counting / drawing more than five objects in a group - because they lose count if trying to count and draw at the same time (middle group). Need more practice with this.

Learning objectives:
Pupils should be able to:
- Add 'one more' to numbers 1–10 (or 1–5 for lower ability group).
- Begin to count up to 10 objects to solve addition problems (1–5 for lower ability group).
- Identify numerals 1–10 (or 1–5 for lower ability group).

NC, ELG and NNS references:
NC KS1: Ma 2, 3a
ELG: p. 76
NNS: p. 14 – reception

Resources: • Selection of toys for counting out objects. • Worksheet (×10). • Small dice (×20). Paper (×10). • Puppet for demo. • Washing line – numbers 1–10	**Health and safety:** • Children to sit in a circle during introduction but individuals doing action to stand in the middle. • Adult support for each group of up to 10 children.

Mental/oral starter (10-15 mins):
Activity A: Children to sit in a circle and in turn say the numbers 1, 2, 3, … 10. Stop the children on a number – the child involved is then invited to select the number from the washing line and to count this many objects.
Aim to stop the lower ability children on numbers 1–5 and the more able children on numbers 5–10 for differentiation. Carry out activity for 5 minutes.

Activity B: Children to sit in circle as before. Invite children not involved in the last activity to come up and quietly tell the teacher what the number is that she shows them. The child then has to do an action this many times (e.g. clapping, hopping) and the rest of the class have to guess what the number is by counting the number of actions.
Aim to have the lower ability children do actions/count numbers 1–5 and the more able children do numbers 5–10 for differentiation. Carry out activity for 5 minutes.

Introduction to main activity (5 mins):
Explain and demonstrate how we can use our counting skills to solve addition. Show them if it is an 'add one more' question we can look at the next number in the sequence and if we don't know the next number we can 'count all' the objects to get the answer. Give several examples of inaccurate counting using a puppet to count objects etc. – ask children to watch and see if it counts accurately. Opportunity for children to see errors in counting. Split the children into ability groups and then the adult working with them can explain what the activity is.

Main activity (15 mins):

Lower group activity: Teacher to continue to work with this group at the table setting up various role play situations involving counting and adding numbers 1–5 (e.g. fruit shop, bus stop). Practical activity using both 'counting all' and 'counting on' methods.	*Middle group activity:* Working with EA children to complete worksheet on addition. Involves adding numbers 1–10 together by counting all of the pictures. Children to record their answer by drawing the total number of objects for each question.	*Higher group activity:* Working with EA on independent activity. Children have to roll two dice and add the numbers on each dice together to get the answers up to 12 using the 'counting all' strategy. Record results on blank page in a pictorial form.
Extension: If appropriate for this group extend the activities to include numbers up to 10.	*Extension:* Children to add written numerals next to their pictures – refer to number line for help.	*Extension:* Children to add written numerals next to their pictures.

Plenary/Review:
Children to return to the carpet area and reinforce points made in the introduction to the main activity. Show a few examples of questions – ask children what they would do to work out the answer.

Assessment opportunities:
Can the lower ability group count up to 5 objects and add numbers between 1 and 5 together?
Can the middle ability group work out addition problems accurately using 'count all' and 'count on' methods appropriately?
Can the higher ability group work independently on addition problems using numbers 1–12?
Assessment will take place during main activity with the help of EAs in the room.

Teacher's role: During main activity to work with the lower ability group.	**Use of classroom support:** During main activity to explain to and support up to 10 children in their work.

Trainee's plan for reception lesson in numeracy

Date	Class/Year/Group/Set:
	Sherbourne yr4 3

Previous lesson's work, and errors and misconceptions that need to be addressed:

Recalling multiplication facts and arrays

NC, ELG & NNS references:	**Learning objectives:**
Ma 2, 1g, 2c, 3d, 4a NNS 2,6,40,52,54,58,64, **Level descriptors:** 82-89 between 2-5, approx level 3	Place value and multiplying integers by 10, 100 or 1000

Resources:	**Mathematical language:**

Mental/oral: Place value cards
     and list
 	
 Main acitvity: White board
     worksheets
 	
 Plenary:
	multiply, times, columns, abacus diagram, thousandths, hundredths, tens, units

Mental/oral starter: Activity and questions to ask:	**Assessment:** Can the pupils?
Play the place value circle game using 27 cards with two to four digit numbers on.	Recognise the place value properties of 2-4 digit integers.

Introduction to main activity: Teacher:	Pupils:
Using the 100 square and white board with laminated number cards, demonstrate what happens when we multiply by 10, using the place value abacus diagram. → Then discuss place value for integers multiplied by 100 and 1000.	Listening on the carpet Discuss and answer questions. Demonstrate the numerous methods being taught th h t u = 462

Trainee's lesson plan for numeracy Year 4

Main activity (15 mins): Phase	Less confident	Average	More confident
Work through the class activity togther and discuss the methods used.	1. 4 × 10 2. 20 × 10 3. 36 × 10 4. 19 × 10 5. 82 × 10 6. 94 × 10 7. 16 × 100 8. 2 × 100 9. 6 × 100 10. 12 × 100 11. 4 × 1000	In their maths book, copy out and answer the questions off the board. For each answer, draw an abacus diagram eg. 94 × 10 = 940 Then answer questions off board. 1. There are 8 children with 10 sweets. How many sweets are there altogether? If the sweets cost 10p each, how much should they pay altogether in £ and p? and one more like this one	

Assessment

Observations and marking work.

Extension/challenge

• Worksheet : "What number am I?"
• Use the class computer to work through the multiplication program.

Teacher's role in the main activity:

To work with Sophie, Alex, Joel, Sarah, Alice and Zoe to deal with certain errors being made.

Differentiation/target-setting (IEPs):	Use of class support and instruction:
Questioning and differentiated tasks and extensions.	The SEN co-ordinator to work with Sarah and her IEP program.

Plenary/Review:

Summarise key points of the lesson and finish with the multiplication circle game for the six times table.

Key questions to ask/areas to discuss:

Mental recall of numbers multiplied by 10 or 100.

Note any errors/misconceptions to cover in the next lesson:

Trainee's lesson plan for numeracy Year 4

Differentiation

This is the matching of the teaching and learning activities to the learners in order to ensure that all pupils progress. The ways in which this has been achieved in the classroom has varied. In the past mathematics teaching has resulted in high levels of differentiation with extremes of different work for each member of the class. The general advice from the PNS is to differentiate by no more than three levels within a class. There can be some difficulties with this advice in small schools with mixed-age classes and wide ability ranges. The message, though, is clearly to meet pupils' needs while not creating unmanageable differentiation that is difficult to monitor or to teach, particularly in the main activity phase of the lesson. Pupils on the special needs register from Stage Two and above will have IEPs to which you will need to refer when planning their work. For example, a pupil with specific learning difficulties may have problems reading but be quite able in mathematics. The form of differentiation required may only be in the wording of the instructions, not in the content of the task. This is an important area in relation to the teacher and the school's part in ECM as it helps to break down the barriers to learning.

Differentiation can be achieved through the following:

- *Task*. This is where the task changes. An obvious example in mathematics is keeping to the main objective but changing the range of numbers being used. For example, an objective focusing on subtraction might involve three levels of differentiation with numbers up to 10, numbers up to 50 and numbers up to 100 for each of the groups. It might also mean that the nature of the task changes from a sheet of calculations to an investigation using previous knowledge. Differentiation is not just about catering for the least able but should be seen in terms of inclusion – meeting the needs of all.
- *Teaching*. Setting different questions in the mental/oral phase, who you ask to demonstrate specific examples in the main activity and how you decide upon the support are examples of differentiation through teaching.
- *Interest*. Particularly for groups who might have potential barriers to learning, setting mathematics in a context that has 'real' meaning for pupils can help to motivate and support their learning. A common example would be to focus on gender and, say, use sport to motivate a class that had a large number of boys as opposed to girls. Travelling pupils or pupils who have recently moved to the country can need support in feeling that even in mathematics care is taken of their needs and interests.
- *Outcome*. All pupils can be given the same task but with different expectations of how far or how much they will gain from the task set.
- *Adult support*. The same task may be set for all pupils but the differentiation would be supported by the adult input to ensure that all pupils have equal access to the task set. This support could be you as the teacher or it might be additional adult support in the classroom. The crucial aspect of this is that you need to plan how you envisage this support will enhance the learning and ensure that you convey that to the adult support.
- *Resource support*. This can take a variety of forms but can be an effective way of supporting pupils. If the lesson, say, has a focus on multiplication a resource might be a table square which allows some pupils to engage with the same level of work as the rest of the class and at the same pace.

See Allen et al (2007) **Primary ICT: Knowledge and Understanding** *from Learning Matters.*

- *Technology*. You might have the support of ILS (integrated learning systems) on a computer which are designed for pupils to work on individually. Alternatively you might decide that the use of a calculator could support pupils working with larger numbers than they might be able to manage without such support. For more able pupils it could allow them to focus more on the patterns in investigative work than on the calculations involved.

- *Grouping*. Not always grouping according to ability can provide a different approach to differentiation. Mixed ability groupings can provide pupils with peer support in tasks.
- *Recording*. Asking pupils to record in different ways can provide support and add challenge. Sometimes asking pupils to record without words can be a challenge. Not recording everything but asking pupils to record their favourite number sentence, the most difficult question they may have been asked and why can also be alternatives for differentiation.
- *Role within group*. Pupils need to be 'trained' to work in groups rather than just sitting together, but when they are they can be assigned different roles in the group which again either support their strengths or challenge them to do things they usually avoid. Clearly you do need to know the pupils well to work in this way and they need to be familiar with this approach. Don't assume that you can walk into a class and immediately make this run smoothly – any class will need time to build up to this approach.

It is important when planning three groups' work for the main activity that you don't assume that when the lower attaining group finish their work they can go on to the middle group's work and they in turn can go on to the higher attaining group's work. The result of this may only be one group for whom to plan extension work but it may not meet the needs of pupils for extension and challenge. The ability range of the groups may be close but they could also be quite far apart. This would result in a mismatch between the learners in the groups and the work given as extension. Extension and challenge requires as much preparation and thought as every other part of the pupils' work.

For more detail see Chapter 3 of Jacques and Hyland (2007) **Professional Studies** *from Learning Matters.*

PRACTICAL TASK PRACTICAL TASK **PRACTICAL TASK** PRACTICAL TASK

Select a task, worksheet or other activity and look at how you can make it easier or harder, and how you could add support to the activities to enable you to offer different versions of the same task to different pupils.

Resources

In order to look at resources you need to be thinking about the resources that you will use to teach and the resources that the pupils will use as separate parts of your preparation for teaching. The preparation of resources can directly affect how a lesson will go both in terms of the learning and in terms of the organisation and control of any class.

Resources for the teacher

You need to ask yourself some questions before deciding upon appropriate resources for your teaching.

For more information on resources see p. 29, Chapter 3.

- **What do I need to demonstrate and which is the best way to do this?**
- **How can I offer a range of different images to support pupils' learning of mathematics?**

The following are some suggestions:

Arrow cards

Large arrow cards can help to demonstrate place value and how reading numbers differs from writing numbers. So 800 and 70 and 3 are condensed when we write 873.

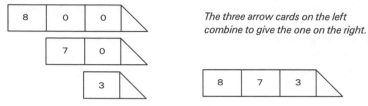

The three arrow cards on the left combine to give the one on the right.

In terms of planning for their use, first have you or the school got a set of arrow cards? Check their condition and the number and size. Resources have to look right so that they can be clearly read, not faded or too small for the whole class to see. If you only have one set then you can't, for instance, make more than one number requiring the same digits. While this might appear obvious, it is easy to grab resources at the last minute without checking and find yourself in difficulties with the questions you have planned because you haven't checked. You might decide that if you are going to use these then the pupils all need access to the same resources for follow-up activities in which case again you need to check availability.

Counting stick

These have become very popular with teachers since the introduction of the NNS and they provide a focus for pupils' attention when counting. They also provide one way of assisting visualising the pattern of numbers along an unmarked number line. You can make numbers to attach to the number line and depending upon what your number line is made of you also need to experiment with what will keep numbers attached to it during a teaching session.

Number lines and tracks

These are quite different things – in a number track the numbers appear in the spaces whereas in a number line the numbers are on a line.

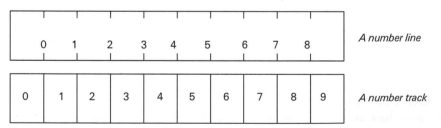

A number line

A number track

One of the biggest problems with planning to use these as resources is where to put them. Many schools do not have a long enough wall to put up a continuous number line from 1 to 100. Alternatives need careful planning and preparation but do not always provide the same image for pupils or the same opportunities for teaching. For example, it is far easier to model the difference between two numbers by attaching pegs or something similar to a number line that is standing proud from the wall than it is with a flat number line. You can make a number line to stand in a wooden base that could be moved into an appropriate position for teaching in the classroom and then put away again.

The other issue to be planned in terms of number lines is the range of numbers that the line covers. For younger pupils a short number line can give the impression that counting stops at, say, 10 or 20. These also don't give pupils an opportunity to look at the patterns within our number system.

Number squares

If space is an issue another way of exploring number patterns is by using a number square, preferably as a permanent display. This can either be on a display board or as part of one of the free-standing boards which many schools have introduced with the NNS. Some of these have pockets for numbers so you can move the numbers around or remove them, some have disks that can do the same. Others are on write-on wipe-off material. With the latter it is important to plan that you have the right kind of pens that will wipe off rather than damage the board by grabbing a pen at the last minute. All these can be used for modelling aspects of the number system, number patterns, odds and evens and place value.

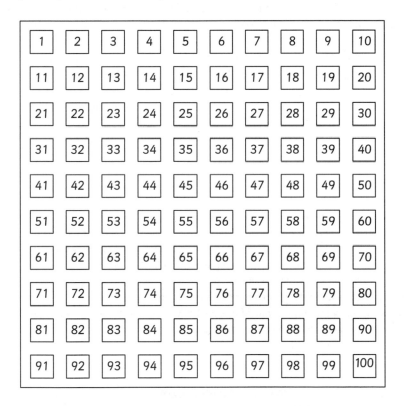

White board/chalk board

Although these are in common use in most classrooms they still need to be considered when planning. First, make sure that you have either sufficient chalk or markers that are appropriate to the surface and the work and are a colour that can easily be seen from anywhere in the classroom. You also need to plan either that all pupils sitting at their tables can see the board and/or there is enough space in front of the board for the whole class to sit comfortably during whole-class teaching time.

It is easy to think of a board to write on and display examples but if you want to use the board several times during the lesson you need to plan ahead. An example of this from a student's lesson is as follows. The lesson was about angles and the student wanted to draw angles with a board protractor to demonstrate its use. This was all right but the board was small and therefore these initial illustrations had to be rubbed off in order that the board could be used again. A useful piece of planning would have been to pre-draw some angles on a large sheet of paper/ card. These could have been measured in the lesson but removed from the board during times when this was needed for other illustrations of work but still available as a resource during the rest of the lesson.

There is also a real skill in organising the data on your board so that pupils can easily follow the instructions etc., particularly for dyslexic pupils who require structure in order to follow work on boards. Planning the space on your board can be a helpful part of lesson preparation: displaying the date and the lesson objectives and sectioning off part of the board for notes and setting tasks. If using an overhead projector you also need to think about these aspects in relation to projecting any images during the lesson. Check how much space the overhead will need and maybe mark it out.

Using the same resources every day can make lessons dull and uninspiring. If pupils are not sure what you might use in each lesson it adds to interest and motivation and can assist with class-room control, as they want to behave in order to see what you will offer next. It also makes it much easier to move away from worksheets in the main activity if you have plenty of practical resources as starting points for activities. It is also easier to plan specific and appropriate exten-sion activities for groups that end up being less time-consuming once you have the resources available.

Resources for pupils

Small boards, either chalk or white
These can be an alternative to the number cards and paddles so that everyone can show an answer and be involved, particularly in the mental/oral phase, though they can also be used in the rest of the lesson. First, availability and the right kinds of pens need to be planned for. Then you need to think about what the learning objectives are and how using the boards will assist you in achieving them. If, for example, one of the objectives is writing numbers either in digits or words then this can be a good way of practising these skills and a way of your spotting pupils who have difficulties with numeral formation, recording numbers involving place value or writing number names correctly.

Digit cards
These can have limitations if the pupils only have 0–9 digit cards, as you can't show some two-digit numbers like 22 or three-digit numbers. This means when planning your questions you need to take this into consideration. Some two- and three-digit numbers, though not all, can be shown if pupils work in pairs. Alternatively you need to plan for more digit cards to be available for each pupil if using them in the mental/oral phase. Cards with words like 'odd' and 'even', 'less than', 'more than' can be used instead of just digit cards in the same way. There are also commer-cially produced cards for money, fractions and decimals which you could consider planning to use.

Arrow cards
As described above, these can assist pupils in understanding place value and how to read and write numbers from ten. When teaching using arrow cards it can be helpful for pupils to have the same resources to repeat your modelling for reinforcement.

Fans or paddles

There are lots of different types of these now available including those which show decimals, money, shapes and fractions as well as digits. They can be limiting for the same reason as the digit cards. Some of the money ones only have one coin of each denomination in a set. This clearly limits the questions you might plan to ask pupils if only one set is available.

Individual number lines

These can be on strips of paper/card or attached to table tops to assist pupils in calculating during any part of the lesson. A quick alternative would be to use metre rulers if available though you do have to make sure they will be kept on the tables and not used for sword fights!

Individual counting sticks

Again this is a new piece of equipment which enables pupils to remodel what you are doing on a counting stick at the front for themselves on one of their own. They could also be used to support activities where the pupils might look at patterns of multiples by attaching small numbers to their sticks, possibly as a means of differentiating the task through the support of resources.

Mathematics dictionaries

The last of the practical resources here for you to think about is a mathematics dictionary. We think about making dictionaries available in English lessons more often than mathematics ones, but they can be a useful planning tool for extension work. You can set challenges for pupils to find out about a topic or a definition and report back to the rest of the class. Or pupils could produce a poster to explain a concept either to the rest of the class or possibly for a younger age group, though you need to look at the dictionary before planning the challenge/task. Alternatively a class might aim to make its own dictionary of terms and definitions over the length of your school placement. In addition, they are very useful for checking that you have the right definition of terms as there is too much content to remember in all areas. If pupils ask questions that you are unsure of then looking it up together can help you if you are not confident about your answers. So having one available in the classroom when you are teaching can be a support to you as well as the pupils.

Information Communications Technology
Computers

This is the most obvious use of ICT and can be the most difficult for you to think about in terms of planning. Many people feel that they have not gained sufficient experience for their own use of computers. It can be a problem but this can sometimes be overcome by using the expertise of the pupils who often have more positive attitudes to their use. The first issue is preparation and with computers this means being familiar with the software and hardware available if possible. You do need to think through the kinds of software or packages that you will use and why. Table 4.1 provides an introduction to the kinds of items that are available in most schools with some examples.

For more information on ICT Allen et al. (2007) **Primary Knowledge, Understanding and Practice** *from Learning Matters.*

Once you have decided that you wish to use computers you then need to plan the organisation. This will be different according to the topic and the availability of machines. If you have one computer, for example, you may feel that demonstrating the use of the software to the whole class may be the most useful method. Each group in turn then works on the computer with you or other adult support during a single lesson, or maybe over a sequence of lessons, depending upon the content of the program.

Category	Examples
Drill and practice	*Hooray for Maths* *The Number Works* *Mighty Maths* Also a number of programs that are part of commercial maths schemes
Integrated Learning Systems (ILS)	*Success Maker* *Global Learning Systems*
Maths adventure and problem solving	*Crystal Rainforest*
Logo	*Logo,* screen turtle and *Roamer world* With links to programmable robots like *Roamer/pips/pixies*
Number specific	*ATM Developing number* *Counting machine*
Data handling	*Black Cat* software *Excel* Databases, e.g. *Findit* *Junior Pinpoint*
Miscellaneous Small software	*My World* *Fun School Maths* *Maths Explorer*
Other devices	OHP calculator
Websites: some of these have activities on that you can use in maths lessons either on or off line	ATM Enrich Ofsted VTC Schools sites such as Ambleside
Interactive whiteboard	A number of programs available, e.g. **http://www.nwnet.org.uk/pages/maths**

Table 4.1 Classifications of ICT

Planning for working in a suite of computers is quite a different prospect. You obviously need to check the software available and find out how it works, as sometimes the software can operate much more slowly on a network. The other issue in terms of planning for teaching in a suite is the organisation of the room and how you will gain pupils' attention at specific times during the lesson. This might sound very basic but control of pupils in front of computer screens can be problematic. You need to agree ground rules and establish a signal, for example, for when you want pupils to stop work and give you their attention.

If working in a suite where you have projection facilities, or even facilities for looking in on their screens, then you can check on what each pupil or small group of pupils are doing. In these circumstances the software you choose to work on needs to be accessible by all pupils. If there are issues about the ability of pupils to read instructions on the screen, you might consider mixed-ability groupings or paired work to allow access to all. Pupils working at a terminal on their own means that they are not discussing the mathematics and any strategies they are using. If this is the case you may want to plan in times when you ask pupils to join together and discuss their work either within the suite time or in a following session by using printouts of work completed.

Pupils working individually through drill and practice exercises is not the most productive use of suite time which might only be available to the class on a limited basis, particularly during numeracy lessons.

The advantage of the suite is that all pupils can be introduced to and make initial explorations with programs that you might then use with groups in the classroom when fewer machines are available. So ICT can form part of the strategy for an individual lesson or for a sequence of lessons where you are planning to develop the pupils' mathematical skills. A good example of this would be Logo, which could be introduced in the context of a suite and followed up with differentiated challenges in the classroom.

Suggested activities for a numeracy lesson in a suite

The following is a very brief overview of some ideas for working in a suite. It is necessarily general, as the idea is to show the potential rather than a specific plan for an age group. The intention is to get you thinking about how you could use computers in numeracy if the opportunities are available and what this means for planning a lesson.

Mental/oral

1. With the whole class use a counting machine which you can set to count in different sized steps. Stop the count and ask for predictions of the next number. You might try one or two of these and then show the class how to change the steps. In pairs/small groups they could challenge each other to find the rules predicting what the next number will be in the sequence.
2. With the whole class, if pupils have a machine each, you could choose a table from the ATM Developing Number software to complete within a time limit. This task could be given to pairs or small groups working against the clock where one person is inputting the answers.

Main activity

Using Complements part of the ATM Developing Number software package, look at complements of numbers that are appropriate for the year group. Demonstrate different ways of working out the complements of the given number. Ask pupils for strategies they would use, e.g. bridging through ten, count up, using known facts. Then set pupils a challenge to use the same strategies to solve complements for different numbers. Here you could differentiate with the size of number but still use the same strategies.

Plenary/review

Here you could use the developing number software again and go over some of the questions that have been answered by a range of pupils. Pick up on any errors and misconceptions. Then take the pupils on further, introducing larger numbers where the same strategies could apply hence extending their learning.

Interactive whiteboards

Interactive whiteboards have taken over from the use of overhead projectors in schools. They also provide more interaction with the programs. Teachers and pupils can make things happen on the board. The following is an example of a 1–100 grid that can be used to show patterns of multiples, in this case 6.

1	2	3	4	5	6	7	8	9	10
11	12	13	14	15	16	17	18	19	20
21	22	23	24	25	26	27	28	29	30
31	32	33	34	35	36	37	38	39	40
41	42	43	44	45	46	47	48	49	50
51	52	53	54	55	56	57	58	59	60
61	62	63	64	65	66	67	68	69	70
71	72	73	74	75	76	77	78	79	80
81	82	83	84	85	86	87	88	89	90
91	92	93	94	95	96	97	98	99	100

The board can be set up so that the colours of the squares will change if touched with a marker or with a finger.

Cameras

Digital cameras can provide opportunities to focus on patterns in the environment, symmetry and, when rescaling images, ratio and proportion. The planning stage of using a camera might have to be spread over several sessions as you have to plan time for pupils to take the photographs before being able to work with them in a numeracy lesson. Pictures taken with ordinary cameras can also assist pupils in looking at patterns and shapes, though again time needs to be spent collecting the images.

Photocopiers

These can be a useful resource for enlarging worksheets displayed for a class/group to work from if an overhead projector is not available. It can also be used for demonstrating enlargements, ratio and proportion. If images of different sizes are copied before the lesson then they can be given to groups to investigate the relationships between the images as part of one of the activities, say in the main activity phase of the lesson. Or you could plan part of a lesson for pupils to work with an adult to produce images of particular sizes.

Calculators

At present the guidance on using calculators focuses on Years 5 and 6 yet there has been evidence from the SATs at the end of Key Stage 2 that pupils are not using them effectively on the papers where calculators are allowed. There are therefore two strands to planning for using calculators in the lesson. The first is the use of a calculator and the second is using it effectively as a tool to support more open-ended activities. This is where the focus of the activity is looking for the pattern or the methods of solving a problem rather than the arithmetic, which if not completed with a calculator would get in the way of extending the pupils' mathematical thinking.

Calculators come in different kinds, though most modern ones are all scientific. Check that all the calculators operate in the same way and that there are sufficient for the whole class. If you can, use an overhead calculator that is the same as the pupils' to demonstrate procedures.

Evaluating the teaching and learning

Lesson and weekly evaluations

This should be completed as soon as possible after the lesson. The two main areas to focus on are the pupils' learning and your teaching. In the area of pupils' learning you will want to note those pupils who did not achieve the objectives for the lesson and why you think they had difficulties, specific errors and misconceptions that did not allow them to achieve. You will also want to know if pupils have exceeded your expectations and specifically what they demonstrated in terms of their understanding during the lesson that could be used to take them further. This will be part of your assessment evidence that you will later transfer to records of progress and attainment.

You will also need to consider your own performance in the lesson. The danger here is to dwell on things that go wrong and not think about the positive aspects of the lesson you have just taught. A good strategy is to consider the positive aspects first and note two or three things that were good and that you will continue to include in your teaching. Then turn to thinking about those aspects which you want to improve. You do not need to give a blow by blow account of what has occurred in the lesson. Again try to select two or three things that you are going to work on in the next lesson or lessons. In this way you are using your evaluation like the formative assessment you carry out in relation to the pupils' learning and alter the next lesson as a result.

Pupils not reaching objectives:	Pupils exceeding the objectives:
Notes for next day/week focusing on teaching	
Good aspects for development:	Areas:

Since you are also planning on a weekly basis it is useful to evaluate the week as well, drawing upon your individual lesson evaluations in order to feed into the next weekly plan.

Objectives attained:	Objectives not attained:
Children not reaching objectives covered: Target:	Children exceeding objectives covered: Target:
Action for next week/half term:	
Teacher's targets:	

A SUMMARY OF **KEY POINTS**

> Planning effective learning for mathematics takes place on four levels:
  - long-term planning often constructed by the whole school and taken from the PNS so not usually an activity that trainees are involved in;
  - medium-term planning often constructed by groups of year teachers or individual class and again not usually an activity that trainees are involved in;
  - weekly planning constructed by all teachers from the medium-term plans;
  - daily lesson plans not always constructed by classroom teachers except when being observed but are usually expected of trainee teachers.
> The long- and medium-term plans may merge in some schools, particularly when following the PNS.
> Careful planning for lessons can assist you in delivering effective mathematics lessons where there is clear progression in pupils' learning, and its importance cannot be overestimated.
> Planning should always focus on the learning first, through clear objectives.
> Key elements in a lesson plan include:
  - a clear three-part structure with a mental/oral starter, main activity and plenary/review phase;
  - use of appropriate mathematical vocabulary;
  - effective use of questioning and opportunities for mathematical discussion;
  - making explicit connections between aspects of mathematics for pupils;
  - direct teaching throughout the lesson to whole class, groups and individuals;
  - effective use of resources;
  - clear differentiation to meet the diversity of pupils' needs;
  - appropriate choice of activities to match the mathematical content and pupils' age and needs;
  - assessment of learning;
  - evaluation of teaching;
  - set targets for the future in terms of learning and teaching.

Moving on

In order to develop your planning and evaluation during your NQT year you may consider arranging to discuss this area with colleagues including teaching assistants. You could also gain feedback from observations of your teaching during this year and you and your mentor should discuss supporting the development aspects of planning teaching and learning of mathematics.

REFERENCES REFERENCES **REFERENCES** REFERENCES REFERENCES

DfEE (1999) *The National Numeracy Strategy: Framework for Teaching Mathematics*. London: DfEE.

DfEE/QCA (1999) *Mathematics: the National Curriculum for England*. London: HMSO.

Skelton, M. (1995) 'Schemes of work', *Primary File*, no. 25, pp. 35–7.

FURTHER READING   FURTHER READING   FURTHER READING

Allen, J., Potter, J., Sharp. J. and Turvey, K. (2007) *Primary ICT: Knowledge, Understanding and Practice*. Exeter: Learning Matters.

Briggs, M. and Pritchard, A. (2002) *Using ICT in Primary Mathematics Teaching*. Exeter: Learning Matters.

DfES (2001) *Guidance to Support Pupils with Specific Needs in the Daily Maths Lesson*. London: DfES.

Fox, B., Montague-Smith, A. and Wilkes, S. (2000) *Using ICT in Primary Mathematics: Practices and Possibilities*. London: David Fulton.

Hayes, D. (2000) *Handbook for Newly Qualified Teachers: Meeting the Standards in Primary and Middle Schools*. London: Fulton.

Jacques, K. and Hyland, R. (eds) (2000) *Professional Studies: Primary Phase*. Exeter: Learning Matters.

MacGregor, H. (1998) *Tom Thumb's Musical Maths: Developing Maths Skills with Simple Songs*. London: A&C Black.

Useful website

http://www.coxhoe.durham.sch.uk/curriculum/Numeracy.htm#Links%20to%20 Useful%20Sites.

5

Assessment

Professional Standards for the award of QTS

This chapter will support you as you work towards evidencing attainment against the following Standards:

Q11, Q19, Q21, Q22, Q23, Q24

Chapter objectives

By the end of this chapter you will have:

- **considered your role in monitoring pupils learning mathematics;**
- **explored how to share assessments with pupils;**
- **considered how to feed back to pupils on their work and/or responses;**
- **considered the role of recording assessments;**
- **explored the variety of techniques for collecting assessment information;**
- **considered the relationship between the statutory assessment of learning and formative or assessment for learning.**

Introduction

One of the first problems to overcome when looking at assessment is the terminology used. So you need to be clear about what each of the terms mean. The terms you will meet most often are MARRA – monitoring, assessment, recording, reporting and accountability.

- *Monitoring* is the day-to-day monitoring of pupils' progression in mathematics. This is partly completed through evaluations of daily lessons and weekly programmes.
- *Assessment* is the use of a variety of assessment techniques to collect evidence upon which to make judgements about attainment and progress.
- *Recording* can be the informal jotting of notes by the teacher as they work with pupils and it can also apply to class and individual records of progress and attainment intended for a wider audience.
- *Reporting* is the process of writing parental reports and discussing progress and attainment at parent consultations.
- *Accountability* can be seen partly as the reporting to parents but also the aggregation of information from testing that is used to produce league tables of schools.

Further terms related to assessment are as follows:

- *Formative* – this type of assessment is completed to inform planning, teaching and learning. This is now referred to as assessment for learning.

  Assessment for learning is the process of seeing and interpreting evidence for use by learners and their teachers to decide where the learners are in their learning, where they need to go and how best to get there. (Assessment Reform Group, 2002)

- *Summative* – this type of assessment is completed at the end of a series of lessons on one topic, or at the end of a term, year or key stage. Although the assessment outcomes may be used for target-setting and inform longer-term planning, it gives you a picture of a pupil's attainment at a particular point in time.
- *Diagnostic* – this type of assessment enables you to find out what a pupil can do and also where specific difficulties lie in order for you to plan effectively for future teaching and learning. It can also be seen as formative though the formative assessment may not give you the specific level of detail about difficulties and whether they are errors or misconceptions. A very useful example of diagnostic assessment is a clinical interview (Ginsburg, 1981). This might sound a daunting challenge for a trainee but what it means in practice is getting an individual to do some mathematics and talk to you while they are completing the task. You would need to record the dialogue either by completing notes and/or making an audio recording.
- *SATs* – the term use for the assessments at the end of each key stage.

There are a few other terms that you might come across when reading about assessment which you will find useful to know about:

- *Ipsative* – this is assessment based on past attainment. An example of this would be a portfolio of a pupil's work where you could identify progress over time.
- *Criterion referenced* – assessment referenced against specific criteria.
- *Norm referenced* – assessment referenced against expected norms for populations.

RESEARCH SUMMARY RESEARCH SUMMARY RESEARCH SUMMARY

The Assessment Reform Group (2002) have developed the following principles for assessment for learning from their research, including Black and Wiliam's (1998) *Inside the Black Box*, to guide classroom practice. This will involve all the adults working with children in schools and Early Years settings.

Principles for assessment for learning to guide classroom practice: 10 principles

Assessment for learning should:

- be part of effective planning for teaching and learning;
- focus on how pupils learn;
- be recognised as central to classroom practice;
- be regarded as a key professional skill for teachers;
- be sensitive and constructive because any assessment has an emotional impact;
- take account of the importance of learner motivation;
- promote commitment to learning goals and a shared understanding of the criteria by which pupils will be assessed;
- provide constructive guidance for learners about how to improve;
- develop learners' capacity for self-assessment and recognising their next steps and how to take them;
- recognise the full range of achievement of all learners.

The reason why you will be assessing pupils' learning of mathematics is to plan effective teaching and learning for the future for all pupils. Assessment must also provide feedback to the pupils in order to motivate them and target their learning. Pupils must be aware of what the focus of any assessment will be for each piece of work and who will be assessing their work.

See Chapter 4 of Jacques and Hyland (2007) **Professional Studies** from *Learning Matters.*

PRACTICAL TASK PRACTICAL TASK PRACTICAL TASK PRACTICAL TASK

Read the PNS's Day-to-Day Assessment in Mathematics, which outlines guidance for all teachers working with the strategy. Make a summary of the guidance to keep in your teaching placement file.

Do remember that more detail is expected from your assessment and record-keeping than from an experienced teacher. In your placements towards the end of your course you will be required to keep records of the whole class's progress and attainment in number. Clearly, you will not be able to build up the kind of detailed picture that the class teacher has simply because your placements will not be long enough to enable you to identify every feature of a pupil's mathematical ability. However, you will be able to work with some aspects of answering problems orally, calculation strategies, their written methods, known facts and areas of error or misconception. On earlier placements in your course you will have kept records for mathematics of the pupils with whom you have been working. This may have started with a small group and worked towards records for the whole class. In this way you will have been building up your experience of using ways of assessing pupils' number work and methods of recording that provide you with sufficient information in order to make judgements about their progress and attainment.

One major issue of assessment is the difference between identifying the work that an individual, group, class or set has covered and their attainment and progress. You will need to be able to keep a check on both these aspects. Coverage, however, is not sufficient alone for assessment purposes though it is essential for monitoring pupils' access to the curriculum.

You will be making judgements about pupils' work through marking and by considering responses to questions posed all the time in the classroom. What you will need to do is to think about ways to record this information to assist future planning and/or discussions with the class teacher/your mentor about teaching and learning in mathematics.

RESEARCH SUMMARY RESEARCH SUMMARY RESEARCH SUMMARY

Cowie (2005), in his article entitled 'Pupil commentary on assessment for learning', suggests that assessment for learning is different from other forms of assessment as it aims to enhance the learning rather than measure it. Pupils and all adults involved in their learning share the criteria by which pupils are being judged and include opportunities for pupils' self-monitoring in the process in order that assessment for learning can be successful. A key part of this article is the focus on the barriers to success of the assessment. This links with the current agenda of breaking down the barriers to learning through the five outcomes of ECM.

Are there any barriers to success with assessment for learning? This type of assessment practice relies on teachers developing in their pupils an orientation towards 'learning' as distinct from 'performance'. The study also highlighted the further complication that pupils are motivated by social goals (such as establishing relationships with teachers and peers) as well as academic goals. The author suggested that pupil dispositions are not fixed and can be changed by, for example, the way teachers give feedback and the type of feedback given.

The following techniques will provide you with information about assessments for learning.

Assessment during the lesson

During the main activity of the daily mathematics lesson you could be working with a group and choose to assess specific skills, knowledge and/or understanding of the topic taught. One trainee achieved this by developing her own sheet on which she recorded the information to assist her in future planning.

Date	Group
Objectives	
Notes including specific barriers to learning – attitudes, behaviour as well as match of work to the pupils' needs	
Objective(s) achieved	
Targets	
Review	

PRACTICAL TASK PRACTICAL TASK **PRACTICAL TASK** PRACTICAL TASK

During a lesson plan to sit with a group to carry out in depth assessment in the main activity phase of the lesson.

Assessment at the end of the lesson

One way to assess a number of pupils at the same time is to map out the progression expected in order that you can identify specific difficulties. The following is a blank template that you could use to begin this process. This is followed by one already filled out for a specific objective.

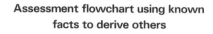

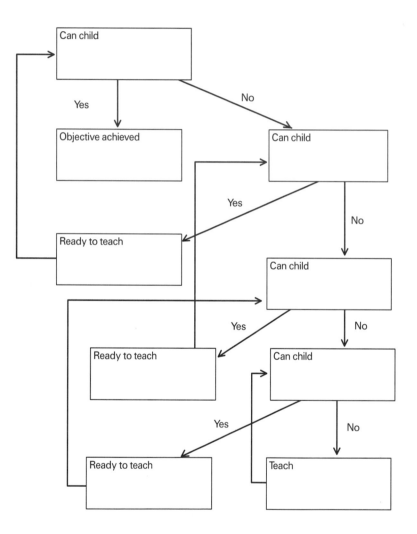

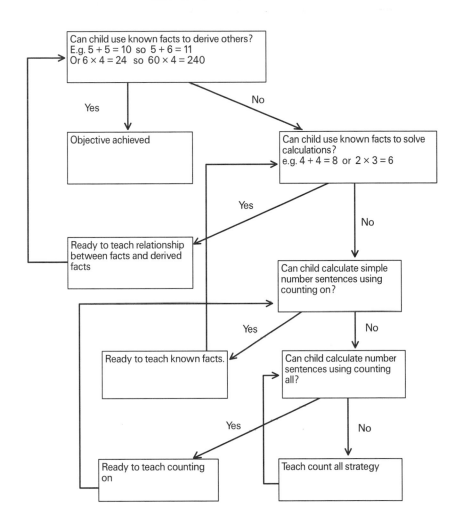

**Assessment flow chart using known
facts to derive others**

PRACTICAL TASK PRACTICAL TASK **PRACTICAL TASK** PRACTICAL TASK

Produce your own flow chart for an objective you will be teaching, which will help you assess.
Then use the information to plan the next lesson.

Marking

Schools often have clear policies on marking, or at least guidance in relation to the style of marking, and it is worth asking your class teacher/mentor about your placement school's views about this issue. The following focuses on some general issues about marking for you to consider alongside school-specific guidance.

Try to mark the work by a pupil called John shown below and, as you do so, think about what you can tell from it:

John Y3

1.	30 + 57 **87**	6.	21 - 15 **14**
2.	47 + 15 **1⁰⁷1**	7.	82 - 24 **82**
3.	12⁵7̷4 + 159 **13⁶1̷2**	8.	2⁸9̷3 - 185 **108**
4.	5 + 135 **648**	9.	438 - 21 **417**
5.	11 + 696 **29**	10.	687 - 47 **640**

At this stage there are no specific comments about this example of pupil's work. The idea is to get you to think about what kinds of assumption you are making about the work as you mark.

- Before pupils are asked to hand in work they should know that you will be marking this specific task rather than it being self-marked or peer-marked.
- Pupils should know what you will be focusing on when marking and it should relate to individual targets set where appropriate. Some schools have adopted the WILF acronym of 'What I Look For' in each piece of work so all pupils know what is expected of them.
- Pupils should have been reminded about any layout or presentation issues.
- When receiving the work you will want to look for successes as well as aspects that will need to be developed and may well form some future targets for the individual.
- Indicate which answers are correct and which are not. (Make sure you get it right!) Do not mark a whole page of work wrong but see the pupil separately. Make sure that you indicate if there are any corrections to be completed and why.
- Try to write comments that inform the pupil and that are in legible handwriting; try to

avoid writing 'good' or 'well done' on their own – say why a piece of work is good.

- Set pupils between one and three targets as a result of marking this piece of work.
- Choose a colour of pen that is in contrast to the pupil's work. There may be a school policy about not using red.
- If you are not sure what is going on when you look at a pupil's work, do not mark it. Set aside time to talk to the pupil individually. We can make assumptions about difficulties based upon the recording we see and that can lead us to plan intervention that is not appropriate.
- This type of marking can assist you as a teacher in collecting evidence of pupils' progress and attainment. You can use this as formative assessment, which will inform the next stage of planning. It will give you and others an indication of the amount of help needed to complete a task if this information is added to your comments on the work, e.g. 'Robert worked with James on this problem' or 'Amy used a calculator for this work'. You can use it as the basis of pupil conferences and it will assist you in compiling summative reports for parents. Table 5.1 will help you think about the type of feedback that you give when marking.

	Type A Rewarding	Type B Approving	Type C Specifying attainment	Type D Constructing achievement	
Positive feedback	Rewards	Positive personal expression Warm expression of feeling General praise Positive non-verbal feedback	Specific acknowledgement of attainment/use of criteria in relation to work/behaviour Teacher models More specific praise	Mutual articulation of achievement Additional use of emerging criteria Child role in presentation Praise integral to description	Achievement feedback
	Punishing	Disapproving	Specifying improvement	Constructing the way forward	
Negative feedback	Punishing	Negative personal expression Reprimands Negative generalisations Negative non-verbal feedback	Correction of errors More practice given Training in self-checking	Mutual critical appraisal	Improvement feedback

Table 5.1 Feedback from marking strategies

Source: Adapted from Gipps (1997), cited in Conner (1999)

The following are examples of assessment and recording, including target-setting, for pupils. They are designed to be used in conjunction with schools' marking and MARRA policies and also provide you with some potential strategies if the school has not fully developed this area yet.

From Cowie's (2005) research with pupils in relation to assessment for learning it is important to note that pupils did not find comments like 'very good' helpful and preferred feedback in the form of suggestions of what to do next. They also found it helpful if teachers used a language that they understood and if teachers revisited ideas and explanation in the class time as well as giving individual feedback. Black and Wiliam (1998) pick out specific issues that relate to marking and giving feedback which you need to consider as you mark children's mathematics work. They found that teachers:

- **valued quantity and presentation rather than the quality of learning;**
- **lowered the self-esteem of pupils by over-concentrating on judgements rather than advice for improvement;**
- **demoralised pupils by comparing them negatively and repeatedly with more successful learners;**
- **gave feedback that serves social and managerial purposes rather than helping pupils to learn more effectively;**
- **worked with an incomplete picture of pupils' learning needs.**

The final point is something that ECM is trying to address with information sharing across all professionals working with a pupil so a 'holistic' picture is possible of the individual's needs to ensure that barriers to learning are removed.

Monitoring the development of mental calculation strategies

Below are lists of the strategies you might expect pupils to use, against which you can check their achievement and progress. If you add dates to this form of assessment record you can begin to identify progress over time. Often this is the most difficult area for trainees as the length of some placements can be quite short. The examples are of specific records focusing on the mental/oral strategies but you may wish to amend something like this to fit more closely your needs for recording attainment and progress of a specific class.

An example of a student's work using this type of grid is shown opposite.

Observing an individual/group working

Below is an example of the observations made of a pupil's working and annotated work.

Name _Dale De_   3th November

Adding and subtracting of two digit numbers

1) $14 + 11 = 25$

Explain how you worked it out.

$10 + 10 = 20 \quad 4 + 1 = 5 = 25$

In adding the numbers, Dale uses the written strategy, breaking each number down into 'tens' and 'units':
$10 + 10 = 20$
$4 + 1 = 5$
25

2) $11 + 14 = 25$

Explain how you worked it out.

Counted back from 25

Here, Dale started on 25 and counted back 11 – he used his fingers to help him. He did not think about the correspondence between sum 1 and sum 2.

Foundation Stage strategies	Y/N	Notes	ELG ref.
Can repeat a number rhyme accurately with appropriate actions			
Recite the number names in the correct order (say up to what number)			
Count accurately objects using one-to-one correspondence (say up to what number)			
Find a specific digit and say what it is (e.g. asked to find a number 5 can do so)			
Find a number of objects to match a numeral or carry out an action a number of times (e.g. asked to find four objects can do so, or can hop five times)			
Uses count all to find total of small numbers of objects			
Uses count on from either number in a calculation			
Uses count on from the largest number			
Can subitise small numbers of objects without counting (know from the pattern of objects how many there are without counting, e.g. ⠖ is five)			
Has some known facts (note what they are like, e.g. 1 + 1 = 2)			

Key Stage 1 strategies	Y/N	Notes	NC level
Count on or back in 10s or 1s (say how far)			
Find a small difference by counting up from the smaller number to largest			
Reorder numbers in calculation			
Add 3/4 small numbers by putting largest number first			
Finding pairs that total 9, 10, 11			
Bridge through a multiple of 10 then adjust			
Use knowledge of number facts and PV to add/subtract pairs of numbers			
Partition into 5 and a bit when adding 6, 7, 8, 9			
Add/subtract a near multiple of 10 to or from a two-digit number			
Identify near doubles			
Use patterns of similar calculations			
Say a subtraction statement corresponding to a given addition statement			
Multiply a number by 10/100 shifting its digits one/two places to the left			
Use knowledge of number facts and PV to multiply or divide by 2, 5, 10, 100			
Use doubling or halving			
Say a division statement corresponding to a given multiplication statement			

Key Stage 2 strategies	Y/N	Notes	NC level
Count on or back in 10s or 1s or 100s.			
Count using decimals and fractions			
Count from any number in whole numbers and decimals steps extending beyond zero			
Find a small difference by counting up from the smaller number to largest			
Count up through the next multiple of 10, 100, 1000			
Reorder numbers in calculation			
Add 3 or 4 small numbers, finding pairs that total 9, 10, 11			
Bridge through a multiple of 10 then adjust			
Partition into tens , units and hundreds , adding tens first			
Bridge through 100			
Use knowledge of number facts and PV to add/ subtract pairs of numbers			
Partition into 5 and a bit when adding 6, 7, 8, 9			
Add/subtract a near multiple of 10 to or from a two-digit number			
Identify near doubles			
Use patterns of similar calculations			
Say a subtraction statement corresponding to a given addition statement			
Multiply a number by 10/100 shifting its digits one/two places to the left			
Use knowledge of number facts and PV to multiply or divide by 2, 5, 10, 100			
Use doubling or halving single digits			
Use doubling and halving of two-digit numbers			
Say a division statement corresponding to a given multiplication statement			
Use known facts and PV to multiply or divide by 10 and then 100			
Partition to carry out multiplication			

An example of a student's work using this type of grid is shown opposite

Identifying Children's Mental Strategies in Mathematics.

Key objectives Year 5	Anthony (Low ability →)	Rachel	Adam	Ashley (→ High ability)
Count on or back in units, tens or hundreds.	✓	✓	✓	✓
Explain the value of each digit in a four-digit number.	not really. After prompting, not confident	✓	✓	✓
Write in figures numbers like fifty-six thousand and nine.	✗	✓	✓ ok	✓
Order a set of decimals with the same number of decimal places: all positive numbers.	✓	✓	✓	✓
...With negative numbers and zero.	not zero – did not include ✗	✓	✓	✓
Round a number to the nearest integer. 10s, 100s, 1000s	✓	✓	✓	✓
Mentally add or subtract any pair of two-digit numbers.	weak	✓	✓	✓
Double two-digit numbers. Halve numbers	weaker on halving ✓	✓	✓	✓
Add several small numbers – reordering numbers to make calculations easier.	yes – needed prompting to reorder	✓	✓	✓
Find a small difference by counting up from the smaller to larger number.	✓	✓	✓	✓
Work out how many to make the next 100 (e.g. 651 + □ = 700)	✗	✗	✓	✓
Work out how many to make the next 1000.	✗ N/A	✗	✓	✓
Use a written method to add or subtract three or four-digit numbers, explain it...	+ evidence in wit but – weak, issues with pv ✗	✓	not tested	not yet
...and check by approximating.	✗	✗		✓
Say a subtraction statement corresponding to a given addition statement (the 4 facts).	yes – evidence in work book	✓	✓	✓

The same can be done for written strategies. The following has been completed in a different way to demonstrate the variety of possible formats for different purposes.

	Written recording and calculation strategies	Y/N	Notes
R	Recording in the context of play, e.g. marks, stamps, physical objects		
Yr 1	Record in the context of practical activities and when solving simple number problems, e.g. number sentences		
Yr 2	Develop recording in the context of practical work and explaining how problems were solved, e.g. how much money there would be if there are 5 coins in a box		
	Use the symbols +, −, ×, ÷ and = to record and interpret number sentences involving all four operatons. Calculate the value of an unknown in a number sentence (square shape divided by 2=6 and 30− square shape = 24)		
Yr 3	Use informal paper and pencil methods to support, record and explain mental addition and subtraction of number to 1,000, e.g. using an empty number line to show how 301−45 was calculated		
	Begin to use column addition and subtraction, using expanded form, e.g. 456 + 63: 400 + 50 + 6 + 60 + 3 400 + 110 + 9 = 519		
Yr 4	Refine and use efficient written methods +/−2 digit and 3 digit whole numbers and £p.		
	Develop and refine written methods for TU × U and TU ÷ U including division with reminders		
	Choose and use appropriate ways of calculating (mental, mental with jottings, pencil and paper) to solve problem		
Yr 5	Extend written methods to column addition and subtraction of two integers less than 1,000 and decimals with up to 2 decimal places e.g. 456 +362		
	Short multiplication of HTU by U		
	Long multiplication of TU by TU		
	Short division of HTU by U		
	Choose and use appropriate ways of calculating (mental, mental with jottings, written methods, calculator)		
	Explain methods and reasoning in writing		
Yr 6	Use efficient written methods to add and subtract integers and decimals, and x and divide integers and decimals by 1 digit integers and to multiply 2 digit and 3 digit integers by a 2 digit integer		
	In solving mathematical problems and problems involving 'real life', explain methods and reasoning in writing		
	Begin to develop from explaining a generalised relationship in words to expressing it in a formula using letters and symbols		

Try to make notes of what is happening when a group is working, and think about what you gain from doing this. What are the difficulties/disadvantages of trying to assess pupils in this way?

To assist you in observing in classrooms you may find it useful to read Wragg (1994). Observation is often used as a technique in the early years where pupils may be in play or less structured situations than a numeracy lesson in Key Stages 1 or 2. If you have the opportunity you may be able to observe in an Early Years setting. If you are able to observe in both situations you will be able to reflect on the relative appropriateness of the technique in each situation.

Remember to note verbal and non-verbal behaviours that may give you more information about barriers to learning.

Concept mapping

An alternative way of finding out about pupils' understanding is to use a technique more often associated with science teaching and that is to ask pupils to construct a concept map. These can range from simple labelled diagrams and drawings to more complex maps, which involve asking pupils how they connect a wider range of words. Arrows can be added to show the direction of the relationship between items.

Below are simple examples of this technique from a Year 1 and a Year 6 pupil. The Year 1 pupil was asked to think about 5 and what she thought of when she saw the numeral 5. As you can see, her thoughts range from the face of a dice to thinking about 5 as the answer for number sentences. You would need to know the context and prior experience of the pupil to know whether or not they are making connections from what they have been taught or new connections by themselves.

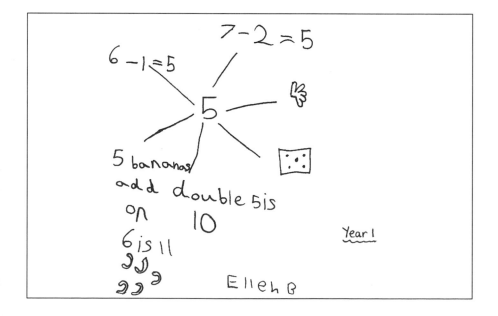

The Year 6 pupil was asked to think about fractions and what they meant to him. Although he started with drawing the cake which is often the first image that people think of when asked about fractions he moves on to see the connection between sharing a cake and decimals and percentages.

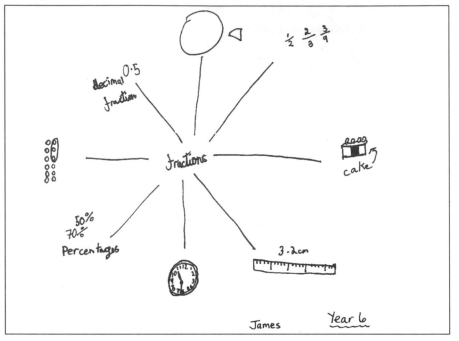

PRACTICAL TASK PRACTICAL TASK **PRACTICAL TASK** PRACTICAL TASK

Before you start to teach a topic, while in school ask the class to spend a few minutes constructing a concept map. You can use this to see any obvious errors and misconceptions about the topic. This will be valuable information on which to base your planning.

The other thing you can do is to ask the pupils to draw a concept map at the end of the series of lessons on the topic, then compare the items included and the connections between them.

Probing questions

The NNS developed probing questions as part of the Assess and Review lessons folder from the NNS for teachers to use as part of their direct teaching of the objective in order to:

- **get pupils to think about the new learning;**
- **make links and so develop a more secure understanding;**
- **explore whether pupils have any misconceptions which can then be addressed at the beginning of the main activity part of the lesson.**

Probing questions may also be used as part of the plenary/review in order to:

- **collect evidence of pupils' understanding to inform effective planning of future lessons;**
- **identify and rectify misconceptions.**

An example of probing questions for Year 4 from the forthcoming materials is as follows:

> *Key objectives: find remainders after division.*
> Do all your divisions have remainders?
>
> Make up some division questions that have a remainder of 1 etc.
>   How did you get your answer?
>
> Make up some division questions that have no remainder.
>   How did you do this? Why won't they have a remainder?
>
> Tell me a number that has no remainder when you divide it by 2, 3 or 5.
>   Are there any others?

You may find it useful to look at the Assess and Review materials (DfES, 2001) in order to assist your planning and assessment in the review lesson in each half term (see **http://www.standards.dfes.gov.uk/primary/publications/mathematics/assess.review**).

Target setting

The context for the following example is a specifically targeted task during which the teacher makes notes about a group of pupils:

Name	Comments/notes
Joe	Shows good understanding of four rules for two-digit numbers in all cases – confident.
Laura	Makes careless mistakes – often masking her lack of understanding. Focuses on the procedures for calculating rather than using knowledge of numbers.
Jenny	Lacks knowledge of odd numbers – this was apparent in lesson on halving and identifying numbers that could not be halved into two equal groups of whole numbers.
Lee	Some work needed on the operation of division – does not see division as sharing.
Jean	Reasonable awareness – some confusion over place value. Need to spend time with her while she calculates in order to find out exactly what the problems are.
Leon	Not sure of multiplication facts – needs support with different ways to help him learn facts.

This will give the teacher notes about the pupils' achievement during a specific task and will often include comments about attitudes. How easy would someone else find it to interpret these records? What do you understand might be the next step for each of these pupils? How might you change these records to make them easily interpreted by another teacher?

Assessment conference with an individual pupil

PRACTICAL TASK PRACTICAL TASK **PRACTICAL TASK** PRACTICAL TASK

Plan to spend 10 minutes with a pupil to talk about their mathematics, review their progress and together set targets for the next few weeks' work. In setting targets you need to choose ones that are achievable both in quality and in content. Concentrate on one area at a time so the pupil doesn't feel swamped. Always pick out things the pupil has achieved as well so the conference doesn't dwell on negative issues alone – praise success. Remember this process is not just for SEN pupils but for all and target setting can be a good way of raising expectations for the higher attaining pupils. Set a time by which you will review these targets. The main purpose of this conferencing and target setting is to give pupils some goals to aim for against which they can measure their own success. It may be possible for some pupils to conference in small groups but there will be pupils for whom it is better to work on an individual basis.

You will need to keep a record of targets set, for example:

Pupil's name:	Year:
Term:	Class:
Date of assessment:	Date of review:
Targets set:	Comment on achievement:
1. 2. 3.	

Diagnostic assessment

Below is an example of closed diagnostic assessment for errors in subtraction.

This form of assessment is often used when you can see that a pupil has a problem but perhaps can't identify exactly what is going wrong. It can take the form of setting a pupil/group specific questions and observing how they tackle these and/or asking pupils to talk you through their method of working on questions. This commonly occurs when pupils are using algorithms without understanding. They do not remember the method sufficiently to succeed at answering the

Source: Resnick (1982) (adapted from Brown and Burton, 1978), quoted in Dickson et al., 1984.

questions and errors are the result. The examples opposite are of errors in subtraction. Try to identify the error in each case.

What does each example reflect about the pupils' understanding of the method and how would you rectify it?

Here is the analysis of what is happening:

1. The pupil has subtracted the smaller digit from the larger digit regardless of which is on top.
2. The pupil has 'exchanged' from zero (that is, has not continued the 'exchanging' from the column to the left of the zero).
3. The pupil has missed out the column with the zero and 'exchanged' instead from the next column, disregarding the middle column.
4. The pupil has 'exchanged' but has not decremented either column.
5. The pupil has 'exchanged' from the correct column and decremented that column but not the column containing the zero. The pupil has then subtracted zero from 12 instead of 1.
6. The pupil has written 0 as the answer in any column in which the bottom digit is larger than the top.
7. The top digit in the column being 'exchanged' from is zero, so the pupil has 'borrowed' from the bottom digit instead.

These errors all indicate a misunderstanding of the subtraction algorithm and aspect of place value.

> **PRACTICAL TASK** PRACTICAL TASK **PRACTICAL TASK** PRACTICAL TASK
>
> Try observing one pupil or a group using a formal algorithm. What does the pupils' writing tell you about their understanding?
>
> Ask a pupil to explain how they did one of the questions. What assessment can you make of their understanding?

Records

The NNS produced some class and individual record sheets to support teachers' recording of assessment.

Year records

Many schools use the year group records at the end of a half term or term to highlight the objectives that most pupils have achieved in green, those that some have had some difficulties with in orange and those not achieved or not addressed in red. These are then used to plan the next half term/term's objectives. This process gives an overview of achievement within a set or class (pp. 84–85).

Records for a group/class

These are blank record sheets, which can be used for a group/class. The idea is that you write in your learning objectives for the lesson and then assess if the pupils have achieved them. Where pupils have specific difficulties then the second sheet is used to record these in greater detail (pp. 84–87).

Key Objectives Year 2

| Solve problems involving addition, subtraction, multiplication or division in contexts of numbers, measures or pounds and pence |
| Identify and record the information or calculation needed to solve a puzzle or problem; carry out the steps or calculations and check the solution in the context of the problem |
| Follow a line of enquiry; answer questions by choosing and using suitable equipment and selecting, organising and presenting information in lists, tables and simple diagrams |
| Describe patterns and relationships involving numbers or shapes, make predictions and test these with examples |
| Present solutions to puzzles and problems in an organised way; explain decisions, methods and results in pictorial, spoken or written form, using mathematical language and number sentences |
| Read and write two-digit and three-digit numbers in figures and words; describe and extend number sequences and recognise odd and even numbers |
| Count up to 100 objects by grouping them and counting in tens, fives or twos; explain what each digit in a two-digit number represents, including numbers where 0 is a place holder; partition two-digit numbers in different ways, including into multiples of 10 and 1 |
| Order two-digit numbers and position them on a number line; use the greater than (>) and less than (<) signs |
| Estimate a number of objects; round two-digit numbers to the nearest 10 |
| Find one half, one quarter and three quarters of shapes and sets of objects |
| Add or subtract mentally a one-digit number or a multiple of 10 to or from any two-digit number; use practical and informal written methods to add and subtract two-digit numbers |
| Understand that subtraction is the inverse of addition and vice versa; use this to derive and record related addition and subtraction number sentences |
| Represent repeated addition and arrays as multiplication, and sharing and repeated subtraction (grouping) as division; use practical and informal written methods and related vocabulary to support multiplication and division, including calculations with remainders |
| Use the symbols , ·, and to record and interpret number sentences involving all four operations; calculate the value of an unknown in a number sentence (e.g. 2 6, 30 - 24) |
| Visualise common 2-D shapes and 3-D solids; identify shapes from pictures of them in different positions and orientations; sort, make and describe shapes, referring to their properties |
| Identify reflective symmetry in patterns and 2-D shapes and draw lines of symmetry in shapes |
| Follow and give instructions involving position, direction and movement |
| Recognise and use whole, half and quarter turns, both clockwise and anticlockwise; know that a right angle represents a quarter turn |
| Estimate, compare and measure lengths, weights and capacities, choosing and using standard units (m, cm, kg, litre) and suitable measuring instruments |
| Read the numbered divisions on a scale, and interpret the divisions between them (e.g. on a scale from 0 to 25 with intervals of 1 shown but only the divisions 0, 5, 10, 15 and 20 numbered); use a ruler to draw and measure lines to the nearest centimetre |
| Use units of time (seconds, minutes, hours, days) and know the relationships between them; read the time to the quarter hour; identify time intervals, including those that cross the hour |
| Answer a question by collecting and recording data in lists and tables; represent the data as block graphs or pictograms to show results; use ICT to organise and present data |
| Use lists, tables and diagrams to sort objects; explain choices using appropriate language, including 'not' |

Year record sheet

Calculation Strand		Name	
Year 4	Year 5	Year 6	Progression from Year 6 to Year 7
Add or subtract mentally pairs of two-digit whole numbers (e.g. 47 + 58, 91 − 35)	Extend mental methods for whole-number calculations, for example to multiply a two-digit number by a one-digit number (e.g. 12 × 9), to multiply by 25 (e.g. 16 × 25), to subtract one near multiple of 1000 from another (e.g. 6070 − 4097)	Calculate mentally with integers and decimals: U.t ± U.t, TU × U, TU ÷ U, U.t × U, U.t ÷ U	Understand how the commutative, associative and distributive laws, and the relationships between operations, including inverse operations, can be used to calculate more efficiently; use the order of operations, including brackets
Refine and use efficient written methods to add and subtract two-digit and three-digit whole numbers and £.p	Use efficient written methods to add and subtract whole numbers and decimals with up to two places	Use efficient written methods to add and subtract integers and decimals, to multiply and divide integers and decimals by a one digit integer, and to multiply two-digit and three-digit integers by a two-digit integer	Consolidate and extend mental methods of calculation to include decimals, fractions and percentages
Multiply and divide numbers to 1000 by 10 and then 100 (whole-number answers), understanding the effect; relate to scaling up or down	Use understanding of place value to multiply and divide whole numbers and decimals by 10, 100 or 1000	Relate fractions to multiplication and division (e.g. 6 ÷ 2 = 1/2 of 6 = 6 × 1/2); express a quotient as a fraction or decimal (e.g. 67 ÷ 5 = 13.4 or 132/5); find fractions and percentages of whole-number quantities (e.g. 5/8 of 96, 65% of £260	Use standard column procedures to add and subtract integers and decimals, and to multiply two-digit and three-digit integers by a one-digit or two-digit integer; extend division to dividing three-digit integers by a two-digit integer
Develop and use written methods to record, support and explain multiplication and division of two-digit numbers by a one-digit number, including division with remainders (e.g. 15 × 9, 98 ÷ 6)	Refine and use efficient written methods to multiply and divide HTU × U, TU × TU, U.t × U and HTU ÷ U		Calculate percentage increases or decreases and fractions of quantities and measurements (integer answers)
Find fractions of numbers, quantities or shapes (e.g. 1/5 of 30 plums, 3/8 of a 6 by 4 rectangle)	Find fractions using division (e.g. 1/100 of 5 kg), and percentages of numbers and quantities (e.g. 10%, 5% and 15% of £80)	Use a calculator to solve problems involving multi-step calculations	Use bracket keys and the memory of a calculator to carry out calculations with more than one step; use the square root key
Use a calculator to carry out one-step and two step calculations involving all four operations; recognise negative numbers in the display, correct mistaken entries and interpret the display correctly in the context of money	Use a calculator to solve problems, including those involving decimals or fractions (e.g. find 3/4 of 150 g); interpret the display correctly in the context of measurement		

Year record sheet for an individual pupil

NAME	ATTENDANCE REGISTER															TARGETS ACHIEVED									
	☑ = PRESENT 0 = ABSENT															1	2	3	4	5	6	7	8	9	10

A = ACHIEVED   HD = HAD DIFFICULTY WITH   NA = NEEDS ATTENTION   U = UNFINISHED

TARGET 1 -
TARGET 2 -
TARGET 3 -
TARGET 4 -
TARGET 5 -
TARGET 6 -
TARGET 7 -
TARGET 8 -
TARGET 9 -
TARGET 10 -

Evaluation and assessment record sheet after each lesson

Assessment :- Needs Attention

Name: **Subject:**   **Date:**

Objectives of lesson:

Problem(s):

What needs to be done:

Evaluation:

More detailed assessment sheet for a specific individual

These are designed to give an overview. You will want to supplement them with daily and weekly notes on individuals/groups as a result of observation and marking to provide information for diagnostic purposes, to enrich reports to parents and to assist in individual target-setting:

Topic: <u>Calculations – pencil and paper procedures Week Commencing: 20th November</u>
<u>addition/subtraction</u>

National Numeracy Strategy: 49. 51 "Use informal paper and pencil methods to support, record or explain additions and subtractions. Extend written methods to column addition / subtraction of integers, and decimal fractions."

Name	20.11	21.11	22.11	23.11	24.11	
	1	2	3	3	4	Additional Notes, including overall grasp of topic.
Anthony						
Scott						
Morgan						
Chelsey						
Liam						
Natalie						
Emma						
Nicola						
Nicola						
Becky						
Mellissa						
Ashley						
Harleen						
Ben						
Thomas						
Lauren						
Jody						
Hannah						
Hollie						
Sonia						
Tannia						
Stacey						
Laura						
James						
Rachel						
Natasha						

Key

*	**Achieved target - firm understanding of concepts.**
+	Struggled with a few aspects, would benefit from further practise.
=	**Had difficulty with, needs reinforcement.**
-	Needs attention, understands some elements.
.	**Has not understood key concepts.**
O	Absent.

Target

1	Calculate additions in columns, including setting them out correctly in HTU columns – awareness of place value.
2	Adding numbers with 1 or 2 decimal points.
3	Calculate subtractions in columns, including setting them out correctly in HTU columns - awareness of place value.
4	Subtracting numbers with 1 or 2 decimal points.

Supplementary daily/weekly record sheet

One of the difficulties about these type of records is the key that is used to differentiate achievement against the objectives. A clear key can make the records accessible to all but sometimes the key could be interpreted in a range of ways. Look at the examples of students' records shown overleaf. Which is clearer to understand and why?

Mathematics record Sheet

School

Key Objectives Year 1

Key Objectives	RAVINDER	KAMRAAN	ADAM	JACK	JOSHUA	CHRISTOPHER	ANDREW B.	NISHA	JASPREET	ABIGAIL G.	ABIGAIL T	STEFAN	FAY	JASKRAN	DANIEL	STEVEN	MATTHEW	SARAH	KATIE	SOPHIE	ANDREW F.	ALEX	HOLLIE	NORINA	LEAH	SHANNON	CARLA	VICTORIA
Count reliably at least 20 objects.																												
Count on and back in ones, twos, fives from any small number, and in tens from and back to zero.																												
Read, write and order numbers from 0 to at least 20; understand and use the vocabulary of comparing and ordering these numbers.	√	√			√	√	√		√	√	△	√	√	√	△	√	△	√	√	△	△	△	△	√	√	√	√	△
Within the range 0 to 30, say the number that is 1 or 10 more or less than any given number.	√	√	√	√	√	√	√																					
Understand the operation of addition, and of subtraction (as 'take away' or 'difference'), and use the related vocabulary.																												
Know by heart all pairs of numbers with a total of 10.	√	√	√	√	√	√	√	√	√	△	△	√	√	√	△	√	△	√	√	△	△	△	△	√	△	△	△	△
Use mental strategies to solve simple problems using counting, addition, subtraction, doubling and halving, explaining methods and reasoning orally.	√	√	√	√	√	√	√	√	√	√	√	√	√	√	√	√	√	√	√	√	△	△	△	△	△	△	△	△
Compare two lengths, masses or capacities by direct comparison.	√	√	√	√	√	√	√	√	△	△	√	△	△	△	△	△	△	△	△	△	△	△	△	△	△	△	△	△
Suggest suitable standard or uniform non-standard units and measuring equipment to estimate, then measure a length, mass or capacity.	√	√	√	√	√	√	√	√	√	√	√	√	√	√	√	√	√	√	√	√	△	△	△	△	△	△	△	△
Use everyday language to describe features of familiar 3-D and 2-D shapes.	√	√	√	√	√	√	√	√	√	√	√	√	△	√	△	△	△	△	△	△	△	△	△	△	△	△	△	△

MATHS

NAME	ATTENDANCE REGISTER ✓ = PRESENT O = ABSENT										TARGETS ACHIEVED 1	2	3	4	5	6	7	8	9	10
RED																				
BILLY	✓	✓	✓	✓	✓	✓	✓	✓	✓		A+	HD	HD	A	HD	A	A	HD	A	A
FAIZ	✓	✓	✓	✓	✓	✓	✓	✓			A	A+	A+	A	HD	A	HD	NA	A	A
JANINE	✓	✓	✓	✓	✓	✓	✓	✓			HD	A	HD	A	HD	A	A	HD	U	A
KATRINA	✓	✓	✓	✓	✓	✓	✓	✓			A	A	A	A	HD	A	A	HD	A	HD
TOM	✓	✓	✓	✓	✓	✓	✓	✓			A	A	HD	A	HD	A	A	A	A	A
KIRAN	✓	✓	✓	✓	✓	✓	✓	✓			A	A	A	A	A	A	A	HD	A	A
BLUE																				
SOPHIE	✓	✓	✓	✓	✓	✓	✓	✓			A	A	A	A	A	A	A	A	A	A
LIAM	✓	✓	✓	✓	✓	✓	✓	✓			A	A+	A	A	A	A	A	A	A	A+
LIAM	✓	✓	✓	✓	✓	✓	✓	✓			HD	HD	A	A	AU	HD	A+	A	A	A+
LYDIA	✓	✓	✓	✓	✓	✓	✓	✓			A	HD	A	A	A	A	A	NA	A	A
MOLLY	✓	✓	✓	✓	✓	O	✓	✓	✓		A	HD	A	A	A	✗	A	A	A	A
FIONA	✓	✓	✓	✓	✓	✓	✓	✓			A	A	A	A	A	A	A	A	A	A
LAUREN	✓	✓	✓	O	✓	✓	✓	O	O	O	A	A	A	✗	A	A	A	✗	✗	
SARAH	✓	✓	✓	✓	✓	✓	✓	✓			A	HD	HD	A	AU	A	A	A	A	A
GREEN																				
FAHMIDA	✓	O	✓	✓	✓	✓	✓	✓			A	✗	AU	A	A	A	A	A	HD	A
JASKAREN	✓	✓	✓	✓	✓	✓	✓	✓	✓		A	A	A	A	A	A	A	A	A	A
DANNY	✓	✓	✓	✓	✓	✓	✓	✓			HD	A	HD	A	HD	A	A	A	A	A
ALEX	✓	✓	✓	✓	✓	✓	✓	✓			A	A	HD	A	A	A	A+	A	A	A+
NEEL	✓	✓	✓	✓	✓	✓	✓	✓			A	A	A	HD	A	A	A	A	A	A
HANNAH	✓	✓	✓	✓	✓	✓	✓	✓			A	A	HD	A	A	A	A	HD	A	A
YELLOW																				
HANNAH	✓	✓	✓	✓	✓	✓	✓	✓			A	A	A	A	A	A	A	A	A	A
HANEEFH	✓	✓	✓	✓	✓	✓	✓	✓			A	A+	A	A	A	A	A	A	A	HD
DAYLION	✓	✓	✓	✓	✓	✓	✓	✓			A	A	A	A	A	U	A	A	A	A
CHARLOTTE	✓	✓	✓	✓	✓	✓	✓	✓			A	HD	A	A	A	A	A	A	A	A
SAM	✓	✓	✓	✓	✓	✓	✓	✓			U	A	NA	A	AU	A	A	HD	A	A
LIA	✓	✓	✓	✓	✓	✓	✓	✓			U	HD	A	A	A	O	A	NA	A	HD
NIKHOLAS	✓	✓	✓	✓	✓	✓	✓	✓			U	U	A	HD	AU	U	A	NA	A	A
SAGE	✓	✓	O	✓	✓	✓	✓	✓			U	HD	✗	A	A	HD	A	NA	A	A

A = ACHIEVED   HD = HAD DIFFICULTY WITH   NA = NEEDS ATTENTION   U = UNFINISHED

20/11/	**TARGET 1 -** TOP: ABLE TO DO SUBTRACTION WITH MONEY MIDDLE: ABLE TO DO SUBTRACTION BOTTOM: ABLE TO DO SUBTRACTION
24/11/	**TARGET 2 -** TOP: ABLE TO MAKE UP VALUES AND WRITE A SUM NAME MIDDLE: MAKE UP VALUES (beginning with money) BOTTOM: COUNT VALUES
27/11/	**TARGET 3 -** TOP: MIDDLE: MAKE UP VALUES WITH A SET NUMBER OF COINS BOTTOM: COUNT VALUES
28/11/	**TARGET 4 -** COMPLETE P.7 & 8 IN NHM BOOK 1 CORRECTLY
29/11/	**TARGET 5 -** MEASURE OBJECTS USING HANDS, FEET OR CUBES
30/11/	**TARGET 6 -** MEASURE OBJECT USING WHICHEVER METHOD APPROPRIATE, ACCURATELY
4/12/	**TARGET 7 -** COMPARE TWO OBJECTS WEIGHTS USING BALANCE SCALES
4/12/	**TARGET 8 -** CHOOSE CRITERIA FOR TWO SETS
7/12/	**TARGET 9 -** PUT OBJECTS INTO TWO SETS
	TARGET 10 - ABLE TO USE THE COMPUTER EFFICIENTLY TO PRACTICE + and −

Summative assessment or assessment of learning in mathematics

Profile for the end of the Foundation Stage

Since 2000 the assessment at the end of the Foundation Stage has been the Profile which is based upon detailed observation of the children throughout the Foundation Stage of 3–5. (It is worth noting that the Early Years Foundation Stage will cover 0–5 from 2008.) The Profile is a document that all adults working with the children will contribute to and forms a summary of achievements during this phase of their education. Children may achieve some or all by the end of the Foundation Stage. The items are not to be seen as a hierarchy and children may achieve them in any order. The following are the items for mathematical development only. The Profile covers all six areas of learning and is shared with parents and carers.

Mathematical development

Numbers as labels and for counting

Says some number names in familiar contexts, such as nursery rhymes.

Counts reliably up to three everyday objects.

Counts reliably up to six everyday objects.

Says number names in order.

Recognises numerals 1 to 9.

Counts reliably up to 10 everyday objects.

Orders numbers up to 10.

Uses developing mathematical ideas and methods to solve practical problems.

The child has achieved all the early learning goals for numbers as labels and for counting. In addition, the child:

Recognises, counts, orders, writes and uses numbers up to 20.

Calculating

Responds to the vocabulary involved in addition and subtraction in rhymes and games.

Recognises differences in quantity when comparing sets of objects.

Finds one more or one less from a group of up to five objects.

Relates addition to combining two groups.

Relates subtraction to taking away.

In practical activities and discussion, begins to use the vocabulary involved in adding and subtracting.

Finds one more or one less than a number from 1 to 10.

Uses developing mathematical ideas and methods to solve practical problems.

The child has achieved all the early learning goals for calculating. In addition, the child:

Uses a range of strategies for addition and subtraction, including some mental recall of number bonds.

Shape, space and measures

Experiments with a range of objects and materials showing some mathematical awareness.

Sorts or matches objects and talks about sorting.

Describes shapes in simple models, pictures and patterns.

Talks about, recognises and recreates simple patterns.

Uses everyday words to describe position.

Uses language such as 'circle' or 'bigger' to describe the shape and size of solids and flat shapes.

Uses language such as 'greater', 'smaller', 'heavier' or 'lighter' to compare quantities.

Uses developing mathematical ideas and methods to solve practical problems.

The child has achieved all the early learning goals for shape, space and measures. In addition, the child:

Uses mathematical language to describe solid (3-D) objects and flat (2-D) shapes.

National Curriculum tests

At the end of Key Stage 1 the use of the tests is under the control of teachers who can decide when to use them with their children and there is a greater emphasis on teacher assessment. This does mean that if you are teaching in Key Stage 1 you will need to keep detailed notes about the children in order to make judgements about their learning and report this as part of the statutory assessment and to parents and carers.

During Key Stage 2 there are optional or QCA tests for Years 3, 4 and 5 and most schools use these to monitor progress before the statutory assessments in Year 6. The QCA tests are used to aid target setting and decide which pupils would benefit from the use of Springboard and booster materials in order to reduce the barriers to learning and achievement at nationally expected levels.

At the end of Key Stage 2 in Year 6 the pupils sit two papers, one of which allows for the use of a calculator and one of which does not. In addition the children sit a mental mathematics test. These tests allow for demonstrating attainment throughout the level 3–5 range.

RESEARCH SUMMARY RESEARCH SUMMARY RESEARCH SUMMARY

Cooper and Dunne (2000) have researched the SATs (National Curriculum Tests) questions for mathematics at Key Stages 2 and 3. Their focus was that some of the questions selected to use in the tests produced unintended difficulties for pupils as a result of the ways mathematical operations were embedded in textually represented 'realistic' contexts. Understanding the rules of the game could be the reason why some groups of pupils performed poorly on this type of question. In test items with 'realistic' elements pupils are required to draw upon their everyday experiences as well as their previous knowledge and understanding of mathematics. At the end of Key Stage 2 working-class and intermediate-class pupils perform less well than service-class pupils on 'realistic' items and the effect is large enough to make a considerable difference to pupils' futures. Differences between the genders are similar though smaller. Cooper and Dunne's research suggests that, as teachers, we need to be aware of the predisposition and effects of prior knowledge of our pupils when they respond to test items that have 'realistic' elements

Reporting to parents

Reports cover the whole of the primary curriculum and the report for mathematics is only a very small section.

When writing reports to parents you need to remember who the audience is and what they expect to read about their child. Written reports should be supportive and meaningful (i.e. not full of education jargon), and should include positive remarks, but also they should not hide any difficulties. They should include aspects of knowledge, skills, understanding and application. Sometimes it is appropriate to mention presentation and/or attention to tasks by some pupils.

See Chapter 4 of Jacques and Hyland (2007) **Primary Professional Studies** *from Learning Matters.*

Reports can come in different formats. They can be computerised and generated from a bank of suggested phrases, they can be tick sheets, full written reports or any combination of these. Computerisation can lead to quite impersonal reports though it can save time. Written reports usually include targets for the next term/year. They are also usually written when the teacher has had the class for a considerable part of the year so they know the pupils well.

Consider this example of a pupil's mathematics report:

> I am delighted in Sam's progress this year. He has worked hard, always concentrates well and seems to have gained in confidence. He is now happy to work independently and has been imaginative and thoughtful in his approach to investigative work.

This particular report could have been about any subject and for any pupil. It is not specific, and it does not really tell you what the pupil can and cannot do.

Now consider this second example:

Mathematics

Sarah understands place value and can read, write and order whole numbers. She is beginning to have more confidence in developing her own strategies for solving problems. She has a good grasp of the four rules and with help can use inverse operation. She needs to become more independent in this field. She is competent in using decimal notation for money and measurement, and can relate simple fractions with whole numbers. She needs to speed up her mental recall of tables and number bonds. She can construct and interpret information from graphs and use the computer to represent her data. She enjoys the practical aspects of mathematics and can work equally well as a member of a group or as an individual and is presenting her work in a neater and more orderly fashion. She needs to have more confidence in her own ability.

This report is much clearer. It could only be referring to mathematics and there are clear statements of what the pupil can and cannot do.

> ## A SUMMARY OF **KEY POINTS**
>
> > **Assessment is an integral part of the teaching and learning process.**
>
> > **Formative assessment is used to plan effective teaching and learning of mathematics.**
>
> > **A variety of different techniques can be used to collect information upon which to base judgements about progress and attainment.**
>
> > **Marking pupils' work requires careful planning and must include feedback to the pupils.**
>
> > **Record-keeping is a summary of other assessment information that you will have as the teacher.**
>
> > **Reporting to parents needs to be informative and accurate, and to set targets for future learning.**

Moving on

Assessment is not an easy area and is one you are likely to continue to develop throughout your career as a teacher. One area that you may want to develop further during your NQT year is the use of observation by yourself and other adults working in the classroom to inform teaching and learning and to enable more personalisation of learning opportunities, particularly for those who have significant barriers to learning.

REFERENCES REFERENCES **REFERENCES** REFERENCES **REFERENCES**

Assessment Reform Group (1999) *Assessment for Learning: Beyond the Black Box*. University of Cambridge, Faculty of Education.

Assessment Reform Group (2002) *Principles of Assessment for Learning: 10 Principles*. University of Cambridge, Faculty of Educatrion.

Black, P. and Wiliam, D. (1998) *Inside the Black Box: Raising Standards through Classroom Assessment*. King's College, London.

Conner, C. (ed.) (1999) *Assessment in Action in the Primary School*. London: Falmer Press.

Cooper, B. and Dunne, M. (2000) *Assessing Children's Mathematical Knowledge: Social Class, Sex and Problem Solving*. Buckingham: Open University Press.

Cowie, B. (2005) 'Pupil commentary on assessment for learning'. *The Curriculum Journal*, Vol. 16, no. 2, pp. 137–61.

Desforges, M. and Lindsay, G. (1998) *Infant Index*. London: Hodder & Stoughton.

DfEE (1999) *The National Numeracy Strategy: Framework for Teaching Mathematics*. London: DfEE.

DfES (2001) *Using Assess and Review Lessons*. London: DfES.

Ginsburg, H. (1981) 'The clinical interview in psychological research on mathematical thinking: aims, rationales, and techniques', *For the Learning of Mathematics*, 1, 3, pp. 4–10.

Gipps, C. (1997) *Assessment in Primary Schools: Past, Present and Future*. London: British Curriculum Foundation.

Resnick (1982) (adapted from Brown and Burton, 1978) quoted in Dickson, L., Brown, M. and Gibson, O. (1984) *Children Learning Maths: A Teacher Guide to Recent Research*. London: Holt, Rinehart & Winston.

Wragg, E. C. (1994) *An Introduction to Classroom Observation*. London: Routledge.

Useful websites:

www.qca.org.uk
www.aaia.org.uk

http://www.standards.dfes.gov.uk/primary/publications/mathematics/assess_review/

FURTHER READING   FURTHER READING   FURTHER READING

Askew, M. and Wiliam, D. (1995) 'Effective questioning can raise achievement', in *Recent Research in Mathematics Education 5–16*. London: HMSO/Ofsted, pp. 15–16.

Clarke, S. and Atkinson, S. (1996) *Tracking Significant Achievement in Primary Mathematics*. London: Hodder & Stoughton.

Jacques, K. and Hyland, R. (eds) (2007) *Professional Studies: Primary and Early Years*. Exeter: Learning Matters.

Torrance, H. and Pryor, J. (1998) *Investigating Formative Assessment: Teaching, Learning and Assessment in the Classroom*. Buckingham: Open University Press

6
Early mathematics

Introduction

Before children arrive in school they will have had a range of experiences which introduce them to, and require them to use, mathematical concepts. Some are quite overtly mathematical, such as singing number rhymes or creating patterns with objects; others involve mathematical concepts more subtly, such as sorting the washing or laying the table. As teachers it is important to acknowledge and extend the pre-school experiences of the children within the classroom. Maths 'talk' needs to be developed from the early years, so that children are confident to share and discuss their methods and outcomes rather than silently internalising the language of maths. Mathematics is a subject where there is a great danger of rapidly moving towards the silent approach, producing pages of written work and formal algorithms from a young age. It is important that classroom practice reflects a far more active approach. The mathematical experiences of young children should be active, multi-sensory, challenging, practical and relevant.

RESEARCH SUMMARY RESEARCH SUMMARY **RESEARCH SUMMARY**

Some of the current research into Early Years mathematics is cited here. Mathematics education journals and Early Years journals are a useful source of further papers.

Influences on mathematics development
The introduction to this chapter acknowledges the home mathematical experiences children will have had before coming to school, and also during the evenings, weekends and holidays while they are at school. Geary (1994) attempted to model the possible influences on mathematical development. His model recognises the part played by mathematics at home, without which it is incomplete.

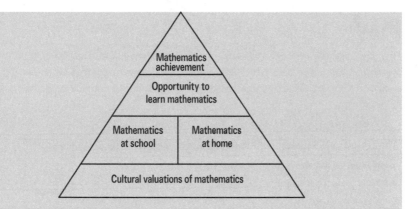

The reality rhetoric gap

Stephen and Wilkinson (1999) researched the curricula offered within a range of Early Years settings. They evaluated how far the particular curriculum met the identified goals for mathematical learning within the setting. They concluded there was a need to engage in careful, focused monitoring of the experiences of children in order to decide if the curriculum was actually meeting the goals. They felt that an acknowledgement of the potential for a gap between the rhetoric and reality was a necessary first step towards reducing it.

Early Years Foundation Stage

From September 2008 the Early Years Foundation Stage (EYFS) is due to come into force. This will be a merger of the Foundation Stage (currently the first Key Stage of the National Curriculum) with the *Birth to Three Matters* Framework. The EYFS will be a single framework for care, learning and development for children in all Early Years settings from birth to the August after their fifth birthday. One outcome of the implementation of this development will be the removal of the Foundation Stage from the National Curriculum. However, the EYFS builds closely on the existing Curriculum Guidance for the Foundation Stage as well as other documentation concerning the care and development of young children. The EYFS will play a key role in setting clear expectations for the care, learning and development young children will receive, whatever the setting they attend. It is intended that the EYFS will mirror the existing guidance and expectations for mathematics as set out in the new framework for literacy and mathematics.

One Area of Learning and Development identified within the Foundation Stage is that of Problem Solving, Reasoning and Numeracy (PSRN). The Primary National Strategy states that this area includes

> *seeking patterns, making connections, recognising relationships, working with numbers, shapes, space and measures, and counting, sorting and matching. Children use their knowledge and skills in these areas to solve problems, generate new questions and make connections across other Areas of Learning and Development.*

The mathematical areas to be developed throughout the Foundation Stage are reflected in the seven strands of the Primary Strategy for Literacy and Mathematics (2006).

Useful resources to support the planning, teaching and learning of PSRN across the Foundation Stage can be downloaded from: **http://www.standards.dfes.gov.uk/primaryframe works/foundation/psrnplanning/**.

Play

One of the key ways children learn in the Early Years is through play. The *Curriculum Guidance for the Foundation Stage* details the opportunities presented to children when playing within a secure environment. Table 6.1 below links these opportunities to possible mathematical situations or outcomes.

Through play, in a secure environment with effective adult support, children can:	Possible mathematical context or outcome:
• explore, develop and represent learning experiences that help them make sense of the world	Children need the opportunity to explore numbers, shapes, patterns and measures and to develop appropriate representations as they start to make sense of these mathematical concepts.
• practise and build up ideas, concepts and skills	Consolidation and practice will enable children to increase their mathematical knowledge and skills, e.g. counting, recognising numbers and shapes.
• learn how to control impulses and understand the need for rules	As children progress in their mathematical learning the need for mathematical rules will become apparent. In the Early Years an understanding of the need for rules in play is a vital first step.
• be alone, be alongside others or cooperate as they talk or rehearse their feelings	These are all contexts that children will work in during their mathematics learning as they progress throughout their primary schooling.
• take risks and make mistakes	Investigating and problem solving in mathematics involves a great deal of risk-taking and learning from your mistakes. Being confident to take risks and to learn from mistakes is an important part of a child's mathematical development.
• think creatively and imaginatively	Mathematics can be, and should be, an extremely creative and imaginative subject that conjures up ideas and images to be used or explored further.
• communicate with others as they investigate or solve problems	Communication is the essence of mathematical investigations or problem solving in order to share discoveries with others.
• express fears or relive anxious experiences in controlled and safe situations	Mathematics anxiety is a well-known reality for some children in school. Being able to articulate this and express fears within a supportive context should ensure mathematics anxiety occurs less often for children.

Table 6.1 Linking play and the teaching of mathematics

The range of mathematical play activities children should experience might include: telling, listening to and creating stories; listening to, singing and adding actions to songs; games and imaginative play, including role play; construction activities; communicating mathematical information to others, e.g. producing labels for the 'class shop', menus for the 'class café'; and so forth. These activities will give children the opportunity to use, explore and experiment with numbers, patterns, shapes and measures.

The *Curriculum Guidance for the Foundation Stage* (p. 25) rightly describes the role of the practitioner as crucial in play, particularly in:

- **planning and resourcing a challenging environment;**
- **supporting children's learning through planned play activity;**
- **extending and supporting children's spontaneous play;**
- **extending and developing children's language and communication in their play.**

Some of these areas will be developed further in this chapter as we look more at teaching and learning mathematics in the Early Years.

Teaching

The *Curriculum Guidance for the Foundation Stage* highlights certain prerequisites for effective mathematics teaching.

- **Practitioners who help children see themselves as mathematicians, and develop positive attitudes and dispositions towards their learning.**
- **Practitioners who maintain children's enthusiasm and confidence when they begin to record their mathematics.**
- **Planning a range of mathematical opportunities.**
- **Making good use of opportunities to talk 'mathematically' as children play or take part in normal daily activities.**
- **Practitioners encouraging children's mathematical development by intervening in their play.**
- **Practitioners who develop children's thinking by showing an interest in methods, not just solutions.**
- **Practitioners who understand that mathematical development does not depend on specific resources.**
- **Practitioners who are confident about themselves as mathematicians and understand the links between different areas of mathematics.**

There are many implications for us as teachers implicit in these statements. First, let us consider the children as they arrive in school. Young children are innately curious and come to school with a great deal of knowledge and understanding in a range of mathematical areas. Their interaction with their physical environment and with other people, as well as the conclusions they have drawn and the ideas they have established from these interactions, form the starting point as they enter the classroom. Their enthusiasm is boundless and their capacity to enjoy new experiences offers teachers a wonderful opportunity to continue the children's mathematical development in a very positive and stimulating manner.

Clear scaffolding to ensure children feel supported as they learn is vital; using real-life contexts and not letting children feel exposed or vulnerable is also crucial. This has clear implications for planning, monitoring, assessment and recording. Knowing exactly where each child is, and what they know, understand and can do is clearly vital if we are to plan meaningful activities that support and extend the children's mathematical learning. This is a very big task for any teacher. It is important to remember that you do not have to do all of this on your own. In Early Years classrooms, teachers should have the help and support of an Early Years assistant. There are currently many initiatives to support the training and development of the role of Early Years assistants and these professional colleagues play a vital role in any Early Years classroom. They can be used to record observations and assessments of children's learning to support your planning for further development. It is important to remember that it is your responsibility as the teacher to ensure your assistant knows the intended outcomes for the children when engaging in activities. It is also your responsibility to ensure they know how, when and where to record their observations. Using classroom support in this way is invaluable in ensuring you have a full and detailed picture of the children's knowledge and understanding of mathematics.

Maths 'talk' is also vital in ensuring children continue to develop a precise and accurate understanding of the technical mathematical vocabulary. Capitalise on every opportunity throughout the day, as part of the classroom or playground organisation and during play activities, as well as clearly planning opportunities to develop the full range of mathematical vocabulary through specific activities.

There are clear links here to p. 44 on planning and to Chapters 3 and 5.

From all of the above it is apparent that teachers of Early Years children need to have a very clear understanding of mathematical subject knowledge themselves. The demands of an Early Years classroom are such that you need to be able to respond flexibly to any situation and capitalise on every learning opportunity as it presents itself. In order to do this effectively and maximise the mathematical learning opportunities for the children a very good personal subject knowledge is required.

PRACTICAL TASK PRACTICAL TASK PRACTICAL TASK PRACTICAL TASK

When you are in school in a nursery or reception class, watch the class teacher when s/he is engaged in interactive oral work. What strategies does s/he use to:

- **involve the children?**
- **ensure a brisk pace?**
- **monitor the learning of children?**
- **tackle errors and misconceptions?**

Think back to the features of effective teaching detailed above. How are these features evidenced within the strategies you have observed?

Learning

The *Curriculum Guidance for the Foundation Stage* also identifies what constitutes effective learning:

- **children initiating activities within a carefully planned environment that promote learning and can be extended;**
- **children enjoying mathematical learning because it is purposeful;**
- **learning which is consolidated and extended through games and gives children opportunities to practise their mathematical skills and knowledge;**
- **children who are confident and enthusiastic about joining in with or talking about mathematical activities.**

See also p. 55, Chapter 4.

Implicit in all of this is effective teaching as outlined above. Capitalise on the children's enthusiasm and curiosity and ensure the environment allows for children to initiate activities that will extend their mathematical learning. Make sure children have access to things such as coins, tills, calculators, different objects and shapes, numbers, different-sized containers and rules, stacking toys, wooden bricks and construction toys, paper, card, labels, pencils, pens, crayons and so forth. All of these resources allow children to initiate activities that can promote their learning of mathematics. Having pencils and paper freely available allows children to record, if they wish, in a way that is meaningful for them. They are far more likely to record if they understand the purpose of the record, and if it is self-initiated there is no question that they understand the purpose.

Children will see themselves as mathematicians if they are encouraged to develop positive attitudes, increase in confidence and enjoy their mathematical experiences. It is the role of the teacher to ensure that this happens.

Organisation within the Primary Framework for Literacy and Mathematics

You may well find yourself delivering the Early Learning Goals of the Foundation Stage within the Primary Framework for Literacy and Mathematics. These two documents have been written so that by working to the Foundation Stage requirements of the Primary Framework, the Early Learning Goals for mathematics can be addressed. The Primary Framework offers detailed advice on planning, organising and assessing mathematical learning in the Foundation Stage.

See Chapter 2, page 10.

The Primary Framework also offers advice on appropriate teaching strategies. One strategy it suggests is based on the amount of mathematics that can be found in a great deal of children's fiction. Books such as *Kipper's Toy Box* by Mick Inkpen are good for counting or *I Don't Want To Go To Bed* by Julie Sykes which is good for ordinal number. Lots of books offer the opportunity to discuss comparatives in size, *Guess How Much I Love You* by Sam McBratney, *Thud!* by Nick Butterworth or the *Large Family* books by Jill Murphy (e.g. *Five Minutes Peace* or *A Piece of Cake*) are a few. There are some lovely stories that introduce children to the passing of time and the sequencing of events, *We're Going on a Bear Hunt* retold by Michael Rosen (sequencing events), *The Very Hungry Caterpillar* by Eric Carle (days of the week) and *The Bad Tempered Ladybird* also by Eric Carle (o'clock time). Take the opportunity to capitalise on the children's enjoyment of books and stories and use them as a stimulus for mathematical activity.

By utilising a range of strategies appropriate to the subject content and children being taught, you will be able both to sustain and develop the enthusiasm, curiosity and confidence of the children as they learn mathematics.

For more information on using ICT in your teaching, see page 59.

Parents and carers as partners

A good relationship with parents and carers with everyone working together has a very positive impact upon the children. Children need to feel secure and confident. Where they recognise that there is consistency and mutual respect between home and school this is most successful. An open and ongoing sharing of information from home to school and vice versa is vital to a successful partnership. It is important that parents are kept informed about the mathematics that their children will be studying. A display about the curriculum for the term/half-term/week can be very useful. But do not forget working parents who may rarely be able to visit the school and see the board. Make sure there are sufficient written communications to keep them suitably informed about, and involved in, the mathematics their child is studying. A mathematics evening can be a useful event, especially at the beginning of the year, when you can outline the curriculum for mathematics and share together the expectations that you have.

Parents and carers need to feel welcome in the classroom and, as a teacher, you need to acknowledge the expertise and skills of the parents and utilise them to support the children. Parents are often very willing to be involved with supporting in class. In order to ensure you make best use of them, plan for their involvement. An activity where children are exploring, maybe using different sized containers in water play and sand play, is enhanced dramatically by appropriate intervention to question and challenge the children's thinking. It is not always possible for you, the teacher, to be there, you may be working with another guided group at this time. If you know you are going to have a parent in the class, share the intended outcomes of the session with the parent and use them to support this independent group.

Equally there may be parents who are very concerned about their own level of mathematical understanding and worried about further supporting their child's mathematical development. Some schools have found it useful to run mathematics evenings for parents which focus more on the subject content in order to enable the parents to support their children successfully. These evenings work when there is a relationship of mutual respect and trust. The Basic Skills Agency has a range of publications and programmes to help support parents and carers as they support the mathematics development of their children. A current catalogue of these can be accessed at the Basic Skills Agency website: **http://www.basic-skills.co.uk**.

In any Early Years setting it is important to recognise the important role parents and carers have played in the child's mathematical development before arriving at school. It is equally important explicitly to encourage this role in the future to ensure you really are working together in partnership to develop the child's mathematical learning.

The Early Learning Goals for mathematics closely match the Primary Framework for literacy and mathematics Key Objectives for reception. The other 'subject-based' chapters in this book (Chapters 7–12) detail a progression in each of these areas throughout Key Stages 1 and 2. This chapter will now move on to consider the progression throughout the Early Years before children enter Key Stage 1 as they work to attain the Key Objectives for the Foundation Stage and the Early Learning Goals.

Unpicking the progression

Counting

In a reception class a teacher is considering the counting strategies of the class. Tom is asked to count the number of crayons on his table.

He clearly counts out loud, 'One, two, three.' When asked by the teacher, 'So, how many crayons are there?' He immediately starts to count out loud again, 'One, two, three.' Straightaway this tells the teacher a great deal about Tom's understanding of counting and the experiences he needs to extend and support his development.

> **PRACTICAL TASK** PRACTICAL TASK PRACTICAL TASK PRACTICAL TASK
>
> What do you know about Tom's understanding of counting? What do you think is the next step in his learning? How might you enable him to achieve this?

Counting is something that we, as adults, do without thinking. It is a completely internalised and automatic action. Yet for a child there are three clear prerequisites before they can start to count meaningfully.

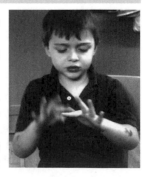

First, they need to know the number names in order. Before they arrive at school many children will have learnt quite a range of number names, some consistent and accurate, others less so. Being able to recite the names consistently in order is sometimes referred to as the 'stable-order principle'. The use of songs and rhymes encourages the learning of the number names in order within an enjoyable and appropriate context. *1, 2, 3, 4, 5, once I caught a fish alive* and *1, 2 buckle my shoe*, along with many other rhymes, encourage learning the number names in ascending order, whereas other rhymes such as *5 little speckled frogs* and *10 fat sausages* encourage descending order. Children can show the numbers on their fingers while singing or reciting the songs and rhymes.

Secondly, they need to have an understanding of matching one-to-one (also called one-to-one correspondence). When children can do this they point to, or touch, an object as they count, to show that they have included it. They say one name for each item counted, making sure they count all objects and don't count any more than once. Children who cannot yet match one-to-one may well point or touch, however, their pointing and the reciting of the number names do not coincide leading to inaccuracies.

Finally, children need to understand that the last number spoken in the count represents the number of elements in the set. This is the cardinal aspect of number. This is the aspect of counting that Tom does not yet understand. He repeats his count every time he is asked how many there are and is unable to state that the last number, i.e. 3, is equivalent to the number of crayons he has counted.

As an extension to these fundamentals for counting Gelman and Gallistell (1978) (cited in Cockburn, 1999) outline two further principles which are a part of our counting skills. The first of these is the 'order irrelevance principle'. This basically means that we don't have to count left to right, we could count right to left or start in the middle, the sequence is irrelevant to the number in the count. This might seem so obvious that it does not seem necessary to state it. However, consider children's reading: r-e-a-d and d-a-e-r are two very different things, so here the order is extremely relevant. Children are rarely told that in some situations the order is vital and yet they still manage to learn when it is the case.

The other principle of Gelman and Gallistell is the 'abstraction principle'. It has been claimed that children can only count objects that are perceptually similar, so in order to be able to count they must first be able to sort. Gelman and Gallistell suggest that children are not this limited in their counting and can in fact count groups of 'things'. The extension of this principle allows counting of unseen objects, e.g. how many people live in your house?

What experiences do you need to provide to develop counting skills?

- **Rhymes and stories that encourage counting in sequence.**
- **Games that involve counting, e.g. clapping games.**
- **Counting the number of children present today, the lunch numbers, etc.**
- **Playing dominoes or board games, e.g. snakes and ladders.**
- **Sets of counting materials, e.g. in the class shop.**
- **An accessible number line/frieze.**
- **In the playground, e.g. counting the number of skips with a skipping rope, the number of bounces with a ball.**
- **Hopscotch – the number names in order.**

Number

There are three areas that require consideration under this heading: the reading and writing of number, the manipulation of number, and calculating.

First, reading and writing number. Many children enter school able to recognise some written digits. It may be the number that represents their age or their house number. In order to be able to progress within written number work, children eventually need to be able to identify and write the digits from zero to nine. The starting point for many children will be the use of their own symbols or tallies to 'label'. For example, they might write their own price labels in the class shop, or label how many of a particular object is in each box. In order to move from this towards writing numbers children need lots of opportunity to encounter and recreate the digits. Here you might use cut-out digits that you can place different textures behind for them to trace with their fingers, e.g. fur, sandpaper, etc.; you might write in the air tracing the shape of the digit together (remember if you are facing the children you will need to 'mirror write!'); you can encourage the children to make the digits in a range of different media, e.g. play dough, salt dough, paint, traced in sand, etc. All of this encourages greater familiarity with the digits. As children start to recognise the digits you can ask them to match the number to the set, play games with number cards, produce their own number lines, and so forth.

As children learn to recognise and record number, it is important that they become confident with the manipulation of number. This will support the development of a 'number sense', an understanding of the size of a number and where it fits in our number system. This will be invaluable as the children become more and more confident with calculations and develop a range of effective and efficient strategies. To encourage this from the Early Years upwards children can be presented with number lines with missing numbers to find, with jumbled numbers to sort into consecutive numbers, then jumbled numbers to sort into order but not containing consecutive numbers. These activities will encourage children to explore, investigate and discuss: greater than or less than; before, after, between; largest, smallest; and so on.

Whether or not children can recognise written numbers when they arrive in school, many children can engage in simple calculations. If given a number problem within a real-life context, a significant number of children have already developed strategies to solve the problem. For example, if you have a teddy and you give him two sweets, then you tell the child the teddy actually wants three sweets, many children are able to give the teddy one more sweet and solve the problem. They can respond with similar success to simple subtraction, multiplication and division problems. In teaching calculation strategies you need to move the children on from their level of understanding on entry to the class. One of the first calculation strategies children will employ is a counting strategy. Many children will be dependent upon this strategy for a great number of years throughout Key Stages 1 and 2. Children begin by 'counting all' when combining, i.e. adding, two or more sets. This is extended to a 'counting on' strategy, where the second set is counted on from the last number in the first set. For example, there are four sweets in the bag, if I add three more how many are there all together? The child then counts on from the 4, saying 5, 6, 7.

Similarly for subtraction, children develop counting strategies to enable them to calculate. They can partition a set of objects and take some away, they then count how many are left to achieve an answer. This is extended to a 'counting back' strategy, which is the inverse of 'counting on'. For example, there are seven sweets in the bag, I eat two, how many are left? Counting back from the 7, the child says 6, 5.

What experiences do you need to provide to develop an understanding of number?

- **Number labels in classroom, both numerals and child written.**
- **A range of media in which to create digits.**
- **Number card games.**
- **Board games, e.g. snakes and ladders.**
- **An accessible number line/frieze.**
- **Sets of counting materials, e.g. In the class shop, to count and label.**

Shape and space

PRACTICAL TASK PRACTICAL TASK **PRACTICAL TASK** PRACTICAL TASK

There is quite an interesting debate associated with early spatial development. It centres on whether children should be taught about 2-D or 3-D shapes first. Before reading on think about this and try to decide what you feel the advantages and disadvantages are of 2-D first or 3-D first.

The argument for 3-D shapes is as follows: as children live in a 3-D world and have therefore encountered a great number of 3-D shapes, these shapes are realistic. Three-D shapes also allow children to consider more than one property at a time, thus improving their knowledge and understanding of the properties of shapes and also leading them to consider the shape of individual faces, and thus to a study of 2-D shape. However, children also encounter plenty of 2-D shapes, often as patterns, for example bonding patterns in brick work, panes of glass in windows, wallpaper, tiling patterns and so forth. In society today, with much increased access to technology, many children entering school will be very used to 2-D representations on computer screens and games machines. This means that 2-D shape is also a realistic context for young children. Some people might argue that resourcing 2-D shape is cheaper and easier; others would argue that there are plenty of 3-D shapes in every home, including cylinders, cubes, cuboids, prisms, spheres, etc. What is clear from this is that encountering and exploring both 2-D and 3-D shapes is very important for children in the Early Years.

Free practical exploration is an important part of the process of children learning about the properties of shapes. Using wooden blocks allows them to explore which will stack, which will roll, which have flat faces, which have curved faces and so on. This can lead to sorting shapes and thus to early classification activities.

PRACTICAL TASK PRACTICAL TASK **PRACTICAL TASK** PRACTICAL TASK

Gather together some 3-D shapes (about 20 if you can) – packaging boxes are usually very good. How many different ways can you sort them? Do not immediately go for the obvious mathematical criteria. Try to think how you might classify them if you were a child, for example shapes I like, shapes I've seen before, and so on. Record the criteria you have used for your sorting. Try this activity with some children in an Early Years setting if you get the opportunity. Observe their discussions and interactions as they make their decisions.

Shapes can be used appropriately to begin to develop the idea of pattern in mathematics. Mathematically patterns repeat, this might not always be the case socially. Children need to have the opportunity to talk about, recreate and extend patterns. This can be done using both 2-D and 3-D shapes. For example:

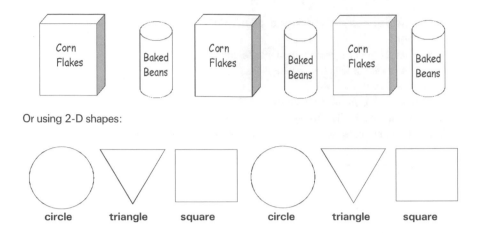

Or using 2-D shapes:

circle   triangle   square   circle   triangle   square

When introducing patterns to children do not launch straight in with specific 'mathematical' resources, e.g. multilink, but start by using objects which are familiar to the children, for example the boxes in the diagram above. Gradually refine the experience until children become confident extending and creating patterns within a mathematical context.

Equally important is the opportunity to describe shapes. This gives children the chance to use everyday language alongside their developing mathematical vocabulary. 'Feely bags' are a very useful resource here, allowing children the opportunity to feel what is in the bag and describe it to someone else to see if they can recognise it. Another useful activity is to put a range of shapes in front of the child and ask them to close their eyes. You can then describe one of the shapes, and when the child opens their eyes they see if they can pick out the shape you were describing. These activities support the progression from using everyday language towards using precise mathematical vocabulary.

A further important aspect of spatial work is that of position. In the Early Years children can begin to develop their understanding of where something is located in space alongside their understanding of prepositions. For example, you might choose to set up an 'assault course' with the PE apparatus. You can then give instructions for the children to follow, e.g. 'Jess, I want you to go under the bench, over the box and sit on the mat.' The children can then give instructions to each other. This development of prepositional language is fundamental to children developing an understanding of location in space, and ultimately to the use of Cartesian coordinates to describe transformations.

What experiences do you need to provide to develop spatial understanding?

- Building, e.g. building bricks, lego.
- Sorting both 2-D and 3-D shapes, by their own chosen properties.
- Sets of shapes to explore and compare.
- Describing shapes, e.g. using feeling bags.
- Developing prepositional language, e.g. in PE or the playground.

Measures

In the Early Years children will use a great deal of comparative language when working with measures. They will explore to see if something is longer than or shorter than, heavier than or lighter than, holds more than or less than. Initially with direct comparison the children will need to compare just two things, for example the length of two pencils, the mass of two teddies, the capacity of two bottles. They can then move on to a comparison of three things. They also need the opportunity to apply their understanding of comparison to find something which is longer than…, wider than…, lighter than…, and so forth.

The development of appropriate and accurate language is crucial in all mathematical areas. In the study of measures there is a great deal of language to be developed right from the Early Years. Use of 'social' language can lead to confusion as children develop an understanding of more and more measurement concepts. For example, 'bigger' can mean a multitude of things: in length – longer, wider, thicker; in mass – heavier; in capacity – holds more; and so forth. The implication of this is the need for detailed planning of activities and structured play situations to ensure the introduction and development of accurate and meaningful language.

In the study of time children need to start with a consideration of the passing of time. They can make a class 'timeline' of the day, each morning when the register is taken. This 'timeline' can be located on a board at child height and they can put pictures and word labels on it to detail the progression in activities throughout the day. At different times throughout the day you can refer the children back to the timeline to explain that 'before' play we did music, 'after' lunch we will do PE, and so forth. This understanding of the passing of time needs to include an introduction to the days of the week. There are songs that can be sung to help children learn the names in order, just like the counting songs which aid learning the number names in order. The Foundation Stage is the ideal time to start considering the passing of time and the ordering of events as these are vital underpinnings in learning to tell the time. As children move from the Foundation Stage into Year 1 they will be expected to start telling the time to the hour and half-hour.

What experiences do you need to provide to develop an understanding of measurement concepts?

- Rhymes and stories in which children encounter measurement concepts.
- Opportunities to develop comparative language.
- Focused sand and water play to compare capacities.
- Balances and sets of objects to balance.
- Pieces of string, laces, dowel, etc., some of the same length, some different, for comparing within the set and against other objects.
- A class timeline.
- 'Cog' clocks to explore telling the time on an analogue clock.

A SUMMARY OF **KEY POINTS**

In order to support the mathematical development of children throughout the Early Years it is important to ensure:

> that positive and productive relationships are developed with parents and carers;

> that you have a good personal subject knowledge of mathematics in order to understand the links between different areas and also to respond flexibly to situations;

> that you undertake careful monitoring, assessment and recording of progress to inform clear and appropriate planning for learning;

> that children have access to well planned and structured play opportunities with appropriate adult intervention;

> that 'maths talk' forms part of the normal daily routine;
> that there are opportunities for children to initiate activities that promote mathematical learning;
> that children are given the opportunity to develop positive attitudes and increase their confidence in mathematics due to a secure and positive environment and role model for mathematics learning;
> that you capitalise on the boundless enthusiasm of children and their capacity to enjoy new experiences.

Moving on

The development of the EYFS has resulted in many new documents and resources being published. Talk to your university tutors and/or colleagues in school to ensure you can keep as up to date as possible. The Children's Workforce Development Council, Sure Start and the British Association for Early Childhood Education are all useful organisations involved in the education of young children.

Also consider speaking to the subject leader responsible for mathematics within the Foundation Stage. They will be able to support you by giving you ideas or pointing you in the direction of additional resources.

REFERENCES REFERENCES **REFERENCES** REFERENCES REFERENCES

Cockburn, A. D. (1999) *Teaching Mathematics with Insight*. London: Falmer Press.

Curriculum Guidance for the Foundation Stage (containing the Early Learning Goals). Available at **http://www.qca.org.uk/5585.html.**

Geary, D. (1994) *Children's Mathematical Development*. Washington: American Psychological Association.

Primary Framework for Literacy and Mathematics. Available at: **http://www.standards.dfes.gov.uk/primary/**.

Stephen, C. and Wilkinson, J. E. (1999) 'Rhetoric and reality in developing language and mathematical skills'. *Early Years*, vol. 19, no. 2, pp. 62–73.

FURTHER READING FURTHER READING **FURTHER READING**

Montague-Smith, A. (2002) *Mathematics in Nursery Education*. London: David Fulton.

Pound, L. (1999) *Supporting Mathematical Development in the Early Years*. Buckingham: Open University Press.

Skinner, C. (2005) *Maths Outdoors*. Cheltenham: BEAM.

Thompson, I. (ed.) (1997) *Teaching and Learning Early Number*. Buckingham: Open University Press.

Tucker, K. (2005) *Mathematics Through Play in the Early Years: Activities and Ideas*. London: Paul Chapman.

7
Number

Introduction

The Primary National Strategy's Primary Framework for literacy and mathematics (2006) aims to encourage children to become numerate in order to confidently tackle mathematical problems independently. In order to achieve this children should have a sense of the size of a number and where it fits into the number system. Developing this 'number sense' is crucial if children are going to move on to become effective and efficient at calculating, both mentally and using pencil and paper methods. A clear progression in the development of concepts is important for children to enable them to fully understand the structure of our number system, how to represent numbers and how numbers relate to each other. This chapter will identify the progression, continuing from and extending that already identified in Chapter 6.

The Primary Framework for Literacy and Mathematics

The Primary Framework for Literacy and Mathematics is composed of seven different strands. The second strand identified is counting and understanding number. The areas included within this strand are:

- **counting;**
- **properties of numbers and number sequences, including negative numbers;**
- **place value and ordering, including reading and writing numbers;**
- **estimating and rounding;**
- **fractions, decimals and percentages, and their equivalents; ratio and proportion.**

It is possible to trace a progression within these areas throughout the Key Objectives, found in the 'Core learning in mathematics by strand' section of the Framework. This chapter will focus predominantly on the first three of these areas.

Unpicking the progression

Counting

The principles of counting and learning to count have been clearly detailed in Chapter 6. However, in considering the progression in counting it is important to remember that counting does not solely involve counting on in ones, i.e. 0, 1, 2, 3, 4, 5, 6, ... but can, and frequently does, involve counting in steps of different size, e.g. counting on in twos – 0, 2, 4, 6, 8, 10, 12, ...; starting from a number other than zero, e.g. counting on in twos – 7, 9, 11, 13, 15, 17, ...; counting back, e.g. counting back in 0.5s – 2, 1.5, 1, 0.5, 0, −0.5, −1, ... By practising and becoming familiar with counting on and back in steps of different sizes, children will acquire a knowledge and understanding that will support them a great deal in developing their calculation and problem-solving skills.

The Primary Framework identifies a progression in introducing counting in steps of different size. This introduction takes place from the Foundation Stage right through the primary years.

> *Count in ones, twos, fives or tens.*
> > *Count on from and back to zero in single-digit steps.*
> *Count on from and back to zero in multiples of tens.*
> > *Count from any given number in whole number and decimal steps.*
> *Extend beyond zero when counting backwards.*

It is important to note that the progression in counting involves the introduction of negative numbers and fractions. Counting is extended through zero to negative numbers and counting in fractional or decimals parts is introduced.

The value of counting should not be underestimated. Many children will use counting as their main calculation strategy for a significant period of time whether adding, subtracting, multiplying or dividing. Indeed Effie Maclellan (1997, p. 40) goes further in stating, *There is now little doubt that children's understanding of number is rooted in counting.*

Properties of numbers and number sequences

Odd and even numbers
Besides counting in ones and steps of different size, one of the first properties of number that children are introduced to is that of 'odd' and 'even'. This is often introduced as an extension of counting in twos from zero and one. Practical resources or pairing up groups of children can be used to demonstrate divisibility by two.

Once children can recognise odd and even numbers they can start to consider some of the properties of combining these numbers in different ways. What happens when two even numbers are added? Two odd numbers? An odd and an even number?

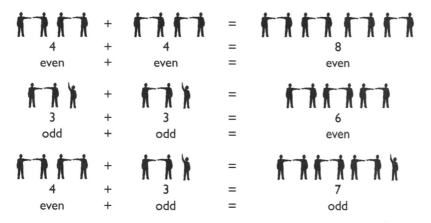

4	+	4	=	8		
even	+	even	=	even		

3	+	3	=	6	
odd	+	odd	=	even	

4	+	3	=	7
even	+	odd	=	odd

A discussion of children's proof of this can be found on p. 119 of **Primary Mathematics: Knowledge and Understanding** *from Learning Matters.*

Exploration of subtraction of odd and even numbers will reveal the pattern in their differences. At the top end of Key Stage 2 children can investigate patterns in the products of odd and even numbers.

Multiples

A further property of numbers which children will start to investigate during Key Stage 1 is recognising multiples.

A multiple is a number which is the product (i.e. achieved by multiplication) of an integer with a given number, e.g. some multiples of 3 are 6 (3 x 2), 15 (3 × 5), 24 (3 × 8).

Children will start by recognising multiples of two (even numbers) and multiples of ten, as they will experience counting in tens from quite a young age. Here again is evidence of the importance of counting. They will then start to recognise multiples of 5, 100 and 50 as they increase their counting and calculation repertoire. By the end of Key Stage 2 they should recognise all multiples up to 10 × 10.

As numbers get bigger it is harder to spot immediately if a number is a multiple of a certain integer. In order to assist this there are certain tests of divisibility which children in upper Key Stage 2 quite enjoy applying, and the Primary Framework identifies in the Year 6 objectives within the 'Knowing and using number facts' strand.

Two

For an integer to be divisible by 2, it must have either 0, 2, 4, 6 or 8 as the last digit, i.e. it is an even number.

Three

For an integer to be divisible by 3, the sum of its digits must also be divisible by 3. For example, is 312 divisible by 3? The sum of the digits is $3 + 1 + 2 = 6$, 6 is divisible by 3 and therefore 312 is divisible by 3, in fact $312 \div 3 = 104$. What about 32,451? The sum of the digits is $3 + 2 + 4 + 5 + 1 = 15$, 15 is divisible by 3 and therefore 32,451 is divisible by 3; $32,451 \div 3 = 10,817$.

Four

For an integer to be divisible by 4, the last two digits must be divisible by 4. For example, is 348 divisible by 4? 48 is divisible by 4 ($48 \div 4 = 12$) and therefore 348 is divisible by 4; in fact 348 $\div 4 = 87$. What about 35,260? 60 is divisible by 4 ($60 \div 4 = 15$) and therefore 35,260 is divisible by 4; $35,260 \div 4 = 8,815$.

Five

For an integer to be divisible by 5, it must have either 0 or 5 as the last digit.

Six

For an integer to be divisible by 6, it must be an even number which satisfies the rule for divisibility by 3.

Eight

For an integer to be divisible by 8, when halved it must satisfy the rule for divisibility by 4. For example, is 432 divisible by 8? First halve the number 432 which gives 216, now check to see if 216 is divisible by 4. 16 is divisible by 4, hence 216 is divisible by 4, and 432 is divisible by 8; in fact $432 \div 8 = 54$.

Nine

For an integer to be divisible by 9, the sum of its digits must be divisible by 9. For example, is 792 divisible by 9? The sum of the digits is $7 + 9 + 2 = 18$, 18 is divisible by 9 and therefore 792 is divisible by 9; in fact $792 \div 9 = 88$. What about 42,453? The sum of the digits is $4 + 2 + 4 + 5 + 3 = 18$, 18 is divisible by 9 and therefore 42,453 is divisible by 9; $42,453 \div 9 = 4,717$.

Ten

For an integer to be divisible by 10, it must have 0 as the last digit.

PRACTICAL TASK PRACTICAL TASK PRACTICAL TASK PRACTICAL TASK

Look at the following numbers and decide if they are multiples of (i.e. are they divisible by) 2, 3, 4, 5, 6, 8, 9 or 10. They may be multiples of more than one number.

5,472   3,564   4,215   2,340   72,432

Factors

In the Primary Framework children are introduced to the term 'factor' in Year 4, despite having known the term multiple from Year 2 onwards. A factor can be defined as any number that divides into another number exactly, e.g. 8 is a factor of 32, but 5 is not. Children can use their knowledge of multiplication tables to find factors of numbers. Factors are usually found as pairs, the exception being square numbers, e.g.

For more on indices see Chapter 2 of **Primary Mathematics: Knowledge and Understanding** *from Learning Matters.*

Factors of 24:

$24 = 1 \times 24$	$24 = 2 \times 12$	$24 = 3 \times 8$	$24 = 4 \times 6$
$24 = 24 \times 1$	$24 = 12 \times 2$	$24 = 8 \times 3$	$24 = 6 \times 4$

So the factors of 24 are: 1, 2, 3, 4, 6, 8, 12, 24

For more information on square numbers see the next section.

Square numbers

Square numbers are introduced in Year 5 of the Primary Framework. A square number is the product of two equal factors, i.e. a number multiplied by itself, e.g. $2 \times 2 = 4$. It can be written as $2^2 = 4$ (i.e. 2 to the power 2). In learning their multiplication tables, children will have already encountered square numbers.

Square numbers can be represented as squares (hence the name!):

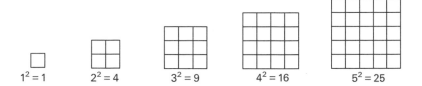

$1^2 = 1$ $2^2 = 4$ $3^2 = 9$ $4^2 = 16$ $5^2 = 25$

Children should also know that square numbers have an odd number of factors, because one factor (i.e. the square root) is multiplied by itself to obtain the answer, e.g.

1	has the factor 1	(one factor)
4	has the factors 1, 2, 4	(three factors)
9	has the factors 1, 3, 9	(three factors)
16	has the factors 1, 2, 4, 8, 16	(five factors)

Numbers that are not square have an even number of factors, e.g.

2	has the factors 1, 2	(two factors)
6	has the factors 1, 2, 3, 6	(four factors)
18	has the factors 1, 2, 3, 6, 9, 18	(six factors)

Another interesting set of numbers, which children can be introduced to as well as square numbers, is the set of triangle numbers. In the same way that square numbers form squares, triangle numbers form triangles!

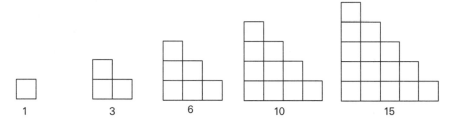

1   3   6   10   15

An interesting feature of triangle numbers that children may notice is that if two successive triangle numbers are added the sum is a square number, e.g.

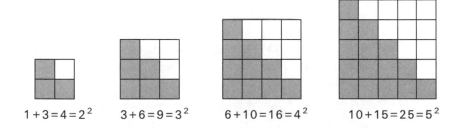

$1+3=4=2^2$ $3+6=9=3^2$ $6+10=16=4^2$ $10+15=25=5^2$

Some numbers are both square and triangular although they are quite rare. Obviously the first number this applies to is 1, the second is 36 (6^2), the next 1,225 (35^2), the next 41,616 (204^2) and the next 1,413,721 ($1,189^2$) getting further and further apart. Children find exploration of 'big' numbers quite fascinating.

Prime numbers

By Year 6 the Primary Framework introduces children to prime numbers. A prime number can be defined as a number that has only two factors, 1 and itself. This means that 1 is not a prime number, as it only has one factor, itself! There are some fascinating ways for children to explore prime numbers.

For further details see p. 148.

One person they might be introduced to is Eratosthenes (c. 276–194 BC). He was a Greek mathematician and a librarian at the University of Alexandria. He used a rather ingenious method for calculating the circumference of the Earth and was also very interested in prime numbers. He worked out a method of finding prime numbers which became known as the Sieve of Eratosthenes. If all the prime numbers up to 150 need to be established, Eratosthenes worked out that it was only necessary to consider multiples of every number up to 13. He knew this because any number up to 150 which is not prime would have a factor of 13 or less (because 13 × 13 = 169). But how does his 'sieve' work?

PRACTICAL TASK PRACTICAL TASK PRACTICAL TASK PRACTICAL TASK

Before reading on to see how Eratosthenes tackled the problem, see if you can establish all the prime number between 1 and 150. Time yourself to see how long it takes, then repeat it using Eratosthenes' 'sieve'. Was the sieve any quicker?

As all the prime numbers up to 150 need to be established, we need to work with a 150 grid. Starting at 2 (1 is not prime – see above), put a ring around it as it must be prime (i.e. have only 2 factors). Now shade in all the multiples of 2 in the table. Then put a ring around the next unshaded number, in this case 3, which must also be prime. Now shade in all the multiples of 3 in the table. The next unshaded number is 5, which is also prime. Put a ring around it and shade in all the multiples of 5. Do the same with the next unshaded number and so on. However, the wonderful thing about the Sieve of Eratosthenes is that it is not necessary to keep going for every unshaded number. If the multiples of all numbers up to 13 are considered, then the remaining unshaded numbers must also be prime, owing to the previously stated fact that any number less than 150 which is not prime will have a factor of 13 or less. Hence the prime numbers are 'sieved' out.

1	(2)	(3)	4	(5)	6	(7)	8	9	10
(11)	12	(13)	14	15	16	[17]	18	[19]	20
21	22	[23]	24	25	26	27	28	[29]	30
[31]	32	33	34	35	36	[37]	38	39	40
[41]	42	[43]	44	45	46	[47]	48	49	50
51	52	[53]	54	55	56	57	58	[59]	60
61	62	63	64	65	66	[67]	68	69	70
[71]	72	[73]	74	75	76	77	78	[79]	80
81	82	[83]	84	85	86	87	88	[89]	90
91	92	93	94	95	96	[97]	98	99	100
[101]	102	[103]	104	105	106	[107]	108	[109]	110
111	112	[113]	114	115	116	117	118	119	120
121	122	123	124	125	126	[127]	128	129	130
[131]	132	133	134	135	136	[137]	138	[139]	140
141	142	143	144	145	146	147	148	[149]	150

The Sieve of Eratosthenes

The Greek mathematician Euclid (c. 330–275 BC) wrote about prime numbers in his *Elements*. It was in these volumes that he proved that there is an infinite number of prime numbers. Some very large primes have been calculated using computers. $2^{756839}-1$ is a prime number, it has 227,832 digits! An even larger prime is $2^{859433}-1$, which has in excess of quarter of a million digits!

Prime numbers lead to the study of prime factors, also introduced in Year 6. Numbers that are not prime numbers are called composite numbers. Composite numbers can be made by multiplying together other numbers, e.g. 16 can be made by multiplying 4×4, 2×8, $2 \times 2 \times 4$, and so on. However, it is possible to mulitply together just prime numbers to obtain a composite number. For 16:

$$2 \times 2 \times 2 \times 2$$

This is called prime factorisation.

The prime factors of 12 are:

$$2 \times 2 \times 3$$

PRACTICAL TASK PRACTICAL TASK **PRACTICAL TASK** PRACTICAL TASK

Find the prime factors of the following numbers:

24   35   18   42   100

Place value and ordering

Place value is used within number systems to allow a digit to carry a different value based on its position, i.e. the *place* has a *value*. By Year 1 the Primary Framework identifies place value as part of a key objective. However, much work needs to go on in Year R to ensure this objective can be met within Year 2. Building on the areas already discussed in Chapter 6, children need to understand what each digit represents in a two-digit number, a three-digit number, a four-digit number and so forth. Partitioning is a very useful strategy to help children develop this understanding. By Year 5 children are expected to multiply whole numbers by 1,000, giving the potential for a very large number of digits. They also need to multiply and divide decimals by powers of ten, thus extending their understanding of our decimal place value system further.

For more on place value, see p. 9 in **Primary Mathematics: Knowledge and Understanding** *from Learning Matters.*

Fundamental to children's understanding of place value is the use of 0 as a place holder. This means that in the number 206, the zero is 'holding' the tens column and showing that there are no tens there. Before our number system used a symbol for zero it would have been necessary to write '2 hundreds and six' as there was no other way of showing the column was empty. A clear understanding of place value is vital if children are to develop effective and efficient mental calculation strategies; yet it is an area in which children can very easily develop misconceptions.

For more on partitioning see the next section.

Misconceptions

Many misconceptions which children develop in the area of Number are related to a poor understanding of place value. The child who reads 206 as twenty-six will have the same conceptual misunderstanding as the child who writes 10,027 when asked to write one hundred and twenty-seven. Both of these errors occur because the child focuses on the zeros as the fundamentally important digits in the numbers 10, 100 and so forth and not on the place value of the

For more on place value, see p. 9 of **Primary Mathematics: Knowledge and Understanding** *from Learning Matters.*

numbers. When asked, 'What is a hundred?' they might well respond, 'It has two zeros.' The child then applies this understanding to the reading and writing of number. Hence 206 is read as 20 and 6, so it is twenty-six.

It is quite clear here that the child has a very limited understanding of place value. In order to correctly read, write and identify numbers children need to understand that the position of each digit is of great significance and that zero can be used as a place holder to show that a column is empty. There are some quite clear implications for teaching to ensure children do not develop this misconception and also to remedy it if it already exists.

Children need to be introduced to the importance of the position of a digit and equally must be able to state what each digit represents in a multi-digit number. This should be reinforced with the partitioning of numbers into, for example, hundreds, tens and ones. Place value cards are a useful resource when partitioning numbers. Using these children can easily partition larger numbers, can identify the value of individual digits and equally can see how zero is used as a place holder.

For example, 325:

Through practical activity, the use of appropriate resources, discussion and an emphasis on correct mathematical vocabulary, children will move towards a much clearer and accurate understanding of these concepts.

The Primary Framework has developed some really useful Interactive Teaching Programs (ITPs) to support the modelling of mathematics for learners. One of these resources is the Place Value program which can be downloaded from: **http://www.standards.dfes.gov.uk/primary frameworks/library/Mathematics/ICTResources/itps/**. From here select the Place Value ITP. This will enable you to manipulate place value cards electronically, an invaluable resource for whole-class or large group modelling.

A further misconception which children can develop related to place value is that of believing a number is larger because it has more decimal digits – for example, stating that 3.125 is larger than 3.14. The child will often state that this is true because, '125 is bigger than 14.' In this situation the child shows no understanding of the place value of digits after the decimal point.

For more on decimals, see p. 26 of **Primary Mathematics: Knowledge and Understanding** *from Learning Matters.*

As in the earlier misconception, children need to know the place value of digits, this time to the right of the decimal point. If they are introduced to the columns as the 1/10 (tenths) column, the 1/100 (hundredths) column, the 1/1,000 (thousandths) column and so forth they will not think of digits to the right of the decimal point in terms of those to the left, i.e. here they will not say '125' and '14', but 'point one two five' and 'point one four' instead. Actually looking at the fractional parts involved leads to a deeper understanding. For example, 3.125 can be seen as 3 and 1/10 (one tenth) and 2/100 (two hundredths) and 5/1,000 (five thousandths) which is the same as 3 and 125/1,000 (one hundred and twenty-five thousandths), whilst 3.14 can be seen as 3 and 1/10 (one tenth) and 4/100 (four hundredths) which is the same as 3 and 14/100 (fourteen hundredths). Expressed in terms of a common denominator this gives 3 and 125/1,000 and 3 and 140/1,000, hence 3.14 is bigger than 3.125.

Teaching to avoid these misconceptions, and remedying them if they do exist, is vital if children are to have a sense of the size of a number and where it fits into the number system. A sound understanding of place value is absolutely fundamental to developing this 'number sense'.

For more on comparing fractions see p. 24 of **Primary Mathematics: Knowledge and Understanding**

A SUMMARY OF **KEY POINTS**

In order to support the development of calculation strategies in the future, it is important that children:

> **recognise odd and even numbers;**

> **count forwards and backwards in steps of different size;**

> **count through zero into negative numbers;**

> **count in fractional and decimal parts;**

> **recognise multiples of numbers;**

> **find factors of numbers;**

> **understand our decimal place value system.**

Moving on

The Standards Site contains a lot of professional development support for teachers in developing numeric concepts. In addition speak to colleagues within your school. The subject leader responsible for mathematics throughout your Key Stage in school will be able to support you by giving you ideas or pointing you in the direction of useful resources.

REFERENCES REFERENCES **REFERENCES** REFERENCES **REFERENCES**

The Primary Framework for Literacy and Mathematics. Available at: **http://www.standards.dfes.gov.uk/ primary/**.

Maclellan, E. (1997) 'The importance of counting' in Thompson, I. (ed.) *Teaching and Learning Early Number.* Buckingham, Open University Press.

FURTHER READING FURTHER READING **FURTHER READING**

O'Sullivan, L. et al. (2005) *Reflective Reader: Primary Mathematics.* Exeter: Learning Matters.

Thompson, I. (ed.) (1997) *Teaching and Learning Early Number.* Buckingham: Open University Press.

8
Calculation

Professional Standards for the award of QTS

This chapter will support you as you work towards evidencing attainment against the following Standards:

Q14, Q15, Q17, Q22, Q23

Chapter objectives

By the end of this chapter you should:

- **understand why pupils should be able to calculate mentally first, before using formal written methods;**
- **be more confident with the progression of calculation from Foundation Stage to Key Stage 2;**
- **know that there are a range of strategies for calculating, and be able to calculate flexibly in a number of ways;**
- **understand how resources such as the empty number line can be used to support pupils' mental calculation skills;**
- **be confident in teaching pupils how to use a calculator to solve problems;**
- **be aware of some of the common misconceptions that pupils exhibit in calculations.**

Introduction

The National Curriculum expects pupils to engage with using and applying number, calculations and solving numerical problems. Within calculations at Key Stage 1, pupils need to understand number operations and the relationships between them as well as be able to calculate mentally. At Key Stage 2 this is extended to written methods and calculator methods. The Framework for teaching mathematics contains a strand entitled 'Calculate efficiently and accurately'.

This chapter will address four main issues: understanding number operations and relationships; mental recall and mental calculation; pencil and paper methods; and using a calculator and checking results.

Throughout the chapter common misconceptions will also be raised and addressed.

Unpicking the progression

Understanding number operations and relationships

'Sum like it not!'

Many teachers incorrectly use the word 'sum' when referring to all calculations. This term should only be used when working with addition calculations. When you are working on subtraction, multiplication or division questions you can refer to them as 'number sentences', 'equations' or 'calculations' instead.

Addition and subtraction

The ability to count reliably is a prerequisite for any meaningful calculation to take place. Counting forwards and backwards in steps of different size is an important skill for young children to develop. In Year 1 pupils need to know by heart all the pairs of numbers that sum to 10. Pupils who can count forwards and backwards to 10 will have little difficulty spotting a pattern and filling in the missing numbers in the following

$$
\begin{aligned}
10 &= 10 + 0 \\
10 &= 9 + 1 \\
10 &= 8 + 2 \\
10 &= 7 + 3 \\
10 &= \square + \square \\
10 &= \square + \square \\
10 &= \square + \square \\
10 &= \square + \square \\
10 &= \square + \square \\
10 &= \square + \square \\
10 &= \square + \square
\end{aligned}
$$

Pupils need to understand the operations of addition and subtraction and the relationship between the two operations. Being able to count forwards and backwards with ease will facilitate the understanding of this inverse relationship. Activities that emphasise the relation between addition and subtraction are important at an early stage. An example of such an activity is shown below:

For more on this see p. 110.

Fill in the missing numbers

8 + 5 = 13	13 − 5 =	13 − 8 =
9 + 6 = 15	15 − 9 =	15 − 6 =
12 + 7 = 19	19 − 12 =	19 − 7 =
46 + 38 = 84	84 − 46 =	84 − 38 =

This familiarity with the inverse relationship between addition and subtraction is an important prerequisite for algebra. Pupils can be given simple problems (see overleaf) to solve that require an understanding of this inverse relationship:

For more on this see Chapter 9.

I am thinking of a number. I add 7 to this number and the answer is 15.
What was the number I was thinking of?

I am thinking of a number. I take away 4 from this number and the answer is 9. What was the number I was thinking of?

Pupils should be encouraged to find the quick way to solve these problems by using the inverse operations.

In the same way that addition and subtraction are introduced to pupils as inverse operations so halving and doubling are introduced. In Year 1 pupils are expected to be able to solve simple problems mentally by doubling and halving. Pupils should be able to do the following.

I am thinking of a number. I double it and the answer is 8. What was the number?

I am thinking of a number. I halve it and the answer is 5. What was the number?

Multiplying and dividing

Just as addition and subtraction were introduced as inverse operations so multiplication and division need to be seen as inverse to each other.

It is, however, more complicated since pupils need to understand the various guises that multiplication and division take. In the first instance, multiplication needs to be introduced as repeated addition. For example:

$5 + 5 + 5$ can be written as 5×3, i.e. it is a mathematical shorthand

$15 \div 5$ can then be seen as asking how many times we can take 5 from 15.

A common misconception that pupils have is that division always makes numbers smaller. It is important that pupils encounter examples where this is not the case. Pupils need to be asked questions such as:

How many times can $\frac{1}{2}$ be taken from 15?

How many times can $\frac{1}{4}$ be taken from 10?

$$15 \div \tfrac{1}{2} \qquad 10 \div \tfrac{1}{4}$$

Meeting examples like this will allow pupils to make correct generalisations. It will allow them to conclude correctly that:

$$15 \div \tfrac{1}{2} = 15 \times 2 \quad \text{and} \quad 10 \div \tfrac{1}{4} = 10 \times 4$$

Next they need to see how multiplication can be used to describe an array. For example:

$$\square\square\square\square \atop \square\square\square\square \qquad 4 \times 2 = 8$$
$$2 \times 4 = 8$$

It is useful spending some time emphasising this aspect of multiplication since it is fundamental for an understanding of long multiplication. Pupils need to understand the distributive property of multiplication over addition if they are to understand long multiplication algorithms. The diagram below helps to show pupils why:

*For more on this see p. 19 of **Primary Mathematics: Knowledge and Understanding** from Learning Matters.*

$$2 \times 13 \qquad\qquad = \qquad\qquad (2 \times 10) \qquad + \quad (2 \times 3)$$

$$\square\square\square\square\square\square\square\square\square\square\square\square\square \;=\; \square\square\square\square\square\square\square\square\square\square \quad \square\square\square$$

$$\square\square\square\square\square\square\square\square\square\square\square\square\square \qquad\quad \square\square\square\square\square\square\square\square\square\square \quad \square\square\square$$

For more on this see p. 19 of **Primary Mathematics: Knowledge and Understanding** *from Learning Matters.*

Pupils need to be able to generalise this rule and see that

$2 \times (\nabla + \square) = (2 \times \nabla) + (2 \times \square)$ is true for any numbers we place in ∇ and $\square$.

From arranging arrays pupils will also be able to see that the operation of multiplication is commutative, i.e. $a \times b = b \times a$.

In order to see division as the inverse of multiplication pupils could be asked to group 26 into 2 rows and that this can be written as $26 \div 2 = 13$.

This grouping can also demonstrate that $26 \div 2 = (20 \div 2) + (6 \div 2)$, i.e. division is right distributive over addition.

It is important that pupils understand this property of division since it underpins the long division algorithm and, later on, work in algebra.

For more on this see p. 10 of **Primary Mathematics: Knowledge and Understanding** *from Learning Matters.*

PRACTICAL TASK PRACTICAL TASK PRACTICAL TASK PRACTICAL TASK

Say which of the following are correct and which are incorrect. Try to do it by looking at the structure rather than calculating the answers.

17×9	$= (10 \times 9) + (7 \times 9)$	15×8	$= (8 \times 8) + (7 \times 8)$
8×23	$= (8 \times 20) + (8 \times 3)$	128×8	$= (120 \times 8) + (8 \times 8)$
$104 \div 4$	$= (100 \div 4) + (4 \div 4)$	$1,072 \div 8$	$= (1000 \div 8) + (72 \div 8)$

In fact they are all correct. The last two examples help to explain why the tests for divisibility by 4 and 8 work.

A common misconception that pupils have is that multiplication always makes numbers bigger. It is not surprising that pupils come to this conclusion since in all the above examples this is the case. Pupils need to be given examples where multiplication makes the number smaller. This is possible if multiplication is understood as a scaling. The following questions place multiplication in this context:

> This tower is 6 cubes high. Make a tower that is 3 times as high.
>
> This line is 4 centimetres long. Draw a line that is twice as long.
>
> This recipe uses 3 eggs. How many eggs will be needed for twice as many people?

Pupils can then be introduced to fractional scalings, for example:

> A tower is 8 cubes high. Build a tower that is half as high.
>
> This line is 12 centimetres long. Draw one that is a quarter of the length.

Pupils can then be shown that these can be written as:

$$8 \times \tfrac{1}{2} = 4 \quad \text{and} \quad 12 \times \tfrac{1}{4} = 3$$

In order to increase pupils' understanding and efficiency in multiplying and dividing they need to reflect on some interesting properties of our number system. Their attention needs to be drawn to the fact that multiplying and dividing by powers of 10 is particularly easy in our number system.

Multiplying by 10, for example, simply moves all the digits one place to the left.

H	T	U			H	T	U
3	2		× 10	=	3	2	0

It is important to emphasise that the numbers have moved rather than say a zero has been added. Pupils who simply add a zero may develop the misconception that $2.3 \times 10 = 2.30$.

Similarly, dividing by 10 simply moves all the digits one place to the right:

H	T	U			H	T	U
4	6	0	÷10	=		4	6

Again it should be emphasised that the digits have moved rather than say a zero has been removed. Pupils who remove a zero may develop the misconception that $203 \div 10 = 23$ or that $.07 \div 10 = .7$

Pupils should be encouraged to investigate what happens when numbers are multiplied and divided by 100.

In this way they will be able to convert pounds to pence and metres to centimetres efficiently.

We have emphasised the inverse relation between addition and subtraction and between multiplication and division. It is also important that pupils can decide when it is appropriate to use each of these mathematical operations. They should have the opportunity of solving word problems involving numbers in 'real life'.

Start with simple one-operation problems, for example:

> How many more is 68 than 42?
>
> Find a pair of numbers with a difference of 15
>
> What is the sum of 24 and 35?
>
> Which three numbers could have a total of 60?
>
> There are 6 eggs in a box. How many in 7 boxes?
>
> A bus seats 52 people. There are 60 people on the bus. How many are standing?
>
> What are the factors of 12?

Lead up to multi-step operations:

> There are 36 children in a class. Half of them have flavoured crisps. One third of them have plain crisps. How many children have crisps?
>
> For her party Asmat spent £2.88 on apples, £3.38 on bananas and £3.76 on oranges. Will a £10 note cover the cost?

Mental recall and mental calculation

Addition and subtraction

Knowing by heart simple addition and subtraction facts is a prerequisite for efficient mental arithmetic. In Year 1 pupils should know all pairs of numbers that add to 10. They should be taught to use these facts to solve related problems, for example:

6 + 4 = 10	What is 6 + 5?
8 + 2 = 10	What is 8 + 3?
5 + 5 = 10	What is 5 + 7?

Similarly pupils should be taught to derive simple subtraction results from known facts:

10 − 6 = 4	What is 11 − 6?
10 − 7 = 3	What is 12 − 7?

They should be taught to use the commutative and associative property of addition to solve problems in efficient ways. They should be taught to rearrange addition problems, for example:

$$4 + 28 \qquad 7 + 8 + 3 + 2 \qquad 26 + 17 + 14 + 13$$

can be calculated more efficiently if calculated as:

$$28 + 4 \qquad 7 + 3 + 8 + 2 \qquad 26 + 14 + 17 + 13$$

Pupils who understand the commutative and associative properties of addition should be able to work out how the trick shown opposite works.

Similarly pupils should be taught to use the properties of subtraction. They should be able to find the following quickly:

$$7 + 9 - 9 \qquad 8 + 7 - 6 \qquad 78 - 25 - 18$$

by considering:

$$7 + 0 \qquad 8 + 1 \qquad 60 - 25$$

They should discover that subtraction is not commutative: $7 - 6$ does not give the same answer as $6 - 7$!

Knowing doubles is useful when adding and subtracting. For example, $8 + 9$ can be derived from knowing double 8. Pupils should be able to derive the following by Year 2:

$$25 + 26 \qquad 38 + 42 \qquad 19 + 21 \qquad 102 - 51$$

from knowing:

$$25 + 25 = 50 \qquad 40 + 40 = 80 \qquad 20 + 20 = 40 \qquad 51 + 51 = 102$$

Using number tracks and number lines

Number tracks can help young children to learn to add by counting on and to subtract by counting back. For example, you may enlist the help of a hand-puppet frog who jumps along the classroom number track, or use a Programmable Robot (such as a Roamer) to go forward three steps (+3) on the carpet number track or back four steps (−4).

REFLECTIVE TASK

Samir has been using a number track to solve some questions. She provides the following answers:

$$3 + 4 = 6 \qquad 2 + 3 = 4 \qquad 8 - 3 = 6 \qquad 6 - 2 = 5$$

What has Samir done incorrectly? How might you help her to remedy this?

Samir has counted on and back and included the number she started at. This could be remedied by asking her to play a board game with some friends. It is unlikely that she will count the same number again in this context, especially if she is trying to reach the end first! You could then talk to Samir about transferring her skills on the board game to the number track.

Older pupils will find number lines a useful aid for mental arithmetic. They may also use a ruler as an aid. Most classrooms display 1–100 number lines on the walls or board as an aid for pupils.

Pupils can be encouraged to imagine a number line when solving addition and subtraction problems. Finding 17 + 8, for example, is more easily found by considering 17 + 3 + 5 on a number line.

Similarly 34 − 8 could be imagined to be 34 − 4 − 4.

Alternatively it could be viewed as 34 − 10 + 2.

Pupils should be encouraged to think flexibly. It is good practice to ask pupils to explain their way of tackling the question so that they can share their approaches and learn from each other.

Some problems are more easily answered by partitioning both numbers. For example, 35 + 24 can be partitioned into (30 + 20) + (5 + 4).

PRACTICAL TASK PRACTICAL TASK PRACTICAL TASK PRACTICAL TASK

Jot down notes to show how you could expect pupils to answer these equations:

$$1)\ 45 + 46 \qquad 2)\ 40 - 19 \qquad 3)\ 101 - 99$$

Try to think of a number of possible ways.

1. A child might know that double 45 is 90 and one more is 91. Alternatively, they might add 40 + 40 (which is 80) and then add 5 + 6 (which is 11), making 91.
2. A child might know that 19 is close to 20, so 40 − 20 is 20. They will then need to add one to compensate for the extra one they took away, making an answer of 21. Alternatively they may take 10 away from 40, leaving 30 and then take the 9 away, leaving 21. Finally, a child may use the inverse calculation, 19 + ? = 40.
3. A child should notice that these two numbers are close together and use a counting on method − (99), 100, 101 − to find the difference of 2.

Multiplication and division

Knowing by heart all multiplication facts up to 10 × 10 is a necessity for pupils. On their own, however, the knowledge of these facts is not sufficient. Pupils need to be able to use these facts to work out related problems. They need to understand, for example, that if 9 × 7 = 63 then this implies that 63 ÷ 9 = 7 and 63 ÷ 7 = 9.

Pupils should be encouraged to relate division facts to the corresponding multiplication facts:

To find out about calculating with decimal numbers see page 26, **Primary Mathematics, Knowledge and Understanding** *from Learning Matters.*

56 ÷ 7 = 8	Tell me a multiplication fact using the numbers 56, 8 and 7.
9 × 6 = 54	Tell me a division fact using the numbers 6, 9 and 54.

They should be able to use the inverse relation between multiplication and division to try the following type of problem:

The problems on the right relate to the statements on the left.
Draw a line between each statement and its corresponding question:

77 ÷ 11 = 7	54 ÷ 9 = 6
9 × 8 = 72	7 × 9 = 63
36 ÷ 4 = 9	11 × 7 = 77
6 × 9 = 54	72 ÷ 8 = 9
63 ÷ 7 = 9	4 × 9 = 36

They should be able to use simple multiplication facts to derive more complicated results. For example, 6 × 3 = 18 can be used to derive 6 × 30 = 180. This is a useful technique when pupils are using grid multiplication. Pupils should be encouraged to try the following type of task: if you know that 6 × 3 = 18, what else can you work out?

For more on grid multiplication see p. 130–131.

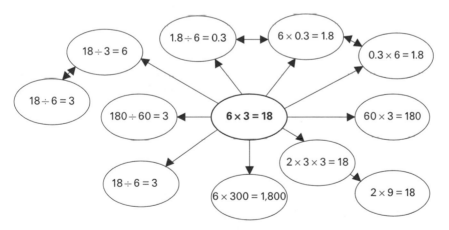

When pupils are completing this task, encourage them to draw the links they can see between the different number sentences they make.

Being able to multiply by 10 and 100 allows pupils to carry out related multiplications. A quick way to multiply by 5, for example, is to multiply by 10 and halve the result. For example, 18 × 5 is a half of 18 × 10 which is 90. The same approach can be used for 25 × 88:

$$25 \times 88 = \tfrac{1}{2} \text{ of } 50 \times 88 = \tfrac{1}{2} \text{ of } \tfrac{1}{2} \text{ of } 100 \times 88 = 2{,}200$$

This method can be generalised and is called halving and doubling. To calculate 14 × 3 we can halve the 14 and double the 3 and find 7 × 6 instead. Pupils should be taught to do the following by using this technique:

16 × 5	48 × 25	18 × 3
4.5 x 4	$7\frac{1}{2}$ × 8	32 × 50

Pupils should be taught to extend their multiplication facts. For example, use the fact that 12 × 12 =144 to find 12 × 13 by adding 12 to 144.

Pupils can then attempt the following type of questions:

26 × 4	18 × 9	16 × 8
49 × 4	99 × 5	89 × 3

and similarly attempt associated division problems:

104 ÷ 4	510 ÷ 5	828 ÷ 4

When pupils understand that multiplication is distributive over addition and subtraction they can be taught how to do the following:

Find the cost of 5 T-shirts each costing £9.99.

Find the cost of 8 articles costing 63p, 8 articles costing 18p and 8 articles costing 19p.

Find $17\frac{1}{2}$% of £80.

For more on this see p. 19 **Primary Mathematics: Knowledge and Understanding** *(2007) from Learning Matters.*

as:

$$5 × £10 − 5 × 1p = £49.95$$
$$8 × (63p + 18p + 19p) = 8 × £1 = £8$$
$$10\% \text{ of } £80 + 5\% \text{ of } £80 + 2\tfrac{1}{2}\% \text{ of } £80 = £8 + £4 + £2 = £14$$

By the time they leave primary school pupils are expected to be able to calculate simple percentages mentally. They should be taught how to find 10% and then make a suitable adjustment.

For example, to find 80% of £90, first find 10% of £90 and multiply the result by 8. Similarly 5% of £90 is half of 10% of £90.

Pupils should be able to use this technique on the following questions:

20% of £60	70% of £80	90% of £60
30% of £40	5% of £120	15% of £40

Pencil and paper methods

Addition and subtraction

For pupils in Key Stage 1 the emphasis is on mental calculation. Initially pencil and paper is used for recording their mental calculations in number sentences.

They should be taught how to use symbols such as □ or Δ to stand for unknown numbers.

REFLECTIVE TASK

It is important for pupils to develop a flexible approach to number from a young age. By introducing symbols such as □ or Δ to represent a missing number, early algebraic foundations are set. However, introducing these does not come without difficulties. How might you encourage pupils to work out the answers to these number sentences?

$$1)\ 7 - 3 = \square \qquad 2)\ \square + 3 = 10 \qquad 3)\ \square - \Delta = 10$$

1. You might want to use a number track to demonstrate the counting back strategy. You might ask the pupil to hold up seven fingers, count down three, then count how many are remaining. (You might also do this with counters, teddies or pop-up people, or any other resource.)

2. This is a more difficult type of question for pupils to answer and research shows that it is often the first stumbling point in written calculations for children. It is essential that you teach the pupil to 'just think of it as $10 - 3$' because although you are highlighting the inverse operation as a method to complete the calculation, you have not actually considered what the question is asking. In this case it is asking, 'I am starting at a number and counting on three to get to ten. What number have I started at?' or 'I am thinking of a number. When I add three more I get to ten. What number am I thinking of?' Alternatively, you may also want to demonstrate by having a plastic cup with seven counters already in it. Count in three more counters and have the pupils count that there are three. Ask them to think about how many were in there to start with. Finally, because this is a number bond to ten, pupils may be able to use their fingers to partition ten into a seven and a three.

3. This is an open-ended question because there are an infinite number of possible solutions. At Key Stage 1 you will probably be expecting the majority of the pupils to come up with the number bonds to ten and find the patterns in that list. You could use Cuisennaire Rods or coloured counters to show the patterns also:

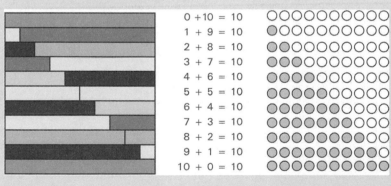

$$0 + 10 = 10$$
$$1 + 9 = 10$$
$$2 + 8 = 10$$
$$3 + 7 = 10$$
$$4 + 6 = 10$$
$$5 + 5 = 10$$
$$6 + 4 = 10$$
$$7 + 3 = 10$$
$$8 + 2 = 10$$
$$9 + 1 = 10$$
$$10 + 0 = 10$$

(At Key Stage 2 you want most pupils to consider answers involving fractions and decimals such as $4\frac{1}{2} + 5\frac{1}{2} = 10$ or $2.35 + 7.65 = 10$ or negative numbers such as $-9 + 11 = 10$.)

When pupils are able to carry out multiplication and division calculations mentally they can use pencil and paper to record their results, for example:

$9 \times \square = 18$	$\square \times 7 = 21$	$\square \times \Delta = 12$
$\Delta \times \Delta = 25$	$\square \div 6 = 7$	$32 \div 4 = \square$

Using a number line to help with addition and subtraction is particularly recommended for pupils.

RESEARCH SUMMARY RESEARCH SUMMARY RESEARCH SUMMARY

Findings from the Third International Mathematics Science Survey(TIMSS) indicate that the way pupils visualise addition and subtraction has a marked affect on their ability to solve problems. Dutch pupils as young as 6 are particularly proficient at solving addition and subtraction problems involving numbers as large as 100. To solve 100˘- 28, for example, Dutch pupils would use an Empty Number Line (ENL), as shown below:

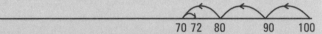

counting back first to 90 then 80 and then down a further 8 to 72.

Alternatively pupils who realise that 28 is 2 less than 30 might count back 30 to 70 and then go forward 2:

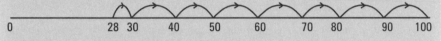

Pupils are also encouraged to count up from 28 to 100 as shown below:

In the Netherlands these three approaches to the same problem are taught at the same time. Pupils are encouraged to appreciate the relationship between the three methods and be able to change between formats.

The last method is particularly useful when we want to give someone change.

Presented with the following problem:

> You are a shopkeeper. A chocolate bar costs 28 pence. Someone gives you a pound coin. Work out how much change you should give him.

a pupil should be encouraged to use an ENL approach counting up from 28 to 100.

Here are some ENLs that some fictitious pupils have used for subtraction problems. Next to each one write the problem the pupil is solving and explain how they have tackled each one.

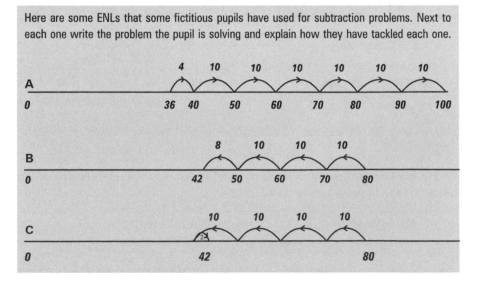

A The problem was to subtract 36 from 100. The pupil has counted on from 36 to 100. The answer of 64 is found by adding the numbers on each arc.

B The problem was to subtract 38 from 80. The pupil counted back 3 tens and then 8 units to find the answer 42.

C The problem was to subtract 38 from 80. The pupil counted back 4 tens and then went forward 2 units.

The ENL is also used for addition. To calculate 34 + 26 a pupil could use the ENL to add 10 and 10 and 6 to 34 as shown:

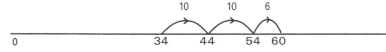

The ENL is a particularly useful aid since it mirrors the way we work mentally. Faced with solving the problem 47 + 29 mentally most people would solve it in one of two ways:

- **first add 20 to 47 giving 67 then add 9 to give 76**; *or*
- **first add 30 to 47 giving 77 then subtract 1 to give 76**

Each of these mental methods can be demonstrated using the ENL.

The two approaches are shown below:

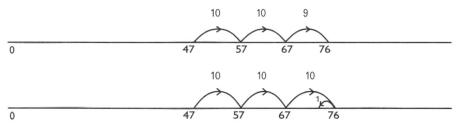

Pupils can be encouraged to use this approach to solve more complicated problems involving addition and subtraction.

> I am thinking of a number. I add 5, subtract 6, add 4, add 7, and subtract 8.
> The answer is 13. What was the number I thought of?

This kind of problem is particularly suited to solving by using the ENL.

In presenting this kind of problem to young children imaginative teachers might wish to present it as follows: 'A bus stops at the bus stop and 5 people get on. At the next stop 6 get off and 4 get on. At the next stop 7 get on and 8 get off. The driver looks round and sees there are 13 people on the bus. How many people were on the bus at the start?'

Pupils could also be encouraged to write their own stories to accompany ENL calculations. Calculating 7 − 6 + 4 is far less interesting than making a story to match 7 − 6 + 4 = 5! Writing a story also helps a pupil to make sense of what the calculation is asking them to do. It is also a useful assessment method for a teacher to check pupils' understanding.

In Year 2 pupils are expected to know that addition can be done in any order. An advantage of using the ENL is that it makes it more obvious that addition is commutative and associative.

Recording the results of the following calculations on the ENL reinforces some of the basic rules of arithmetic:

$17 - 4 - 6$	$17 - 6 - 4$
$12 + 8 + 6$	$12 + 8 + 6$
$12 - 5 + 4$	$12 + 4 - 5$

Multiplication

The Framework for Teaching Mathematics suggests that pupils' introduction to long multiplication should be grid (or tabular) multiplication.

In this multiplication method each part of the first number is multiplied by each part of the second and the products are added. The distributive law is emphasised by this approach. So 35×24 is written as:

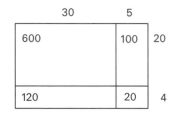

$$600 + 100 + 120 + 20 = 840$$

For more on this topic see p. 15 of **Primary Mathematics: Knowledge and Understanding** (2007) *from Learning Matters.*

As well as illustrating clearly how the multiplication method works, this method provides a foundation for the later idea of multiplying out a pair of brackets: $(30 + 5)(20 + 4) = (30 \times 20) + (5 \times 20) + (30 \times 4) + (5 \times 4)$.

Older children will be expected to multiply a three-digit number by a two-digit number and this method can easily be extended as shown:

$$345 \times 36$$

300	40	5	
9,000	1,200	150	30
1,800	240	30	6

In this example six numbers need to be added together to find the answer:

$$9,000 + 1,200 + 150 + 1,800 + 240 + 30 = 12,420$$

As pupils become familiar with this method they can dispense with the lines.

A popular way for older pupils to record multiplication of larger numbers is to use a variation of grid multiplication called Gelosia (or lattice) multiplication. Examiners have commented for several years that pupils who adopt this approach have a higher success rate.

For more on this topic see p. 15 of **Primary Mathematics: Knowledge and Understanding** (2007) *from Learning Matters.*

To find 345 × 36, the working is set out as follows:

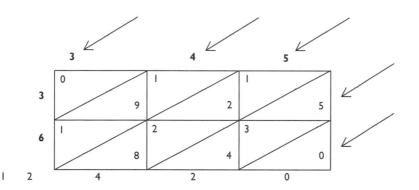

Starting at the right-hand side and adding the numbers inside the grid in the directions of the arrows gives the answer 12,420. This is a modification of grid arithmetic: the six products are found but they are added together more efficiently.

REFLECTIVE TASK

Can you work out how the Gelosia method above works? Explain your answer using correct place value terminology.

Division

Pupils' first introduction to division is repeated subtraction.

This approach can also be used for division by more 2 or 3 digit numbers. Consider the following problem:

> Coaches can transport 53 children.
> How many coaches will be needed to transport 1,300 children?

The method illustrated below makes use of repeated subtraction.

For more on this topic see p. 16 of **Primary Mathematics: Knowledge and Understanding** (2007) *from Learning Matters.*

1,300 530	10 buses
770 530	10 buses
240 106	2 buses
134 106	2 buses
28	1 bus

Total number of buses needed is 25

A pupil doing the problem this way needs to be able to calculate 53 × 10 and 53 × 2 mentally. Research has shown that pupils who adopt this method have a far higher success rate. By keeping the word 'buses' in the working, pupils are far less likely to forget about the 28 pupils who need a bus to transport them! Another advantage of setting the work out in this way is that as pupils' mental arithmetic improves they can adopt quicker and more efficient methods. Once the pupil can calculate 53 × 20 and 53 × 4 mentally the problem can be laid out as follows:

1,300 1,060	20 buses
240 212	4 buses
28	1 bus

As pupils get older and have less need for the context being included in the working they can dispense with 'buses' and simply focus on the arithmetic.

Using a calculator and checking results

Pupils in the latter part of Key Stage 2 are required to use a calculator effectively. Several skills are required to achieve this:

- **to be able to check results by making sensible estimates;**
- **to know how a calculator prioritises operations;**
- **to be able to interpret the calculator output.**

Estimating

Being able to estimate results is an important skill. If the calculator output is of the wrong magnitude it is helpful if a pupil can detect this immediately. Before resorting to the calculator the pupil needs to have some idea what the answer is going to be. If, for example, a number is being multiplied by a fraction less than 1 then the pupil should be aware the result will be smaller.

Before teaching pupils how to use a calculator pupils should be able to do the following type of questions:

Choose the approximate answers to the following:

208 + 305 + 769 + 638	*a* 180	*b* 1,800	*c* 18,000	*d* 18,0000
52 × 49	*a* 250	*b* 2,500	*c* 25,000	*d* 250,000
2873 ÷ 38	*a* 70	*b* 700	*c* 7,000	*d* 70,000
345 × 0.5	*a* 17	*b* 170	*c* 1,700	*d* 17,000
2,001 − 1,998	*a* 3,000	*b* 300	*c* 30	*d* 3

In fact they should not even be resorting to a calculator for the last question!

Prioritising operations

It is important for pupils and teachers to know how a calculator prioritises operations. Most calculators used in primary schools simply work from left to right. For example, $4 + 8 \times 2 - 5$ would be calculated as 19. Scientific calculators used in secondary schools, however, would give 15 for this expression. These calculators give precedence to multiplication and division. It is useful, therefore, for all the pupils to be using the same type of calculator. In order, however, to carry out calculations on a simple calculator pupils will often need to use brackets to prioritise operations. The following type of question is an example where pupils will need this skill:

Adult tickets cost £3.40 Child tickets cost £2.10.
Find the total cost of 37 adult tickets and 68 child tickets.

Pupils should be taught to enter this in the calculator as $(37 \times 3.40) + (68 \times 2.10)$

PRACTICAL TASK PRACTICAL TASK PRACTICAL TASK PRACTICAL TASK

Time needs to be spent on converting word problems into the appropriate format for a calculator. Using a calculator, practise changing the following type of word problems into calculator format as Year 5 or 6 pupils would be expected to.

1. Winston has £8.60 in his piggy bank at the start of the year. Each month he saves the same amount. At the end of the year he has £86.60. How much did he save each month?

2. Emma saves £3.20 each week for 18 weeks. Peter saves £2.70 a week for 26 weeks. Who has saved more and by how much?

3. A plant grows 7 metres in 3 years. If it grows at the same rate each year how much did it grow in the first year? How much will it have grown in 6 years?

4. A bus can carry 53 passengers. How many buses are needed to carry 8,438 people?

Interpreting the calculator output

1. A pupil should enter the calculation as $(86.6 - 8.6) \div 12$ or $(86.60 - 8.60) \div 12$. The calculator output is 6.5. It is important that pupils realise that the answer is £6 and 50 pence and not £6 and 5 pence.

2. A pupil might enter the calculation on a calculator as $(18 \times 3.20) - (26 \times 2.70)$. The calculator output is −12.6 The pupil needs to be able to interpret this negative result as meaning that Peter saves more, by £12 and 60 pence.

3. A pupil might enter $(7 \div 3) \times 6$ to solve the second part of the question. The calculator output on a simple calculator is 13.9999999. Pupils need to be taught why the calculator gives this result and that the result needs to be rounded to 14.

4. $8,438 \div 53$ entered on the calculator gives 159.20754. Pupils need to be taught to consider the context of the question. In this example it is inappropriate to round the answer to the nearest whole number since 11 people would not be transported!

Examiners have commented for several years that one of the greatest difficulties pupils have when using calculators is in deciphering the output. Most calculators display ERROR if an illegal operation is punched into the calculator. Pupils and teachers need to be able to interpret this message. It can mean the calculation is beyond the capability of the memory or that an illegal operation has been carried out. The following inputs would cause a simple calculator to display ERROR:

$$900,000 \times 900,000$$

$$\sqrt{} \ +/\!\!-\ 16$$

The first is beyond the memory capability of a simple calculator and the second is asking the calculator to find the square root of a negative number.

Misconceptions

Several misconceptions had been identified throughout this chapter. Many of these involve pupils' confusion over place value which is why it is essential that pupils have a firm foundation in place value and are able to effectively calculate mentally before moving on to written calculations.

Standard algorithms

Ayesha is asked to add the following numbers:

25, 175, 50, 200, 5

She tackles the problem as follows:

```
  25
 175
+ 50
 200
   5
————
1625
```

What does this tell you about her understanding of addition?

Firstly it is clear that Ayesha does not yet have a sufficient understanding of place value to tackle column addition and should be using a different method. This example really encourages mental calculation. If she wanted to use a written method, an expanded written form would be far more appropriate.

Many of the misconceptions pupils develop in the area of calculation arise as a result of lack of understanding of the standard algorithms. In the past it was assumed that all pupils could learn algorithms by heart and apply them. Research has shown that unless pupils understand the algorithms they use, errors will creep into their work. Their lack of understanding means they find it difficult to detect errors in their working. For this reason far more emphasis is now placed on non-standard algorithms and jottings. Only when pupils are confident should they be moved onto standard algorithms. Many educators would argue that standard algorithms, although more efficient, are of little benefit since pupils should be resorting to calculators for more difficult calculations. For further information on misconceptions in calculation read Fiona Lawton's chapter in Hansen (2005).

A SUMMARY OF **KEY POINTS**

In order to support the development of calculation strategies it is important that pupils:

> **know basic number bonds;**

> **know multiplication tables up to 10 x 10;**

> **are able to use these facts to derive new facts;**

> **practise mental arithmetic regularly;**

> **are able to use a range of resources including the Empty Number Line (ENL) to support their mental calculations;**

> **understand the inverse relation between addition and subtraction and between multiplication and division;**

> **be allowed to continue using non-standard algorithms where necessary;**

> **can use a calculator efficiently.**

Moving on

There are a number of resources in your school and/or university library and on the internet to support your calculations work. These are a useful point of first contact for support. For example, you could look at the two QCA books entitled *Teaching Mental Calculation Strategies: Guidance for Teachers at Key Stages 1 and 2* (1999a) and *Teaching Written Calculation Strategies: Guidance for Teachers at Key Stages 1 and 2* (1999b). These break down into various mental and written calculation methods as well as things to think about when using calculators. They set out clearly expectations for pupils at each year group and give practical examples for you to use in the classroom. In addition to this, the Standards Site (at **http://www.standards.dfes.gov.uk**) contains a lot of professional development support for teachers in teaching calculations. Finally, consider speaking to the subject leader responsible for mathematics in your key stage or your school. They will be able to support you by giving you ideas or pointing you in the direction of school resources.

REFERENCES REFERENCES **REFERENCES** REFERENCES REFERENCES

Hansen, A. (ed.) (2005) *Children's Errors in Mathematics: Understanding Common Misconceptions in Primary Schools.* Exeter: Learning Matters.

FURTHER READING   FURTHER READING   **FURTHER READING**

Askew, M. (1998) *Teaching Primary Mathematics.* London: Hodder & Stoughton.

Frobisher, L., Monaghan, J., Orton, A., Orton, J., Roper, T. and Threlfall, J. (1999) *Learning to Teach Number: A Handbook for Students and Teachers in the Primary School.* Cheltenham: Nelson Thornes.

Haylock, D. (2005) *Mathematics Explained for Primary Teachers,* 3rd edition. London: Paul Chapman.

QCA (1999a) *Teaching Mental Calculation Strategies: Guidance for Teachers at Key Stages 1 and 2.* London: QCA. This highly informative booklet was produced to support the National Numeracy Strategy. It describes approaches to the teaching of mental calculations and the role of calculators. Copies can be obtained for a small price from QCA Publications, on 01787 884444 (tel) or 01787 312950 (fax).

QCA (1999b) *Teaching Written Calculation Strategies: Guidance for Teachers at Key Stages 1 and 2.* London: QCA. This highly informative booklet was produced to support the National Numeracy Strategy. It describes approaches to the teaching of written calculations in Key Stages 1 and 2. Copies can be obtained for a small price from QCA Publications, on 01787 884444 (tel) or 01787 312950 (fax)

Thompson, I. (ed.) (1997) *Teaching and Learning Early Number.* Buckingham: Open University Press.

Thompson, I. (ed.) (1999) *Issues in Teaching Numeracy in Primary Schools.* Buckingham: Open University Press.

9
Algebra

Introduction

It is interesting to note that the Primary Framework for literacy and mathematics (2006) does not make explicit reference to algebra as a specific strand. However, a great deal of algebra is to be found in the objectives identified within the 'Using and applying mathematics' strand.

It might be interesting to speculate why it is not overtly referred to as 'algebra'. This may be due to the experience many people will recount of their own algebra learning with things 'jumping over the equals and changing the sign' or 'change the side, change the sign'. This did little to develop an understanding of algebra and even less to encourage an interest in and enjoyment of the subject! Algebra is firmly rooted in patterns, and the creation, extension and expression of patterns is fundamental to algebra. This needs to be our starting point with children if we are to support them as they develop a clear understanding of algebra and come to marvel at its elegance.

REFLECTIVE TASK

From your own learning of the subject, think of all the words, phrases and activities you associate with algebra. How does your own learning compare to the developmental structure proposed within the following Research Summary?

RESEARCH SUMMARY RESEARCH SUMMARY RESEARCH SUMMARY

Algebra is one area of mathematics where children have traditionally worked in the abstract. This has meant that young children, although very able to cope with patterning, have had limited opportunity to work algebraically. In order to help overcome this Rod Bramald (1993) proposed a developmental structure for algebra in primary schools. This ensures a 'bottom up' approach, resulting in very positive and appropriate opportunities for children to work within algebra.

Stage 1: Copying and continuing patterns
Stage 2: Devising their own repeating patterns
Stage 3: Recording/describing patterns either practically or pictorially
Stage 4: Recording/describing patterns in words
Stage 5: Translating words into patterns
Stage 6: Recording/describing patterns using their own symbols
Stage 7: Knowledge of symbol conventions
Stage 8: Manipulating symbols

This structure closely matches the progression identified within the Primary Framework for literacy and mathematics and may support you as you attempt to unpick the algebraic demands of the teaching mathematics.

The Primary Framework for Literacy and Mathematics and the Mathematics National Curriculum

The Primary Framework for Literacy and Mathematics is composed of seven different strands. The first strand identified is 'Using and applying mathematics'. The areas related to algebra in this strand include:

- **properties of numbers and number sequences;**
- **reasoning about numbers or shapes and making general statements about them;**
- **using letters and symbols to represent unknown numbers or variables.**

As in the Primary Framework, the mathematics National Curriculum does not make explicit reference to algebra within the Programme of Study of Key Stages 1 and 2. However, as the two documents claim to be 'fully aligned', there are very similar references to patterning, expressing patterns and generalising within the National Curriculum. The one place where algebra is given specific mention is in the title given to Attainment Target 2 and the associated Programmes of Study. Attainment Target 2 Number and Algebra makes much more explicit reference to the knowledge, skills and understanding expected for algebra, especially at levels 4 and 5.

Unpicking the progression

Vocabulary

The Primary Framework for literacy and mathematics clearly identifies all the vocabulary children are expected to understand and use. The vocabulary for each year group is subdivided under headings to support planning. As algebra is not mentioned explicitly within the strands it is not identified explicitly within the vocabulary. It is possible, however, to pick out some vocabulary which children need to be able to understand and use, in order to support their learning of algebraic concepts.

Reception and Key Stage 1

problem	solution	inverse
method	explain	predict
reason	pattern	relationship
compare	repeating pattern	show me
puzzle	symbol	equation
diagrams	pictures	odd, even
solve	order	

count in ones, twos, fives, tens . . .

In addition to all this vocabulary, children should understand and be able to use the following by the end of Key Stage 2:

test	reasoning	strategy
sign	operation	rule
sequence	property	formula
criterion/criteria	generalise	general statement
construct	term	represent

From all of this it is evident that, even if it is not mentioned explicitly, there is a very clear expectation that children will study algebra throughout Key Stages 1 and 2.

Number sequences and spatial patterns

The Primary Framework identifies a clear progression in learning about number sequences, starting with counting in steps of different sizes from and back to zero, then one, then any number. This is supported by the expectation that children will learn to recognise multiples of numbers. By the end of Key Stage 2 children are expected to count back through zero into negative numbers, count in steps of fractional size, recognise and extend sequences of square numbers and make general statements about odd and even numbers.

Alongside the learning of number sequences, children also start to investigate patterns within shape and space. They start by recreating patterns, then extending them; they then talk about the patterns and go on to describe them. This gradually leads to a recognition that number patterns can be generated from spatial patterns, and that these patterns can be expressed generally, at first in words and then using symbols.

An example of this move from spatial pattern to number sequence to generalised rule is shown below, with possible expectations for children at different stages.

For more on counting see p. 110, and for more on the properties of numbers and number sequences see p. 111.

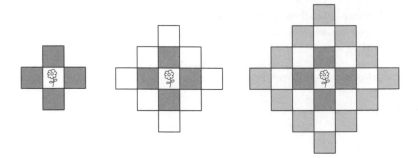

The picture shows the number of slabs around a flowerbed in the garden. Each picture has a different number of slabs depending on how many 'rows' there are. This pattern could be given to children in either Key Stage 1 or 2 but their responses would be very different depending upon their previous experiences and understanding.

PRACTICAL TASK PRACTICAL TASK **PRACTICAL TASK** PRACTICAL TASK

In order to support your own subject knowledge development, before reading on have go at generalising the number of slabs in each new 'row'.

In Key Stage 1 a child might practically reproduce the pattern using a concrete resource like Multilink. They may extend the pattern to produce the next in the sequence:

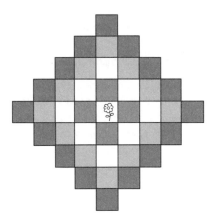

By Year 2 you could expect a child to be able to tell you that the number pattern for the number of slabs in each 'row' is 4, 8, 12, 16 and that the next 'row' would have 20 slabs. By Year 4 you could expect to find children generalising the sequence in words, for example: 'The numbers in the sequence are multiples of 4.' By Year 6 the children should have progressed from generalising in words towards generalising more in symbols. Thus you should find children who are able to find the nth term of this sequence, i.e. the number of slabs in the nth 'row' is equal to $4n$.

Generalising

In the preceding example the children were expected to generalise the pattern, first in words and later using symbols. But how do children learn to generalise? It is certainly true that many people undertaking courses of initial teacher training were never taught to generalise patterns themselves. Those who were tend to have encountered the topic as part of a GCSE syllabus purely in an abstract context. This means that many students are having to teach an aspect of

To support your own subject knowledge development in this area see p. 42 in **Primary Mathematics: Knowledge and Undestanding** *(2007) from Learning Matters.*

mathematics they have not fully learnt or understood themselves. This can prove quite challenging, but meeting the challenge reaps great rewards.

In order to ensure children develop fully within mathematics, it is important that they encounter a clearly planned progression within algebraic concepts from a young age. In the area of generalising this means they need to start with general statements and find examples to match the statement. Examples include:

(Year 1) All triangles have three sides:

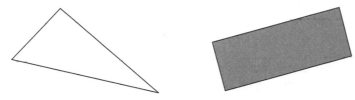

The white shape is a triangle but the grey shape is not a triangle

(Year 3) Any odd number is one more than an even number:

$$23 = 22 + 1 \qquad\qquad 15 = 14 + 1$$

The general statements that children encounter get more and more challenging throughout the Key Stages. By Year 6 you should expect children to be able to find examples to match statements such as:

If you add three consecutive numbers, the sum is three times the middle number:

$$4 + 5 + 6 = 15 = 3 \times 5$$

Or:

Any square number is the sum of two consecutive triangular numbers:

$$4 = 1 + 3 \qquad 25 = 10 + 15 \qquad 64 = 28 + 36$$

For more on triangle numbers see p. 113.

As children become increasingly confident in finding examples to match general statements they need to be given the opportunity to start to express general relationships in words (about Year 4). This might be within a real-life context, e.g. finding the number of days in any number of weeks, or within a purely mathematical context, e.g. explaining a number sequence. Into Year 5 children should start to record the general relationships they express in writing. For example, if given the sequence:

$$1, \quad 4, \quad 9, \quad 16, \quad 25, \quad \dots$$

you might expect a child to express the relationship as follows:

This is the sequence of square numbers. A square number is when a number is multiplied by itself, for example $2 \times 2 = 4$. To find the 10th square number you would need to multiply 10×10 and to find the 27th square number you would need to multiply 27×27.

By Year 6 you can expect children to be able to express their relationships in symbols. For example, in order to find the formula for the nth term of the sequence:

$$3, \quad 6, \quad 9, \quad 12, \quad 15, \quad \dots$$

they will first need to recognise that the numbers are multiples of three and that the sequence starts at 1×3. Once they have seen this they need to express the nth term as $3 \times n$ or $3n$.

From this it can be seen that it is vital for children to encounter a gradual and progressive development in being introduced to algebraic concepts. If they start in the Early Years and build on previous learning, then algebra should not be an abstract mathematical mystery to them.

Misconceptions

One possible misconception that children might develop when encountering symbolic representation within algebra occurs when children interpret the algebraic symbols as shorthand for words, for example:

$2a + 3b$ is not shorthand for 2 apples plus 3 bananas.

PRACTICAL TASK PRACTICAL TASK **PRACTICAL TASK** PRACTICAL TASK

Before reading on think about why this might be counterproductive when children are learning algebra.

In fact if the equation was $2a + 3b = 5$, then one possible solution would be $a = 1$ and $b = 1$, i.e. $a = b$, but an apple can never equal a banana!

The easiest way to ensure children do not develop this misconception is not to teach it. Although you may have experienced this yourself when you were being taught algebra, it is just as easy to plan to teach this aspect of the subject in a more meaningful way. By introducing children to the use of letters to represent variables before they start to generalise symbolically, they become familiar with the concept. Using letters which are completely different to the words in the relationship also helps to prevent this misconception, e.g. if generalising the number of days in any number of weeks, using a and b would be better than using d and w, which the children might interpret as abbreviations for days and weeks.

Teaching using strategies that ensure children understand algebraic concepts in a meaningful way supports a fuller knowledge and awareness of the fundamental role algebra plays in mathematical communication. It is not a peripheral area that is encountered briefly then left alone again with relief — it is the essence of all mathematical recording and interaction. It should be brief, elegant and meaningful!

A SUMMARY OF **KEY POINTS**

In order to support the development of algebraic understanding, it is important that children:

> **count forwards and backwards in steps of different sizes;**
> **recognise, recreate and describe number and spatial patterns;**
> **extend number and spatial patterns;**

> find examples to match general statements;
> express general relationships orally in words;
> express general relationships in writing;
> express general relationships symbolically.

Moving on

Make sure you are confident yourself with generalising expressions in order to support you as you teach algebra within school. Check out some of the useful revision sites such as the BBC Bitesize site to practise your own skills in this area. In addition speak to colleagues within your school. The subject leader responsible for mathematics throughout your key stage in school will be able to support you by giving you ideas or pointing you in the direction of useful resources.

REFERENCES REFERENCES **REFERENCES** REFERENCES **REFERENCES**

Bramald, R. (1993) 'A pattern for algebra', *Child Education*, Sept.

National Curriculum for England. Available at: **http://www.nc.uk.net**.

Primary Framework for Literacy and Mathematics.

   Available at: **http://www.standards.dfes.gov.uk/primary/**.

10
Measures

Introduction

Included in the *Primary Framework for Literacy and Mathematics* (DfEE, 1999) is a clear progression in the development of measurement concepts. Alongside this children need to realise that, although we can theoretically talk about measures with great accuracy, in reality all practical measurement is an approximation. As children progress through their primary years, there is an expectation that these approximations will become more and more accurate. This occurs as they become increasingly able to use measuring equipment and read scales with greater accuracy. A good understanding of measures is vital for all children as so many everyday tasks involve either an accurate measure of some thing or an estimate. Shopping, cooking, decorating, driving, arriving somewhere on time, all involve different measurement concepts. It is amazing to think just how many times in the day you encounter measurement without necessarily being consciously aware of it.

PRACTICAL TASK PRACTICAL TASK PRACTICAL TASK PRACTICAL TASK

Note down all the times you encounter a measurement concept during a 24-hour period. Classify your list into different types of measures and identify if the measure was an estimate or accurate. Remember to include time, pints (either milk or beer!), oven temperatures, distances on road signs and so forth. You will probably be amazed!

The Primary Framework for Literacy and Mathematics

The Primary Framework for literacy and mathematics is composed of seven different strands. The sixth strand identified is 'Measuring'. The areas related to measures included within this strand are measurement of: length; mass; capacity; perimeter; area; time.

It is possible to trace a progression within these areas throughout the Key Objectives, found in the 'Core Learning in Mathematics by Strand' section of the Framework.

Unpicking the progression

Vocabulary

Measurement is one area of mathematics where a great deal of vocabulary is developed from the very early stages. The types of activities that can be done to support the development of this language in the early stages have been covered Chapter 6. This chapter will continue with the development of measurement concepts as they advance from that point.

At all times, constant reinforcement of appropriate and accurate vocabulary within measures is very important. Misconceptions can easily develop, with children confusing concepts and using them as if they were interchangeable. In order to help prevent this, careful consideration needs to be given to the selection and use of mathematical vocabulary.

For more on misconcpetions see p. 150 later in the chapter.

As children move through Key Stage 2, they quite enjoy playing with the words used to describe units of measures. It is quite an interesting task to ask them to compare the language of measurement with other words in social usage in order to support an understanding of the size of the units. For example, you could ask them what is a centipede? a century? a centimetre? Or what is a millipede? a millennium? a millilitre?

Our system of measures has been developed over thousands of years. The use of different units and the history of measures make for interesting study at upper Key Stage 2. Moving beyond the minimum stated curriculum allows opportunities for good cross-curricular links. Children can study units of measurement used in the different ancient civilisations and also look at the historical development of units of measure in our own society.

The earliest recorded units of length were based on body parts, for example:

- **the cubit – the forearm from the elbow to the tip of the middle finger;**
- **the span – the tip of the thumb to the tip of the little finger on an extended hand;**
- **the reach – on outstretched arms, the tip of one middle finger to the tip of the other;**
- **the hand – the width of a hand (fingers closed) from the edge of the palm to the edge of the thumb (still used to measure the height of horses);**
- **the foot – the Romans divided this measure into 12 inches, but it was originally based on the length of a foot.**

Prior to adopting the metric system of measures, the UK used the imperial system for measuring. This system was first described officially in the Magna Carta (1215) and is still in quite common usage today. Since the beginning of the year 2000, however, metric units have had to take precedence over imperial units in retailing. Unlike the imperial system, in the metric system there are clear connections between the units. For example:

Imperial units:

12 inches	=	1 foot
3 feet	=	1 yard
1,760 yards	=	1 mile
4 gills	=	1 pint
2 pints	=	1 quart
8 pints	=	1 gallon

Metric units:

1 m = 100 cm = 1,000 mm

1 litre = 100 cl = 1,000 ml

Non-standard and standard units

The Primary Framework suggests that children start measuring by making direct comparisons of lengths, masses, etc. They then move on to use uniform non-standard units to measure (introduced in Year 1). Uniform non-standard units are things like Multilink cubes, yoghurt pots, drinking straws and so forth. These are all objects that are of uniform size/mass, but they are not a standard unit of measurement. At this stage children are also introduced to standard units of measure, initially metres and litres with kilograms and centimetres being added in Year 2. They can be encouraged to use these measures for direct comparison – for example, find something shorter than a metre, something that holds more than a litre, something lighter than a kilogram.

By Year 3 children are generally expected to use the following standard units of length, mass and capacity to estimate, measure and record measurements:

Length:	*Mass:*	*Capacity:*
centimetre	gram	millilitre
metre	kilogram	litre
kilometre		

In Year 4 children start to consider area. Again here uniform non-standard units form a very sound introduction to measuring area. Multilink cubes, coins, sheets of paper, either A4 or newspaper, etc. are very useful units depending on the size of the area to be measured. Another way of using uniform non-standard units when introducing area is to consider tesselations. A tessellation is where a shape fits together with a number of exact copies with no gaps or overlaps; for example:

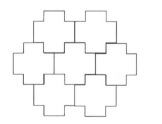 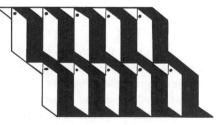

As with all uniform non-standard units, tesselations can be used to encourage children to recognise the need for standard units of measure. By asking simply. 'How many crosses does it take to cover the paper?' and then, 'How many penguins?' children can be guided to the need for standard units if we are to communicate measurement effectively.

By Year 6 the range of standard units children are expected to understand and use has increased to include:

Length:	Mass:	Capacity:	Area:
millimetre	gram	millilitre	square millimetre
centimetre	kilogram	centilitre	square centimetre
metre	tonne	litre	square metre
kilometre			

In addition the National Curriculum states that children should also 'know the rough metric equivalents of imperial units still in daily use.' By Year 6 this should include:

Length:	Mass:	Capacity:
mile	pound	pint
yard	ounce	gallon
foot		
inch		

Having considered vocabulary and standard and non-standard units, this chapter will now briefly outline the expected progression in different areas of measurement.

Length – a progression

- **Use comparative language (e.g. longer than, shorter than) to directly compare two lengths, then more than two lengths.**
- **Measure using uniform non-standard units.**
- **Estimate, measure and compare using standard units: metre, then centimetre, then millimetre, including their abbreviations.**
- **Use a ruler to draw and measure lines to the nearest centimetre, then half centimetre, then millimetre.**
- **Explain the relationship between kilometres and metres, and metres and centimetres, then centimetres and millimetres, and convert between them.**
- **Calculate the perimeters of rectangles and other simple shapes, then regular polygons, then simple compound shapes (shapes that can be split into rectangles).**
- **Know the imperial unit of a mile.**

The word circumference is introduced in Year 6 of the Framework. The circumference is the distance around the edge of a circle and, as such, is closely linked to perimeter. Eratosthenes (c. 276–194 BC) rather incredibly managed to calculate a value for the circumference of the Earth. Having heard of a well at Syene (now modern day Aswan) where sunlight only struck the bottom at midday on the summer solstice, he was able to use this fact together with measurements taken at the same time in Alexandria to perform his calculation, which gave a circumference of about 40,000 km. Present-day calculations give a distance of 40,024 km. So, over 2,000 years ago he managed to calculate the Earth's circumference incredibly closely.

For further details see p. 114.

Area – a progression

- **Calculate areas of rectangles and other simple shapes using counting methods and standard units, cm².**
- **Understand that area is measured in square centimetres (cm²).**
- **Understand and use 'length x breadth' for the area of a rectangle.**

- **Calculate the area of simple compound shapes (shapes that can be split into rectangles).**

Area is first mentioned in Year 4 of the Primary Framework, as indeed is perimeter (see *Length* above). These two aspects of measurement are frequently taught alongside each other as children focus on different measurement properties of shapes. It is interesting to consider if a shape with a fixed area will always have the same perimeter and vice versa. Let us look at a shape with an area of 4 cm^2 – using squared paper will make the task easier.

This shape has an area of 4 cm^2.
Its perimeter is equal to 8 cm.

This shape has an area of 4 cm^2.
Its perimeter is equal to 10 cm.

PRACTICAL TASK PRACTICAL TASK PRACTICAL TASK PRACTICAL TASK

Try doing the same but this time keep the perimeter fixed. Do all shapes with a perimeter of 10 cm have the same area?

Mass – a progression

- **Use comparative language (e.g. heavier than, lighter than) directly to compare two masses, then more than two masses.**
- **Measure using uniform non-standard units.**
- **Estimate, measure and compare using standard units: kilogram, then gram, including their abbreviations.**
- **Suggest suitable measuring equipment and read scales to the nearest labelled division, then unlabelled division.**
- **Explain the relationship between kilograms and grams, and convert between them.**
- **Know the imperial units of a pound (lb) and an ounce (oz).**
- **Know the metric and imperial equivalence of lb and kg, and oz and g.**

Mass can be defined as the amount of matter in an object and weight is the downward force of the object, calculated as the mass multiplied by the force of gravity. Hence the units of mass are kilograms and grams and the unit of weight is the newton.

The newton is named after Sir Isaac Newton (1642–1727). The story frequently relayed involves Newton observing an apple falling in his orchard. He realised that the force pulling the apple towards the Earth was the same force that held the Moon in orbit and, thus was the first to explain gravitational force.

Capacity – a progression

- **Use comparative language to directly compare two capacities (e.g. by filling and emptying containers), then more than two capacities.**
- **Measure using uniform non-standard units, e.g. yoghurt pots.**
- **Estimate, measure and compare using standard units: litre, then millilitres, including their abbreviations.**

- **Suggest suitable measuring equipment and read scales to the nearest labelled division, then unlabelled division.**
- **Explain the relationship between litres and millilitres, and convert between them.**
- **Know the imperial units of a pint, then a gallon.**
- **Know the metric and imperial equivalence of litres and pints and gallons.**

At Key Stages 1 and 2 capacity is studied but not volume. Volume is the amount of three-dimensional space an object takes up, and is introduced in the Year 6 progression to Year 7 of the Primary Framework. Capacity applies to containers and is equal to the amount of liquid a container can hold when full. For example if you are buying a 2-litre bottle of lemonade this means the amount of liquid in the bottle is equal to 2 litres. But is the capacity of the bottle 2 litres?

PRACTICAL TASK PRACTICAL TASK PRACTICAL TASK PRACTICAL TASK

Investigate some containers that you have as a result of shopping. Look at the liquid volume of the purchase you have made, e.g. 2 l of lemonade, and compare this to the actual capacity of the container. How much 'empty space' are you purchasing? (Don't worry, as long as you get the 2 l of lemonade that is advertised, the empty space is free!)

Time – a progression

- **Sequence familiar events.**
- **Know the days of the week in order, the seasons of the year, then months of the year.**
- **On an analogue clock read o'clock time, then half hour, then quarter hour.**
- **Know the relationship between units of time: second, minute, hour, day, week, then month and year.**
- **Read time on a 12-hour digital display.**
- **Use a calendar.**
- **Read the time to 5 minutes on an analogue and 12-hour digital clock, then to the nearest minute.**
- **Use a.m. and p.m.**
- **Read simple timetables.**
- **Read time on a 24-hour digital clock and use 24-hour notation.**
- **Appreciate different times around the world.**

There is a great deal of language associated with time that needs to be developed with children from the Early Years upwards. It is interesting to consider how people have developed these concepts as society has become more and more sophisticated. The most primitive peoples measured time solely in terms of day or night and the passing of the seasons. As calendars were developed the year was divided into months based on lunar cycles. We can now measure time with an incredible degree of accuracy – indeed the most recent addition is the atomic clock which will only gain or lose one second every 1.7 million years. So there is no excuse for being late with one of those!

Misconceptions

Mass and weight

A common misconception held by children is to confuse mass and weight. These words are frequently used socially, as if they were interchangeable. This means that, outside the classroom, children may encounter the language applied to the wrong concept, which will obviously cause confusion.

It is interesting to note here that there is a slight difference between the National Curriculum for mathematics and the Primary Framework for Literacy and Mathematics. Although mathematically and scientifically there is a clear distinction between mass and weight, the National Curriculum specifies *weight* in the programmes of study at Key Stage 1 for Ma 3, *Shape, space and measures*, and identifies the unit as kg. In the programme of study for Key Stage 2 *mass* is specified, this time correctly. The Primary Framework consistently uses weight and kg. If national documents for teachers, such as these, use these two concepts interchangeably, is it surprising that so many children develop misconceptions in this area?

So, how can you overcome this problem and stop this misconception developing? It is clear that using the words as if they were interchangeable will do nothing to address the problem. Equally, being pedantic at all times is also counterproductive. The most straightforward way is the constant 'drip feed' of correct vocabulary associated with the concepts being developed. For example, when you are engaged in practical activity you ask a child to pass you five one hundred gram **masses**, not weights. When using a pan balance, if a child finds their shoe is balanced by 400 g, then you say the shoe weighs the same as the 400 g mass, leading eventually to, 'it has a mass of 400 g'.

There are clear implications for planning here. If you are going to ensure you use the correct vocabulary in your teaching, you need to be confident that you are well prepared. Identifying the vocabulary in advance, and also identifying a clear progression in the development of language, will be vital to ensuring the children acquire a clear understanding of the concepts presented.

Time

Time is another area of measurement where a number of misconceptions can develop. These are due to the amount and use of language associated with time and the quite complex way we measure time and divide our day.

One of the first things to consider is the language of time. Children are frequently told, 'wait a minute' or 'you can play for one more minute', both of which, in reality, are used to represent any amount of time. Other confusion can arise from time-related words such as daytime and nighttime. Children may well establish that they sleep at nighttime and play during daytime – except in the summer they appear to sleep during daytime and in the winter they play at nighttime! We should therefore not be surprised when children have little understanding of the length of time. Time passing is a very ephemeral concept. It cannot be touched or directly seen, it can only be 'seen' through measuring instruments or, longer term, through changes, e.g. from day to night.

Reading time is a further area for confusion. An analogue watch or clock has at least two hands, sometime three. Children are expected to interpret time by reading the display. It is quite interesting to compare our expectations for reading the time with that of the utility companies for reading their meters. When reading an analogue clock face children from Year R are expected to interpret two hands on one dial (Year R – o'clock). If you are not at home when the utility company comes to read one of your meters you are left with a card. On the card you have to write the number if it is a digital display, if not, you simply draw the position of each hand on each dial. There is no expectation that you, as an adult, should 'read' the number represented by the hands on the dials, an expectation we have of four year olds!

When introducing telling the time on an analogue clock face, it is important that the chosen resources accurately represent time passing on a clock face. For example, simply moving the big hand from 12 to 6 to change from 'o'clock' to 'half past' without moving the minute hand will not support children's understanding or ability to tell the time. A 'cog clock', one that links the two hands appropriately so that when one is moved, the other moves proportionately around the clock face, is a very useful resource.

Further confusion can result from the fact that time is not measured using a metric scale; hence if children try to add or subtract time using standard algorithms they are almost guaranteed an incorrect answer. Complementary addition bridging through the hour would be a far more effective method.

*For more on complementary addition, see p. 12 of **Primary Mathematics: Knowledge and Understanding** (2007) from Learning Matters.*

The complex nature of learning to tell the time and appreciate the passing of time has clear implications for planning and assessment. As a teacher you will need to be very clear in identifying the learning, in planning for that learning to take place and in recording your assessments in order to inform future development in this area. In your planning you will need to have clearly 'rehearsed' the lesson in order to anticipate any misconceptions and misunderstandings and have considered how you might address these.

The Primary Framework has developed some useful Interactive Teaching Programs (ITPs) to support the modelling of mathematics for learners. Some of these resources are designed to support the development of different aspects of measures and can be downloaded from: **http://www.standards.dfes.gov.uk/primaryframeworks/library/Mathematics/ICT Resources/itps/**. 'Area', 'Measuring Cylinder', 'Measuring Scales', 'Ruler', 'Tell the Time' and 'Thermometer' alll tackle different aspects of measurement. You are able to manipulate all the resources electronically, invaluable for whole-class or larger group modelling.

A SUMMARY OF **KEY POINTS**

In order to support the development of understanding measurement concepts, it is important that children:
> **recognise that all measure is approximate;**
> **use the appropriate language of measures confidently and accurately;**
> **can estimate and compare as well as measure;**
> **can explain the need for standard units;**
> **understand and can use imperial measures still in everyday use;**
> **understand the relationship between different units of measure.**

Moving on

Make sure your own knowledge and understanding of all aspects of measures is sound. Take some time to look at some of the older measurement systems to see how the concepts and language have developed. This will support you in your teaching by giving you a broader knowledge to draw upon and increasing your own interest in the subject.

In addition speak to colleagues within your school. The subject leader responsible for mathematics throughout your key stage in school will be able to support you in giving you ideas or pointing you in the direction of useful resources.

REFERENCES REFERENCES **REFERENCES** REFERENCES **REFERENCES**

National Curriculum for England. Available at: **http://www.nc.uk.net**.

Primary Framework for Literacy and Mathematics.

Available at: **http://www.standards.dfes.gov.uk/primary**.

11
Shape and space

Professional Standards for the award of QTS

This chapter will support you as you work towards evidencing attainment against the following Standards:

Q14, Q15, Q17, Q22, Q23

Chapter objectives

By the end of this chapter you should:

- **know and understand the spatial expectations of the Primary Framework for Literacy and Mathematics (2006);**
- **understand the progression in the learning of spatial concepts from Early Years to the transition from Key Stage 2 to Key Stage 3;**
- **understand how children's learning can be affected by misconceptions related to shape;**
- **be able to set challenging targets for yourself and for children's learning of shape.**

Introduction

The Primary Framework for Literacy and Mathematics (2006) outlines not only the objectives for developing numerical concepts, but also those for developing spatial understanding as well. A good spatial understanding is important for children as they compare, classify, investigate and solve problems within mathematics. Spatial activities can be the springboard for work in other mathematical areas including number, algebra and handling data.

RESEARCH SUMMARY RESEARCH SUMMARY RESEARCH SUMMARY

Some of the current research in a few spatial areas is cited here. Mathematics education journals are a useful source of further papers.

Angles
Clements and Burns (2000) have used Logo (software in common use in schools in various versions) to research the development of an understanding of angles. They found children learned about turns by integrating two schemes, turn as body movement and turn as number. The children could easily use these two schemes separately, but there was a gradual intertwining and integration of them. This led to the gradual construction of mental images and manipulations of these images to 'stand in for' what was a physical strategy. This is an 'image scheme', that is an 'internalised dynamic mental image acquired through bodily experience'.

Geometric development
The van Hiele model of geometric development (cited in Monaghan, 2000) details a possible progression in developing a geometric understanding. It is probable that most children in the primary years will be working at levels 0 and 1 with some children moving into level 2.

Level 0 (Basic level): Visualisation
> Geometric figures are recognised by their shape as a whole, i.e. physical appearance, not by their parts or properties.

Level 1: Analysis
> Through observation and experimentation children begin to discern the characteristics of figures. These properties are then used to conceptualise classes of shapes. Figures are recognised as having parts and are recognised by their parts. Relationships between properties cannot yet be explained and definitions are not understood.

Level 2: Informal deduction
> Children can establish the interrelationships of properties both within figures (e.g. in a quadrilateral, opposite sides being parallel necessitates opposite angles being equal) and among figures (a square is a rectangle because it has all the properties of a rectangle). Definitions are meaningful. Informal arguments can be followed or given. Formal proofs can be followed, but they cannot construct a proof starting from a different premise.

Level 3: Deduction

Level 4: Rigour
(For definitions of Levels 3 and 4 refer to original paper – see References at the end of the chapter.)

The Primary Framework for Literacy and Mathematics

The Primary Framework for Literacy and Mathematics is composed of seven different strands. The fifth strand identified is 'Understanding shape'. The spatial areas included within this strand are:

- **properties of 2-D and 3-D shapes, including symmetry;**
- **position, including coordinates;**
- **direction, angle.**

It is possible to trace a progression within these areas throughout the Key Objectives, found in the 'Core Learning in Mathematics by Strand' section of the Framework.

The Primary Framework has developed some really useful Interactive Teaching Programs (ITPs) to support the modelling of mathematics for learners. Throughout this chapter you will be directed to certain of these resources, which can all be downloaded from: **http://www.standards. dfes.gov.uk/primaryframeworks/library/Mathematics/ICTResources/itps/**.

Unpicking the progression

2-D and 3-D shape

The issues associated with early development have already been discussed in Chapter 6. This section will consider spatial development as it continues from that point.

Throughout their primary schooling children move from using everyday language to describe shapes (at the lower end of Key Stage 1) to using precise mathematical vocabulary. They also have an ever increasing range of shapes that they can recognise, describe and discuss. By the end of Key Stage 1 they will have encountered:

3-D shapes:
    cube
    cuboid
    pyramid
    sphere
    cone
    cylinder

2-D shapes:
    circle   hexagon
    triangle   octagon
    square
    rectangle
    pentagon

By the end of Key Stage 2 the children will have also encountered:

3-D shapes:
    hemisphere
    prism
    tetrahedron
    polyhedron
    octahedron
    dodecahedron

2-D shapes:
    equilateral triangle   polygon
    isosceles triangle   quadrilateral
    scalene triangle   kite
    rhombus   parallelogram
    oblong   trapezium
    heptagon   semicircle

For more on polygons and 3-D shapes see p. 90 of **Primary Mathematics Knowledge and Understanding** *(2007) from Learning Matters.*

Take the opportunity to look at the Polygon ITP. From the ITPs homepage select the Polygon ITP. This program will enable you to draw and measure a whole range of polygons and to use the dynamic tools to manipulate them.

But what do the children do with these shapes? Again the Primary Framework identifies a clear progression from using them to make models and pictures, ordering them by size, making repeating patterns and so on, to visualising properties such as parallel or perpendicular faces or edges, classifying using criteria such as size of angles, identifying nets, recognising transformations, using coordinates in four quadrants to describe position, using a protractor to draw acute and obtuse angles to the nearest degree and so forth.

For an explanation of these concepts see p. 75 of **Primary Mathematics Knowledge and Understanding** *(2007) from Learning Matters.*

This progression covers concepts from each of the areas of properties, position and angles.

Properties of 2-D and 3-D shapes

When comparing and describing 2-D and 3-D shapes, you should consider certain properties. These include the number of sides, edges, faces, the length of sides and edges, the area of faces, the size of angles, and so on. These properties are often referred to as *Euclidean* properties. They are named after the Greek mathematician Euclid (c. 330–275 BC) who described these properties in his *Elements*.

What other properties might children use to compare shapes?

PRACTICAL TASK PRACTICAL TASK **PRACTICAL TASK** PRACTICAL TASK

Classifying polygons
Given the following shapes, how might they be classified into different sets?

    square   arrowhead
    rhombus   irregular pentagon

| regular hexagon | irregular heptagon |
| equilateral triangle | isosceles triangle |

Symmetry

Children may well first encounter the subject of reflective symmetry when making folded 'butterfly' or 'blob' paintings.

They can extend their understanding through further creative activities such as cutting out paper chains of people. Peg boards and pictures only showing one half can be used to encourage the children to complete the pattern or picture so that there is a line of symmetry. To consider symmetry about more than one axis, paper can be folded into quarters and a 'snowflake' cut to introduce two axes of symmetry. Different shaped paper, with different numbers of folds, can introduce a different number of axes.

For more on reflective symmetry see p. 78 of **Primary Mathematics: Knowledge and Understanding** (2007) from Learning Matters.

2 lines of symmetry

4 lines of symmetry

By upper Key Stage 2, children can be asked to find all the lines of reflective symmetry of any polygon, both regular and irregular.

For more on rotational symmetry see p. 79 of **Primary Mathematics: Knowledge and Understanding** (2007) from Learning Matters.

If a child is to achieve level 5 by the end of Key Stage 2, Attainment Target 3 states they must be able to identify all the symmetries of 2-D shapes. Implicit in this statement is the need to identify rotational symmetry of 2-D shapes. This is not mentioned explicitly as an objective within the Primary Framework until Year 6 progression to Year 7. However, in Year 6 children need to be able to visualise where a shape will be after a rotation through 90° or 180°, hence offering an appropriate opportunity to introduce consideration of rotational symmetry.

PRACTICAL TASK PRACTICAL TASK PRACTICAL TASK PRACTICAL TASK

Children often enjoy mathematics that is associated with them personally. As their understanding of symmetry increases, you could ask them to find all the symmetries of the letters in their name. Have a go yourself with your own name.

Take the opportunity to look at the Symmetry ITP. From the ITPs homepage select the Symmetry ITP. This program enables you to create and reflect simple images in a mirror line. You can predict where you think the image will appear before checking. This is a useful interactive program for children to predict and check on the interactive whiteboard in a large-group teaching situation.

Position and coordinates

The Primary Framework encourages children to describe position from Year R. Initially they use everyday language, but by Year 2 they start to use more mathematical language, for example, 'higher than', 'on the edge of'. In Year 4 games such as Battleships can be used to introduce children to locating squares on grids, prior to introducing coordinates in Year 5. Year 5 introduces the idea of the first quadrant, and during Year 6 children can start to use coordinates in four quadrants to describe position.

In addition to using coordinates to describe position, children also need to use a range of other mathematical language to describe location in space. This includes being able to identify and use horizontal, vertical, diagonal (lines joining opposite corners), perpendicular and parallel.

Knowledge and understanding of the language of position and the use of coordinates will support children as they describe location and solve problems.

Take the opportunity to look at the Coordinates ITP. From the ITPs homepage select the Coordinates ITP. This will enable you to manipulate coordinates on a grid. It is possible to work in only the first quadrant, the first two quadrants or all four quadrants.

For more on Cartesian coordinates see p. 93 of **Primary Mathematics: Knowledge and Understanding** *(2007) from Learning Matters.*

Direction and angles

Building on the idea that angle is a measurement of something dynamic, children are introduced to 'turning' in Year 1 of the Primary Framework. By Year 2 children can recognise whole, half and quarter turns and specify a direction, either left or right, or clockwise or anti-clockwise. In addition they will know a right angle is a quarter turn. Degrees are introduced as a measure of turn in Year 4. Children start to draw and measure angles throughout Years 5 and 6 and use their understanding of these concepts to solve problems.

In Year 3 children are introduced to the four compass directions, North (N), South (S), East (E) and West (W). They are encouraged to make the connection between right angles and the four compass directions by making quarter turns between the points. In Year 4 this is extended to the eight directions N, S, E, W, NE, NW, SE, SW. Development of an understanding of these concepts can be enhanced very effectively by using ICT to support the children's learning. Both floor robots and 'logo' type software are very useful resources.

Why are there 360° in a full turn?

The Greek astronomer Hipparchus of Nicea (c. 170–125 BC) is thought to have first divided a circle into 360. He is thought to have obtained the number 360 from the early astronomers. They believed the Earth was stationary and all the stars rotated about it on a circular band divided into twelve parts. Each part was about 30 days, approximately one lunar cycle, hence 30×12, which gives 360. He did a great deal of work studying the Earth and calculated the length of a year to within 6½ minutes of the figure we accept today!

For more on angles, see p. 71 of **Primary Mathematics: Knowledge and Understanding** *(2007) from Learning Matters.*

At all stages throughout primary mathematics it is important to emphasise the dynamic nature of 'angle' as a measurement of turn. This should help prevent possible misconceptions developing as children progress through Key Stage 2 and into Key Stage 3.

Misconceptions

Many misconceptions that children develop in shape and space can be avoided with careful planning and consideration of how information is presented. If polygons are always shown as regular shapes 'sitting' on one side, then children's conceptual understanding of these shapes may be limited. For example, if a child is always presented with a triangle as in figure (a) below, then, when they encounter a triangle orientated as in (b), they frequently describe it as an 'upside-down' triangle.

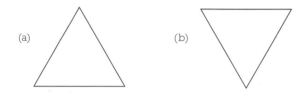

In order to prevent this happening it is important to present a range of different triangles, both regular and irregular, in a variety of orientations, e.g.

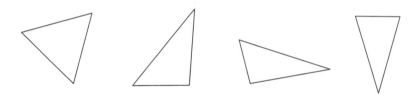

For more on triangles see p. 79 of **Primary Mathematics: Knowledge and Understanding** *(2007) from Learning Matters.*

This will allow children to focus on the characteristics that are important when describing triangles, i.e. number of sides and angles, and not focus on irrelevant details such as orientation. This is also the case when children are learning to distinguish different types of triangle when they need to focus on length of sides and sizes of angles.

This misconception is also revealed when children refuse to accept that any six-sided polygon is a hexagon, e.g.

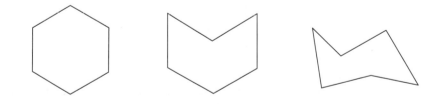

For more on regular and irregular polygons see p. 78 of **Primary Mathematics: Knowledge and Understanding** *(2007) from Learning Matters.*

This is frequently due to the fact that they have always been presented with regular shapes when working with polygons. Again, they focus on specific characteristics that are not necessarily the key ones. It is vital that children encounter a range of polygons, both regular and irregular, in a variety of orientations, in order that this misconception does not develop.

A further misconception children can develop is related to social usage of language that is also used mathematically. An example of this is the child who is asked how many sides shape (a) below has, and replies '2'. When asked how many shape (b) has they also reply '2'. In desperation the teacher shows them shape (c) and asks how many sides, the child replies '3'.

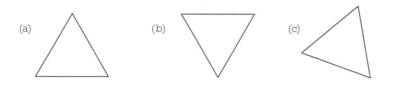

When asked to explain the child says that shape (a) has two sides and a 'bottom', shape (b) has two sides and a 'top' and shape (c) has three sides!

This really demonstrates the importance of planning for the mathematical vocabulary that will be developed when teaching different aspects of shape and space in order to prevent children forming these misconceptions.

In all aspects of shape and space children can develop misconceptions. If they fail to understand that angle is dynamic, they may well be unable to order angles of different sizes correctly because they are focusing on irrelevant pieces of information. For example, looking at angles *a* and *b* below, a child may well state that *a* is larger than *b* because the 'arms' are longer in *a* than in *b*.

In order to avoid this misconception developing, children need to be introduced to angle as a measurement of turn. They need to have plenty of opportunity for practical exploration before encountering angles represented in this way. If they have engaged in these practical activities first, they will be able to apply their knowledge of angle as a measurement of something dynamic, i.e. turn, to this task successfully and not focus on irrelevant details such as the length of the 'arms'.

For more on language in mathematics see p. 133 of **Primary Mathematics: Knowledge and Understanding** *(2007) from Learning Matters.*

A SUMMARY OF **KEY POINTS**

In order to support the development of spatial understanding it is important that children are able to:

> **identify and name a range of polygons and polyhedra;**
> **describe, compare and classify shapes using Euclidean properties;**
> **identify the symmetries of 2-D shapes;**
> **use mathematical language and coordinates to describe position;**
> **recognise angle as a measurement of turn;**
> **specify direction using compass directions.**

Moving on

Ensure that you are absolutely confident in your own understanding of spatial concepts. If you want more support visit the BBC Bitesize website or consult the Shape and Space Chapter in the *Primary Mathematics: Knowledge and Understanding* book from Learning Matters.

In addition speak to colleagues within your school. The subject leader responsible for mathematics throughout key stage in school will be able to support you by giving you ideas or pointing you in the direction of useful resources.

REFERENCES REFERENCES **REFERENCES** REFERENCES **REFERENCES**

Clements, D. H. and Burns, B. A. (2000) 'Students'development of strategies for turn and angle measure'. *Educational Studies in Mathematics*, vol. 41, pp. 31–45.

Monaghan, F. (2000) 'What difference does it make? Children's views of the difference between some quadrilaterals'. *Education Studies in Mathematics*, vol. 42, pp. 179–96.

National Curriculum for England. Available at: **http://www.nc.uk.net**.

The Primary Framework for Literacy and Mathematics.
Available at: **http://www.standarfds.dfes/gov.uk/primary/**.

12
Handling data and probability

Introduction

Within the National Curriculum for Key Stage 1, processing, representing and interpreting data form a subsection of the Attainment Target Ma2. Handling data is extended in Key Stage 2 to its own Attainment Target, Ma4. In this children are expected to use and apply handling data, process, represent and interpret data as well as begin to consider early probability ideas. In addition to this, the National Curriculum highlights that *teaching should ensure that appropriate connections are made between the sections on 'number', 'shape, space and measures', and 'handling data'.*

In the Foundation Stage, learning arises from children's everyday experiences. As a result, developing mathematical ideas to solve problems, talking about, recognising and recreating simple patterns and sorting familiar objects then presenting the results using pictures, drawings or numerals are all aspects of handling data that can be drawn out of their play.

The Primary National Strategy Framework for Teaching Mathematics contains a strand entitled 'Process, present and interpret data to pose and answer questions'. This encompasses the problem-solving nature of handling data at primary level. Handling data allows teachers to embrace the potential to engage children with meaningful problems to solve in creative and cross-curricular ways.

This chapter will focus on the progression through the primary age range in handling data and probability and some of the difficulties that children and teachers might find. For further information about these aspects of mathematics at a higher level of attainment or for your own subject knowledge, readers should refer to the companion book in this series, *Primary Mathematics: Knowledge and Understanding.*

Unpicking the progression

Collecting, sorting and organising data

In order to model the collection of data, tasks are often undertaken by the teacher or jointly as a class in Key Stage 1. As an example consider young children sorting magnetic from non-magnetic material. The teacher has supplied the child with the magnetic and non-magnetic material. The child is asked to sort the data into two groups and organise the data using appropriate diagrams. In this case it is appropriate to use a Carroll diagram, Venn diagram or tree diagram to organise the data. These diagrams are the most appropriate when the data have to be sorted and organised.

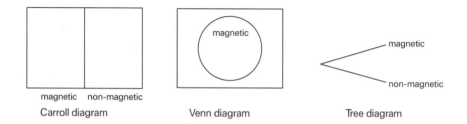

| Carroll diagram | Venn diagram | Tree diagram |

In each case the children physically place the actual magnetic material in one part of the diagram and the non-magnetic material in the other part of the diagram. This kind of activity where the children are sorting using one criterion is the most appropriate for young children in Key Stage 1. Normally, children sort into two sets themselves first and record in their own way before the teacher introduces this formal method of recording.

Progress can be made to sorting using two criteria. Suppose, for example, we wish to find out which materials are magnetic and which are made of metal. We can use the same kind of diagram but, because there are now two criteria, each diagram will have four parts instead of two.

Carroll diagram

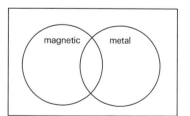

Venn diagram

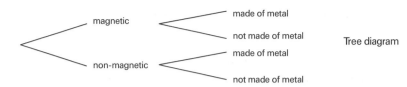

Tree diagram

Again the materials would be placed on the diagrams. These diagrams are useful for answering questions like 'Are all the metals magnetic?' In Key Stage 1 children only classify using one or two criteria. By Key Stage 3 children use similar diagrams to classify using more criteria and to solve problems involving probability.

Representing, extracting and interpreting data

One clear implication of collecting data is how children go on to represent the data. For example, if the class wants to find out the most popular way of coming to school, a simple show of hands from the children is an efficient way of collecting the data. (The teacher will need to limit the number of choices.)

This is called a pictogram or pictograph. They can be drawn horizontally or vertically with each icon representing one child. Questions such as 'How many more children walk than cycle?' can be extracted from this diagram. In turn the diagram is a simple way to interpret the answer.

Once the children realise that drawing icons is very time-consuming, then it is time to progress to **block graphs** where the icons are simply replaced by blocks. These diagrams do not require a side scale since the blocks can be easily counted.

For the purposes of answering the question 'Which is the most popular form of transport?' this is a perfectly adequate diagram.

When the frequencies become larger, however, it is inconvenient to have to count each block. The advantage of using **bar charts** can then be pointed out. A side scale is introduced and the frequencies can be read from the side of the graph.

The progression is from pictogram to block graph to bar chart. In each of these cases the data being handled is categoric, sometimes called qualitative. In other words the horizontal

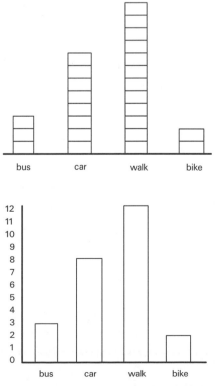

For more detail on pictographs see p. 101 of **Primary Mathematics: Knowledge and Understanding** *(2007) from Learning Matters.*

scale contains categories and not numbers. It is most appropriate at Key Stage 1 to pose questions that relate to categoric data. Examples of appropriate questions are:

- **'What is our favourite cartoon character?'**
- **'What is the most common eye colour?'**
- **'What is the most popular way to travel to school?'**

Another way to represent categoric data is by using a **pie chart**. Creating a pie chart by hand by calculating angles is complicated but with the advent of ICT they are now used extensively in Key Stage 1. Children should be encouraged to use data-handling packages such as *Number Box* to manipulate their data and produce appropriate diagrams. It is important, however, that children are familiar with correct terminology if they are to use the packages correctly.

If we are interested in answering questions such as 'Do more children walk to school than cycle?' then a pie chart is a particularly useful diagram to use. This information can be quickly extracted. Pie charts are appropriate when we are asking questions about relative sizes.

Quantitative data

In Key Stage 2 children can begin to handle quantitative data. This is data that has a numerical value. Suppose, for example, the children want to find out the most common shoe size of the class. Shoe sizes are quantitative data, i.e. numerical. The children will first need to collect this data. This data can be collected quickly by a simple show of hands. A tally chart can then be drawn up:

Shoe size	Number of children
1	‖
2	‖‖
3	卌 ‖
4	卌 ‖
5	卌 ‖‖
6	‖‖
7	‖

A frequency table can then be produced:

Shoe size	Number of children
1	‖
2	‖‖
3	‖‖\ \
4	‖‖\ ‖
5	‖‖\ ‖‖
6	‖‖
7	\

The appropriate diagram to represent this data is a **bar line graph**:

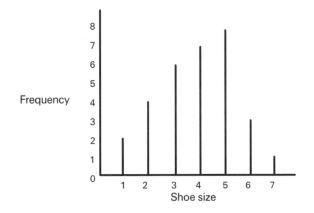

Shoe sizes are an example of *discrete* data. Shoe sizes only come in certain sizes. Other examples of discrete data are dress sizes, hat sizes, the number of children in a family, the number of goals scored in a soccer match. In general a bar line graph is the appropriate way to represent discrete data. This is logical since the vertical line needs to go to exactly that particular numerical value.

Quantitative data can also be *continuous*. This is the kind of data that can take any value within a certain range. Examples of continuous data are time, distance, and speed. In Key Stage 2 children need to be able to interpret **line graphs**. The graph below is a line graph showing how the distance travelled by a car is related to the time it has been moving.

For more detail on line graphs see p. 102 of **Primary Mathematics: Knowledge and Understanding** *(2007) from Learning Matters.*

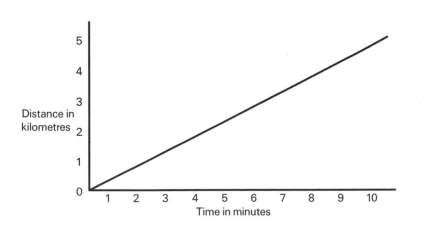

Children should be taught to interpret the graph and be able to answer questions such as:

- **'How far has the car travelled after 8 minutes?'**
- **'How long does it take to travel 3 kilometres?'**

Other line graphs that children can be introduced to are conversion graphs. For example, say that at the current rate of exchange £10 can be exchanged for 16 euros. A conversion graph can be constructed and children asked to exchange pounds into euros and vice versa. Research shows that children find it easier to go from the horizontal scale to the vertical scale rather than vice versa. In the above example they find it easier to find how far the car has gone after 4 minutes rather than finding how long the car took to go 3 kilometres. It is worth spending time on reading conversion graphs both ways.

Using ICT effectively to collect, represent and interpret data

With easy access to wide and varied data on the internet, websites are a useful source of data for children to use in their cross-curricular work. For example, it is possible to search for and track over time the population sizes of villages, towns and cities to study population trends in history or geography.

As mentioned earlier in this chapter, the use of computerised data handling packages has meant that children are able to construct attractive, accurate graphs very simply and effectively. It is also possible to amend data and have an immediately updated graph. The use of the interactive whiteboard has also meant that skills involved in creating and interpreting graphs can be developed with the whole class efficiently. This is very welcome because a regular criticism of lessons prior to ICT inclusion was that children would spend whole lessons *creating* graphs but then did not *use* or *interpret* them, which is of course the main purpose of being able to handle data.

It is important to note, however, that computer packages will present *any* data in *any* way for you. This means that children can produce a line graph using discrete data which is nonsensical. For example, a line graph could be produced on a computer to represent shoe sizes in the class, but reading that 4.5 children wear size 11.75 shoes does not provide accurate data! Equally, when creating and interpreting pie charts, it is necessary for children to realise that they are comparing proportions.

What should all graphs have?

Whether constructing graphs by hand or using a computer package it is necessary to highlight for children what information their graph must contain. Look at the generic bar graph template below. Note the information that must be on it in order to provide all the necessary information for people to interpret it.

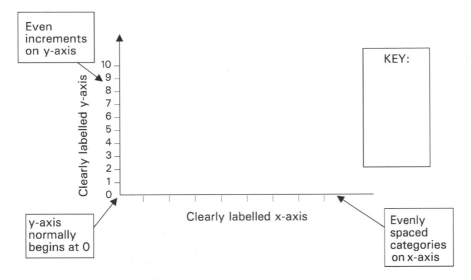

It is important to note that other types of graphs will still require the same precision in layout and presentation.

Constructing block graphs and bar graphs

A common hurdle for children is the move from constructing block graphs to bar graphs by hand. The difference is in the labelling of the y-axis. It might be helpful for you to consider this progression in relation to number lines and plotting coordinates:

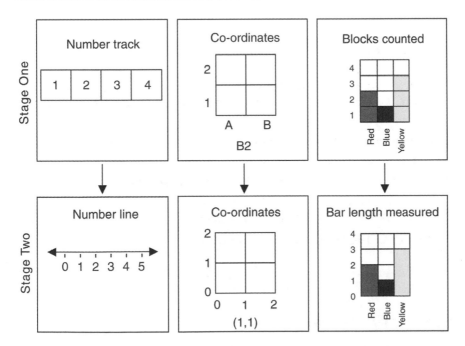

The move from using number tracks to number lines, from labelling squares in co-ordinate geometry to labelling points, and from creating block graphs to bar graphs all happen around similar times in school. By being aware of this shift occurring in several mathematics areas and making the links explicit to children may help their confusion.

How can I be creative in handling data and developing cross-curricular links?

It is not uncommon for children in upper Key Stage 2 to be constructing graphs about their favourite pop stars or their favourite food. Quite frankly, this is no different to the skills required of them when in Reception class they were answering questions about their favourite pets or food. In order to keep children interested and motivated it is necessary for them to see the purpose of their activity. The biggest challenge in setting questions for your children, or supporting them in choosing an appropriate question, is the level of challenge both mathematically and in other areas of the curriculum.

If you wish to consider handling data discretely within mathematics lessons, one way to do this is to create a data handling project with children where they answer a question of their choice in project groups. For example, they may collect data about adults' preferred car colour and present their findings to a car manufacturer. Another example might be to canvas children's preferred pet choices and present this information to a pet shop owner. Projects of this type can also benefit from having a guest speaker or organising visits for the children for them to see the purpose of their data collection, representation and interpretation. Another significant benefit is that the children recognise a purpose and gain a sense of the audience for their work.

If you are going to handle data in subjects other than mathematics lessons you may wish to consider teaching the skills of handling data within mathematics lessons and then use those skills in other lessons. Alternatively, you may use the double lesson time to integrate maths and the other subject together. Be aware of when the children are involved in mathematics and when they are engaged in other subjects, however, to ensure appropriate coverage of the curriculum.

REFLECTIVE TASK

For each of the questions below, consider how your children might gather data, present it and interpret it. Try to be as creative as you can. What cross-curricular links can you make with these ideas?

- **How many tins does our class recycle?**
- **How do we get to school?**
- **Which is the best country performing in the world championships?**
- **What prices should we charge in the school canteen?**
- **What factors encourage people to move house?**
- **What effect does the weather have on wildlife?**

For more detail on when mean, median and mode are best used see p. 106 of **Primary Mathematics: Knowledge and Understanding** *(2007) from Learning Matters.*

Next time you sit down to look at your medium-term plans, think about where you can realistically make creative cross-curricular links in your teaching.

Summary statistics

Older children progress to finding summary statistics. The easiest summary statistic to find is the mode. Indeed even in Key Stage 1 children are finding 'the most common eye colour' and 'the most popular way of travelling to school'. Children should be encouraged to call this the mode.

In Key Stage 2 we introduce other averages such as the mean and median. Care should be taken, however, to find these statistics only when they are appropriate.

Consider the following example. As part of their History project a class of children was collecting data on the wages of miners. The table below (adjusted) shows the annual wages of the miners in their sample:

Miner	A	B	C	D	E	F	G	H	I	J	K
Wage (£)	2,000	2,000	2,000	2,000	2,000	2,500	3,000	3,000	3,000	4,000	5,500

The question the children wanted to answer was: 'Which summary statistic gives a true reflection of the average wage?'

PRACTICAL TASK PRACTICAL TASK **PRACTICAL TASK** PRACTICAL TASK

Before reading on, consider how you might answer this question: Which summary statistic do you feel gives a true reflection?

- **The mode, the most common, is £2,000.**
- **The median, the wage of the middle miner F, is £2,500.**
- **The mean, the total wage bill divided by the number of miners, is £3,000.**

From the management's viewpoint the total wage bill is very important. Consequently the mean is their most appropriate summary statistic because it is linked to the total wage bill. However, from the workers' standpoint what most people earn is of importance. The mode is their most appropriate summary statistic.

It would be misleading, however, for management to say the average wage was £3,000, just as it would be misleading for the workers to say the average wage was £2,000. It is important to state which average is being used.

The National Curriculum says that 'pupils should be taught to recognise when information is presented in misleading ways'.

It is a useful activity for children to find references to averages in newspapers and decide which average, the mode, median or mean, is being referred to.

Misconceptions

The misconception many children have is that the graph is a picture rather than a scaled representation. Teachers need to emphasise that each point on the line (in the graph showing the distance travelled by a car on p. 166) represents a distance travelled in a particular time. In fact it is good practice for teachers to build the graph up from a set of points. Children can be encouraged to fill in missing values in the table (shown below) and then plot the points on a grid. The teacher can then discuss whether or not it is valid to join the points together to make a line. If the car is travelling at a constant speed then it is valid to join the points.

Time (in minutes)	Distance (in kilometres)
2	1
3	$1\frac{1}{2}$
4	2
5	
	3
7	
8	
9	
	5

Children will begin to appreciate that the straight line does not show a car going in a straight line but a linear relationship between distance travelled and time taken.

For further details about misconceptions in handling data you can read the chapter by Surtees in Hansen's (2005) *Children's Errors in Mathematics: Understanding Common Misconceptions in Primary Schools*.

Probability

In the National Curriculum and the Framework for Teaching Mathematics the emphasis is on the language associated with probability. Although probability is only specifically mentioned in upper Key Stage 2 there are opportunities in Key Stage 1 to introduce some terminology. The emphasis in the first instance is on identifying all the *possibilities* or *presenting outcomes*.

As an example consider the following investigation: 'A flag has three stripes. How many different flags can be made only using the colours red and blue? You can use just one colour if you want to!'

Children trying a problem like this for the first time do not usually attempt it in a systematic way. They need to be taught how to be systematic in order to ensure all the possibilities are found. Many of the investigations and problems that children are set in Key Stage 1 require this systematic approach.

After working with possibilities children can progress to the ideas of impossible and certain. For example, children could be asked: 'When two dice are thrown and the numbers added which of the following are possible scores – 7, 10, 1?' or 'Are you certain to get a total less than 12?' The emphasis here is on language and children should be encouraged to consider non-quantitative statements as well. For example, 'Is it possible that you will win the National Lottery?' or 'Is it possible that you will have a birthday in the next year?'

PRACTICAL TASK PRACTICAL TASK **PRACTICAL TASK** PRACTICAL TASK

An interesting way to introduce children to the terminology of probability is to give each pupil a card with a statement on, such as, 'I will throw a 7 on a dice', 'It will rain tomorrow', 'It will snow tomorrow', 'I will throw a total of between 2 and 12 when I throw 2 dice', ' I will see a cat on the way home from school'. Children are then invited to categorise these as impossible,

possible or certain. When children have done this they can then discuss if some of the possible things are more likely than others. Try to produce some more statements yourself and order the statements in order of *likelihood*.

Questions like these will often elicit responses that use words such as 'not likely', and 'extremely unlikely'. The next stage is the idea of *likelihood*: the idea that although two events are both possible one is more likely to happen than the other. For example, 'When an ordinary dice is thrown are you more likely to get 6 or an even number?' or 'Are you more likely to see a cat or a fox on the way home from school?' Children should be encouraged to place events in order of likelihood. Words such as 'good chance', 'poor chance', 'risk', 'doubt' and 'probable' should be introduced. The next stage is to introduce the notion of equal chance, i.e. the chance it will not happen is the same as the chance it will. Questions such as 'Is there an equal chance of throwing a head or a tail?' or 'Is there an equal chance of throwing an even number or an odd number on a dice?' often elicit the response 'Yes – if the coin or dice is fair.' The terms 'fair' and 'unfair' can now be introduced.

From Year 6, we can place a numerical value on the likelihood. We can introduce the idea by saying the probability of obtaining a head or an even number on a dice is a half. We can then progress to finding probabilities other than a half. For example, we could ask 'What is the probability the number on a dice is less than 3?' or 'What is the probability I throw a 6?' The examples we choose are those with equally likely outcomes. When a dice is thrown, there are six equally likely outcomes. When a coin is thrown, there are two equally likely outcomes. We do not yet consider outcomes that are not equally likely.

RESEARCH SUMMARY RESEARCH SUMMARY RESEARCH SUMMARY

An evaluation by HMI (Ofsted, 2002) challenges teachers' questioning in areas of the curriculum such as handling data. They provide an example from a Year 3 classroom where the teacher asked children to answer simple questions such as 'How many children like blue?' but did not ask more challenging questions such as 'How many more children like blue than orange?' The report also found that few schools make regular use of ICT during mathematics lessons. However, timetabled ICT time was commonly used to teach children how to use graphical presentations, data analysis and spreadsheet software.

In addition to this, the 2003 report from Ofsted highlighted the need for regular 'real-life' problems to develop skills such as interpreting data.

A SUMMARY OF **KEY POINTS**

In order to support the development of a child's understanding of handling data, it is important that children:

> **approach statistics as essentially a problem-solving exercise;**

> **progress from collecting, sorting and organising data to representing, extracting and interpreting data;**

> **progress from discrete to continuous data;**

> **understand the difference between discrete and continuous data and know in which ways these should be represented;**

> **are enabled to use measures of average in relevant contexts;**

> are taught with an emphasis on the language of probability;
> only calculate probabilities using equally likely outcomes.

Moving on

There are a number of resources in your school and/or university library and on the internet to support your handling data work. These are a useful point of first contact for support. For example, you could look at the QCA ICT Schemes of Work which contain several suggestions for cross-curricular work.

You may wish to tap into web-based resources such as that run by the Royal Statistical Society Centre for Statistical Education (at **http://www.censusatschool.ntu.ac.uk**/). Finally, the Standards Site (at **http://www.standards.dfes.gov.uk**) contains a lot of professional development support for teachers in teaching handling data and using ICT to handle data.

Finally, consider speaking to the subject leader responsible for mathematics in your key stage or your school. They will be able to support you by giving you ideas or pointing you in the direction of school resources.

REFERENCES REFERENCES **REFERENCES** REFERENCES REFERENCES

Hansen, A. (ed.) (2005) *Children's Errors in Mathematics: Understanding Common Misconceptions.* Exeter: Learning Matters.

Ofsted (2002) *The National Numeracy Strategy: The Second Year. An Evaluation by HMI.* London: Ofsted.

Ofsted (2003) *Mathematics in Primary Schools: Ofsted Subject Reports Series 2001/2*, HMI 806. London: Ofsted.

FURTHER READING   FURTHER READING   FURTHER READING

Askew, M. (1998) *Teaching Primary Mathematics.* London: Hodder & Stoughton.

Haylock, D. (2005) *Mathematics Explained for Primary Teachers*, 3rd edition. London: Paul Chapman.

Hopkins, C., Gifford, S. and Pepperell, S. (1999) *Mathematics in Primary School: A Sense of Progression*, 2nd edition. London: David Fulton.

Hopkins, C., Pope, S. and Pepperell, S. (2004) *Understanding Primary Mathematics.* London: David Fulton.

Suggate, J., Davis, A. and Goulding, M. (2006) *Mathematics Knowledge for Primary Teachers*, 3rd edition. London: David Fulton.

Index

Achieving QTS

The Achieving QTS series continues to grow with nearly 50 titles in 8 separate strands. Our titles address issues of teaching and learning across both primary and secondary phases in a highly practical and accessible manner, making each title an invaluable resource for trainee teachers.

We've updated and improved 13 of our bestselling titles in line with the new Standards for QTS (September 2007). These titles are highlighted with a * in the list below.

Assessment for Learning and Teaching in Primary Schools
Mary Briggs, Angela Woodfield, Cynthia Martin and Peter Swatton
£15   176 pages   ISBN: 978 1 903300 74 9

Assessment for Learning and Teaching in Secondary Schools
Martin Fautley and Jonathan Savage
£16   160 pages   ISBN: 978 1 84445 107 4

***Learning and Teaching in Secondary Schools (third edition)**
Viv Ellis
£16   192 pages   ISBN: 978 1 84445 096 1

Learning and Teaching Using ICT in Secondary Schools
John Woollard
£17.50   192 pages   ISBN: 978 1 84445 078 7

Passing the ICT Skills Test (second edition)
Clive Ferrigan
£8   80 pages   ISBN: 978 1 84445 028 2

Passing the Literacy Skills Test
Jim Johnson
£8   80 pages   ISBN: 978 1 903300 12 1

Passing the Numeracy Skills Test (third edition)
Mark Patmore,
£8   64 pages   ISBN: 978 1 903300 94 7

***Primary English: Audit and Test (third edition)**
Doreen Challen
£9   64 pages   ISBN: 978 1 84445 110 4

***Primary English: Knowledge and Understanding (third edition)**
Jane Medwell, George Moore, David Wray and Vivienne Griffiths
£16   240 pages   ISBN: 978 1 84445 093 0

***Primary English: Teaching Theory and Practice (third edition)**
Jane Medwell, David Wray, Hilary Minns, Vivienne Griffiths and Liz Coates
£16   208 pages   ISBN: 978 1 84445 092 3

***Primary ICT: Knowledge, Understanding and Practice (third edition)**
Jonathan Allen, John Potter, Jane Sharp and Keith Turvey
£16   256 pages   ISBN: 978 1 84445 094 7

***Primary Mathematics: Audit and Test (third edition)**
Claire Mooney and Mike Fletcher
£9   52 pages   ISBN: 978 1 84445 111 1

***Primary Mathematics: Knowledge and Understanding (third edition)**
Claire Mooney, Lindsey Ferrie, Sue Fox, Alice Hansen and Reg Wrathmell
£16   176 pages   ISBN: 978 1 84445 053 4

*Primary Mathematics: Teaching Theory and Practice (third edition)
Claire Mooney, Mary Briggs, Mike Fletcher, Alice Hansen and Judith McCullouch
£16   192 pages   ISBN: 978 1 84445 099 2

*Primary Science: Audit and Test (third edition)
John Sharp and Jenny Byrne
£9   80 pages   ISBN: 978 1 84445 109 8

*Primary Science: Knowledge and Understanding (third edition)
Graham Peacock, John Sharp, Rob Johnsey and Debbie Wright
£16   240 pages   ISBN: 978 1 84445 098 5

*Primary Science: Teaching Theory and Practice (third edition)
Rob Johnsey, John Sharp, Graham Peacock, Shirley Simon and Robin Smith
£16   144 pages   ISBN: 978 1 84445 097 8

*Professional Studies: Primary and Early Years (third edition)
Kate Jacques and Rob Hyland
£16   256 pages   ISBN: 978 1 84445 095 4

Teaching Arts in Primary Schools
Raywen Ford, Stephanie Penny, Lawry Price and Susan Young
£15   192 pages   ISBN: 978 1 903300 35 0

Teaching Design and Technology at Key Stages 1 and 2
Gill Hope
£17   224 pages   ISBN: 978 1 84445 056 5

Teaching Foundation Stage
Iris Keating
£15   200 pages   ISBN: 978 1 903300 33 6

Teaching Humanities in Primary Schools
Editor: Pat Hoodless
£15   192 pages   ISBN: 978 1 903300 36 7

Teaching Religious Education: Primary and Early Years
Elaine McCreery, Sandra Palmer and Veronica Voiels
£16   176 pages   ISBN: 978 1 84445 108 1

Achieving QTS Cross-Curricular Strand

Children's Spiritual, Moral, Social and Cultural Development
Tony Eaude
£14   128 pages   ISBN: 978 1 84445 048 0

Creativity in Primary Education
Anthony Wilson
£15   224 pages   ISBN: 978 1 84445 013 8

Creativity in Secondary Education
Jonathan Savage, Martin Fautley
£16   144 pages   ISBN: 978 1 84445 073 2

Teaching Citizenship in Primary Schools
Editor: Hilary Claire
£15   192 pages   ISBN: 978 1 84445 010 7

Teaching Literacy Across the Primary Curriculum
David Wray
£14   144 pages   ISBN: 978 1 84445 008 4

Achieving QTS Extending Knowledge in Practice

Primary English: Extending Knowledge in Practice
Jane Medwell and David Wray
£16   160 pages   ISBN: 978 1 84445 104 3

Primary ICT: Extending Knowledge in Practice
John Duffty
£16   176 pages   ISBN: 978 1 84445 055 8

Primary Mathematics: Extending Knowledge in Practice
Alice Hansen
£16   176 pages   ISBN: 978 1 84445 054 1

Primary Science: Extending Knowledge in Practice
Judith Roden, Hellen Ward and Hugh Ritchie
£16   160 pages   ISBN: 978 1 84445 106 7

Achieving QTS Practical Handbooks

Learning and Teaching with Interactive Whiteboards: Primary and Early Years
David Barber, Linda Cooper, Graham Meeson
£14   128 pages   ISBN: 978 1 84445 081 7

Learning and Teaching with Virtual Learning Environments
Helena Gillespie, Helen Boulton, Alison Hramiak and Richard Williamson
£14   144 pages   ISBN: 978 1 84445 076 3

*Successful Teaching Placement: Primary and Early Years (second edition)
Jane Medwell
£12   160 pages   ISBN: 978 1 84445 091 6

Using Resources to Support Mathematical Thinking: Primary and Early Years
Doreen Drews and Alice Hansen
£15   160 pages   ISBN: 978 1 84445 057 2

Achieving QTS Reflective Readers

Primary English Reflective Reader
Andrew Lambirth
£14   128 pages   ISBN: 978 1 84445 035 0

Primary Mathematics Reflective Reader
Louise O'Sullivan, Andrew Harris, Gina Donaldson, Gill Bottle, Margaret Sangster and Jon Wild
£14   120 pages   ISBN: 978 1 84445 036 7

Primary Professional Studies Reflective Reader
Sue Kendall-Seater
£15   192 pages   ISBN: 978 1 84445 033 6

Primary Science Reflective Reader
Judith Roden
£14   128 pages   ISBN: 978 1 84445 037 4

Primary Special Educational Needs Reflective Reader
Sue Soan
£14   136 pages   ISBN: 978 1 84445 038 1

Secondary Professional Studies Reflective Reader
Simon Hoult
£14   192 pages   ISBN: 978 1 84445 034 3

Secondary Science Reflective Reader
Gren Ireson and John Twidle
£16   128 pages   ISBN: 978 1 84445 065 7

To order please phone our order line 0845 230 9000 or send an official order or cheque to BEBC, Albion Close, Parkstone, Poole, BH12 3LL
Order online at www.learningmatters.co.uk